FIRST YEAR
ON THE BENCH

Mary Nan Thompson

Cover: Watercolor painting by
Mary Nan Thompson of Courthouse in Fayetteville, North Carolina

Published by Amazon Publishing
ISBN 978-1-48356-701-3 Published in the United States of America

For Katherine, Jack II, Craig, and Rob,

Our legacy.

And their legacy, Jake, Sophia, Jack III, Mary Alex, Guy,

and Zachary

and thereby, ours as well.

A Word To The Reader

These cases are actual, a matter of public record: no content has been changed. While most of the testimony is verbatim, some is paraphrased. I also took the liberty of combining some of the questions and answers to abbreviate the testimony, as sometimes it requires multiple questions to arrive at one answer under the rules of evidence.

I have changed the name of one major character, the rape victim in Chapter Four, to protect her from further public humiliation. I have also changed a few names of peripheral characters for reasons that should become obvious.

These fictitious names are marked by an asterisk the first time they appear.

Any other inaccuracies are not intentional, but what I heard and saw, and subject to human fallacy. I apologize in advance for any mistakes I may have made and trust they are minor.

This book began, not as a true crimes chronicle, but as a journal, a record of Judge Thompson's first year on the bench as I traveled the state with him. But it soon became apparent that this was to be a remarkable year, remarkable in its schedule of significant cases, the diversity of locales, and as a learning experience.

Although I had lived and worked within the legal system most of my adult life, I was surprised by my new perspective: that justice, like everything else, is relative, dependent upon a myriad of variable human factors, and perhaps most significantly, a matter of perception: Idealism vs. realism.

CONTENTS

Preview

One Judge in the State of North Carolina heard the six trials documented in this book in the time span of one year.

Six cases, six victims, each innocent in his or her own way:

Gary Quinn, a private investigator, was caught in the middle of a lover's triangle, perhaps, unaware.

Darla Cline was in the wrong place at the wrong time, filling in at work for someone else. Her husband was sleeping in their apartment upstairs, oblivious to her death screams.

Vivian Whitaker became friends with the wrong person, the mother of a dangerous son, the defective offspring of a family torn by alcohol abuse and mental illness.

*Sherry Wells, young, bright, and engaged to be married, was too trusting, and the system failed her. Her assailant, a known rapist, was free to strike again.

Rosemary Chavis was living in a backwards culture inclined to saving face and settling family disputes by violence. So was her killer, her father's lover.

And Sabrina Buie was the eleven-year-old pawn of four young men in search of instant gratification at any cost. She paid for their lust with her life.

These are their stories as told to each jury in the trials that follow.

But the victims' stories are not the only ones. Each defendant has his own story to tell, and how his or her life intertwines with that of the victim is at times contrived, sometimes accidental, and at times, perhaps, inevitable.

And, finally, this is also the story of how our criminal justice system handles these lives by the complex orchestrated proceedings that we have come to know as trials. Trials are not sterile exercises in intellectual arguments of legal interpretation. Trials are for and about people. Amid the abstract academic principles, what emerges ultimately are multi-plot dramas, studies of human behavior and the consequences wrought upon other lives.

And each trial is unique, never having exactly the same circumstances as another.

Some trials are "just," while others fall short. The degree of fairness varies, dependent on competence, location, political climate, and ability to communicate when all the players come together for the first time in unfamiliar settings to reach unanimous decisions. And the personality of each player--the defendant, the lawyer he chooses, the attorney that counters him, each juror that passes judgment, and the judge who rules on the law--plays a definitive role in the outcome.

The presiding judge is an ordinary person, who brings his degree of legal experience and individual personality with him to the bench.

Lawyers are ordinary people, bringing their degree of expertise and individual personalities with them to the counsel tables.

And jurors are ordinary people, bringing their diverse backgrounds, common sense, and individual personalities with them into the jury box.

Twelve people take their assigned seats. A judge greets them. Lawyers try to persuade them to their side through their witnesses, some more articulate, some more candid, and some more believable than others.

The jurors were not present at the scene of the crime. They do not know the parties involved nor the facts of the case. The evidence they base their decisions on, which may mean life or death, unfolds from the witness stand. They must piece this evidence together, determine the credibility of each witness, and apply the law the judge gives them to the circumstances of the case before them. A formidable task.

In the six cases that follow, you will hear the evidence just as the jury did, witness by witness, and decide for yourself if you would have come to the same conclusion.

While ours is by no means an ideal system, it is a far cry from the obligatory revenge in ancient civilization, feeding on itself until it comes full circle, as Hamlet so amply illustrates.

But we should not expect the moon. The law cannot totally solve our problems--cannot set things back the way they were.

The law cannot resurrect Gary Edwards or Darla Cline or Vivian Whitaker or Rosemary Chavis or Sabrina Buie, nor can it stop Sherry Wells' nightmares. The best the law can do is to ask twelve people from off the street to remove the offender from their midst and stop him from doing more harm.

What we call justice.

PROLOGUE

The year was 1991.

Judge Jack Thompson was new to the bench, having assumed the position of Superior Court Judge in January.

He had been practicing law for twenty-five years, first as a prosecutor, then on the other side, defending the accused and litigating civil cases. His children had grown into young adults, and he now felt free to pursue the life of traveling required by his new job, which he viewed as a challenge, an opportunity to make a contribution in a new way, a cap on his legal career.

His first two months on the bench had been in his hometown, Fayetteville, and consisted of hearing guilty pleas, probation revocations and the standard fare of drug cases. His next assignment was the roving slot, meaning the Trial Court Administrator could send him anywhere in the State of North Carolina, and he did. In the first two months, he had been all the way from the outer banks on the coast to the great metropolis of Charlotte, and now to the mountains.

As a novice judge, he expected to learn. What he did not expect, perhaps, was that in addition to the continuation of the usual court calendar, he was to be cast straightaway into three potential death cases as well as a first-degree murder case, a second-degree murder case, and a brutal rape case, all within his first year.

There were two ways to look at it: baptism by fire, or, given his love of a challenge, the proverbial briar patch.

His adventure began in March in a small mountain town.

We were on our way to Rutherfordton, snug in the foothills of the Blue Ridge Mountains with a name that you couldn't say very fast. A deliberate coordination of brain and mouth is necessary to say Ruth-er-ford-ton without pausing. We would find out that "Ruferten" was the native slurred version.

"We," I say. I was just along for the company, support, entertainment--whatever wives do when they accompany their husbands.

Our destination was a good five to six hours away, and on the road, we talked about the capital case ahead of him. I was reading the transcript from the last trial of this case five years ago.

I also had plenty of time to study this man sitting beside me. Now that he wore a robe, others might look at him differently, some had even started treating him differently, but I knew that I would see him as I always had.

His Scottish roots ran deep, his ancestors immigrating here from Ayr, Scotland. His forefathers settled in North Carolina, but brothers were separated in New York, the two never locating each other again. We had visited that part of the British Isles five years ago, and it was hard to distinguish Jack from the locals. The Scottish people were cordial, purposeful, and fiercely proud, and their physical build was solidly stocky, on the shortish side. If I had ever had doubts about the influence of genes, I never would again.

His eyes were hazel--meaning they looked gray with a white shirt, blue with one of that color, and green at the ocean--and they were the best means by which you could read his mood--serious, a good deal of the time, but they were quick to twinkle. A permanent crease in his high forehead made him look stern even when he wasn't, and his hairline converged in a prominent widow's peak, now streaked with silver.

His personality was complex, a true Gemini. While he was organized and practical with an everything-has-its-place attitude, he loved a good party. He liked people, and they liked him.

Above all, he valued honesty, whether dealing with a client, another attorney, or his children; the latter knowing better than anyone else, that what he would not tolerate was anything less than the truth. His temperament was well suited for his new position, his sense of fairness being the single most important qualification--that and knowing the law.

This assignment was to be his first capital case, and it was a little frightening for a novice judge. He had served as District Attorney for four years, but fifteen years of private practice had intervened, and in the meantime, the Supreme Court had made capital cases more complex from picking a jury to sentencing. It was like comparing the major leagues to sandlot baseball.

This case had been tried before and the defendant sentenced to death; yet five years later, the Supreme Court said the Judge had erred in his charge to the jury, so the defendant was entitled to a new trial.

But when Monday came, the capital case was postponed. Judge Thompson had no choice but to continue the case to a later date because the attorneys had presented motions that the accused be examined by each of their psychological experts to determine if he was mentally competent at this time to stand trial.

The deadlines for motions had long passed, but a man's life was at stake. The Supreme Court would have rapidly reversed if these motions were not granted.

So here we were in this charming one-street town with a court calendar crammed with small cases, mostly misdemeanor appeals. The District Attorney was having to drop back and punt now that this two-week case had been continued, and his method was to choose randomly from a fifty-three-page calendar. When asked why this small town would have so many cases for trial, we received the following explanation: It seems that a previous District Court Judge had given all the defendants she found guilty the maximum sentence. She was running for the office of Superior Court Judge at the time. As a result, of course, the defendants' appealed to Superior Court. It fell to subsequent judges, including Judge Thompson, to clean up the mess.

I strayed from the courthouse, trying to entertain myself.

This didn't last long. By the middle of the week, despite the altered and mundane calendar, I found myself slipping into the courthouse for a few hours on several days to get a flavor of the community.

I quickly learned that being a Judge's wife had its advantages. People are anxious to meet you and talk to you, and you are not a total stranger in the courthouse. I am a friendly person by nature. I not only enjoy the clerks and secretaries and court reporters, but I also understand their problems. As a court reporter, I had been there. I know they work hard and put up with a lot of different personalities, not all of them pleasant, and that the camaraderie in the courthouse is an integral part of their lives and makes their jobs more interesting than many other means of employment. They were congenial and eager to make us feel welcome.

But inside the courtroom, the proceedings were not going that smoothly. Many of the lawyers were unprepared and had to be located when their case was called, and a great amount of time was spent sitting and waiting. At the end of three days, Judge Thompson let it be known that any lawyer who had a case scheduled had best be in the courtroom and ready to proceed.

It was a long week.

We left Rutherfordton for the weekend and headed farther west, deeper into the mountains. Some of the highest peaks were covered with snow from the week before, and a few roads on the Blue Ridge Parkway were still closed with no warning until we reached the roadblocks. What was supposed to be an hour-and-a-half trip up to Beech Mountain turned into four hours.

The drive was not a total waste, however. Rounding a curve, we saw a clock on the top of what looked like a church steeple, but the steeple was on the ground, as if whoever had built it had no way to raise it to its lofty perch. We decided this had to be where they filmed the movie Winter People based on John Eyles's book of the same title. The backtracking and hairpin curves had been worth it. Arriving after dark at a friend's borrowed condo, we retrieved the key from a deposit box and drove straight up the mountain and right into snow.

We spent Saturday discovering the small surrounding towns and watching the skiers having their last fling on the final snow of the season.

We returned to Rutherfordton Sunday afternoon and checked into a small condominium in a complex named Apple Valley, named for the small, squatty, still-bare trees that covered the landscape. Six weeks later, their blossoms would be decorating the hills and valleys like pink frosting.

We were expecting another uneventful week in court and we were right for the first two days. But when you're dealing with the court system, things have a way of changing rapidly. Also pertinent is that the smaller districts do not have Superior Court every week, so the larger cases can be held for a while until a judge returns to their county seat.

The District Attorney decided that he desperately needed to try a second degree murder case while he still had a judge. The main problem was his assistant who was to try it was in another county on a serious case that had run longer than anticipated. The earliest he could start this week would be Wednesday, and that would allow only three days for a trial. Judge Thompson told the chief prosecutor that he would start picking the jury no later than first thing Wednesday morning, with or without his assistant, and that the jurors and witnesses would be kept until seven o'clock each night and, if necessary, brought back on Saturday and Sunday. All witnesses would be present and waiting to go on the stand--no delays. The bottom line was that he would not carry the case into next week. The prosecutor and the defense attorney agreed on the conditions.

CHAPTER ONE

MARCH: STATE v. WALLACE

On Wednesday morning, jury selection began.

Picking a jury is an interesting process. Men and women of every description and from every walk of life and background come together, sit in the courtroom as a group, and are sworn as the "finders of the fact" in a situation they have never heard of, involving parties they have never seen. The judge gives them a short lesson on our system of jurisprudence and instructs them that under our system, guilt must be proved: there is a presumption of innocence until or if the State proves guilt beyond a reasonable doubt.

In this particular case, they were also told there might be long days that could go into nights and there was a possibility of continuing into their weekend. You would think that half of them would have said they had problems with this interference to their lives, but no one did.

What is it that makes people want to sit on a jury in a courtroom and decide the fate of a fellow human being? Was it a genuine concern for justice? Was it the chance to participate in the drama of an unfolding story to which they write the ending? Or simply a diversion, a day away from work or TV or boredom? "Twelve men good and true," and in 1940, the Supreme Court had decided that women were also capable of making a decision.

The standards for being qualified to sit on a jury are minimal: a resident of the county, no convictions of any serious crimes and still on active probation, and not having served on a jury during the last two years.

Jurors come into the box with varied opinions of the courts. Some think that the law shouldn't go to such stringent lengths to protect the defendant's rights. They might not consider that they themselves could be sitting at that table with the entire State and all its help from law enforcement trying to put them away.

Innocent until proven guilty--that a crime has been committed becomes obvious when the State presents its evidence.

The question is: is this the person that committed it? Therefore, it is an innocent man's right, and accordingly, every man's right, and his son's and daughter's and Mom's and Dad's and cousins' right to make someone prove, not just allege, that he has broken the law.

So the jurors sit and learn at least enough to know that there is more to a trial then they suspected. They will learn some new words, hear objections granted or rejected without understanding why, and then have to sort out what they were "allowed" to hear. Most will come away confused by the complexity of the system, but they may acquire a healthier respect for the efforts to uphold the ideals of justice. Those that shun anything they don't understand will continue to belittle the system, while others with more insight may legitimately envision changes that need to be made.

But the desire to serve is probably in large part curiosity, that trait of the human condition that has brought us from the cave to the desire to know, to create and recreate, and also, in our baser moments, to destroy.

At any rate, once they are seated in that box and have a chance to be a part of the system, they all, with few exceptions, try to give the "right" answers that the lawyers want to hear so they can stay in the box. No matter what they've said in the hall ("If he wasn't guilty, the police wouldn't have arrested him."), once in the box, "yes," they can be fair and impartial; "yes," they can keep an open mind until all the evidence on both sides is presented; "yes," they can consider the defendant, who is accused of second degree murder, innocent until the State fully satisfies them through their common sense and reasoning that he is the guilty party.

All of us want to think we can be fair and open-minded, and one of the best testing grounds of who we are is in the jury box.

It took until lunch to pick twelve members and two alternates, and the first statement they heard from the State was that the District Attorney didn't know where the murder weapon was. In other words, it was "lost." *The Judge kept a straight face--this is the same D.A. who insisted this case be tried and then waited until the last three days of his two week session.* His Honor expressed confidence that the D.A.'s office could "find" the weapon by no later than 1:45 P.M. if the staff set their minds to it.

The judge then explained to the jury some of the mechanics of the trial they were to hear. They could examine the exhibits, but without commenting; the attorneys had a right to object to questions, and when he said "Sustained," they were to disregard the question, but when he said "Overruled," the answer could be given, and when something was "stricken," they were not to regard it in their deliberations--in other words, forget what they had heard. He dismissed them for lunch.

They were on their own now. Judge Thompson has told them not to discuss the case with anyone, not even each other, and not to listen to anyone else's version on the radio or television or in the papers. They cannot talk about the case in the jury room while they're waiting for legal issues to be settled--issues that will determine what evidence they can hear and what they are not entitled to hear. Each one will have to carry what he has heard in his head, battle his own battles, and form his own conclusions until everything that's going to be said has been said by both sides and the Judge says, "Okay, now you can talk about it."

Everyone was in their seats at 1:45 and the jury was brought in from the jury room.

The defendant was an attractive looking man with wavy brown hair, a mustache, and an air of confidence, whether he felt confident or not. His attorney, Mr. Burwell, was straight out of the movies, looking very distinguished with his shock of wavy gray hair that immediately bespoke a certain degree of wisdom and experience.

Mike Edwards, the Assistant District Attorney, a tall gangly young man, appeared, looking rushed and haggard. His boss had chosen the jury for him while he had given his final argument in another case in another county and had then left a replacement to wait for the jury so he could speed over here and try this one. The one thing he was sure of this afternoon was that the State of North Carolina wasn't paying him enough.

Whether or not to give an opening argument is the choice of both counsels. It seems odd when they don't because it is usually a summary of what each side intends to show by witnesses and/or physical evidence. The jury hears at least a synopsis of what the case is about. When no opening is given, the jury must patch together the people and the events they testify to like pieces of a jigsaw puzzle, without having the puzzle picture on the box to go by.

Nevertheless, both sides having waived opening arguments, the prosecutor called his first witness.

Mr. Quinn, the father of the victim, showed the jury a framed eight-by-ten color picture of his son, Gary Wayne Quinn. He testified that his son had been an automobile mechanic and a part- time private detective, had been divorced from his wife, and had an eight-year-old son, Christopher. His hobby had been restoring automobiles. He had been twenty-seven years old when he died.

Mary Sue Beam, a sweet-faced, white-haired, and impeccably dressed woman, was the next witness. She was the mother of the woman involved. She said her daughter Alecia had been living with her, but had recently bought a trailer near the house and was planning to spend her first night there on the first of August, the night of the "incident." Mike, the defendant, had helped remodel it. The two had been dating while Alecia and he were in the process of getting divorces. Mike had called Mrs. Beam at a quarter of twelve that night. Mrs. Beam was already in bed, and her son's daughter was spending the night with her. Mike had walked somewhere to use a pay phone because his truck was loaded with furniture and he didn't want to drive it, and his phone had not been connected.

"Where is Lecia? She didn't come by," he asked Mrs. Beam.

"She's not here. I thought she was with you." She added that he sounded angry and was screaming into the phone.

"Who is she seeing?"

"Nobody," Mrs. Beam replied.

"I know she has got to be seeing someone else," he said. "This is driving me crazy."

And then he added he felt like shooting his brains out.

She told him to calm down and go to bed and talk to Lecia tomorrow. She hastily put on some shoes, and taking her granddaughter with her, got into her car and drove the quarter mile to Lecia's trailer. Yes, the lights in the trailer were on; in fact, it was "pretty well lit up."

She knocked on the door and called to Lecia, and when Lecia opened it, Gary was there, and she told her Mike had called and was upset.

Q. Did you know Gary Quinn?

A. Gary had investigated Lecia's husband for the divorce.

Q. Didn't Lecia also work as a private investigator?

A. Yes. But I don't know if they had worked together.

Q. When Lecia opened the door, how did they appear?

A. Lecia was in her nurse's uniform and he was dressed.

Mrs. Beam testified that she had walked back to her car, and when she was halfway there, Mike Wallace arrived in his truck and headed for the trailer.

A. I just kept going because of my granddaughter.

Q. Where did you go?

A. Back home. But I didn't go back to bed. My granddaughter was upset, and I was trying to calm her down. Ten or fifteen minutes later, Mike knocked on my door and said, "Call an ambulance. I shot that man." My granddaughter was scared and told me not to open the door, so I didn't.

Q. Were your daughter and Mike living together or spending nights together?

A. I think so.

Q. Were they sleeping in the same bed?

A. I don't know.

Q. Weren't you involved in conversations about the remodeling of the trailer with Mike as well as Lecia?

A. Yes. In fact, I loaned him a hundred and eighty dollars, and gave him some blinds, an air conditioner, and a stove.

Q. Didn't Mike and his son help Lecia pick out the trailer?

A. Yes.

Q. So wasn't the purpose of Lecia moving out of your house and buying the trailer so that she and Mike could live there?

A. No, sir.

Q. Or if it was, you did not want that to be public knowledge. Isn't that correct, Mrs. Beam?

A. They were still married to other people. Would you?

Next on the stand was Alecia Beam Horton, early thirtyish, with large brown eyes and short, curly auburn hair, and dressed as stylishly as her mother. "Yes," she had been a private investigator on a part-time basis off and on for three years. She had employed Gary Quinn in March of 1990 to investigate the husband she was separated from. She had met with him reference the case, but not very often. Most of their conversations had been by phone. She had met him at a Shriner's Christmas party.

Q. What was your relationship with Mike?

A. I saw him some. He helped me remodel the trailer.

Q. Hadn't you had a previous relationship with him?

A. Yes. We dated in 1986, then broke it off before Christmas of 1987. This was before I married Tommy. Then in April of 1989, Tommy and I were separated, and we were divorced in 1990. I started dating Mike again in May of 1990.

Q. How often did you see him?

A. We were breaking things off at the end of July. It was my decision.

Q. Did you talk to him about ending your relationship?

A. I told him I was still in love with my husband and asked if he wasn't still in love with his wife. His reply was no, he wasn't.

Q. Did you tell him not to come around anymore?

A. Not directly.

Q. Did you have a sexual relationship with Mike?

A. Yes.

Q. And when did that end?

A. The end of July.

Q. Starting from August 1, 1990, when was the last time you saw him?

A. He walked by that day while I was taking a break outside the hospital where I work.

Q. Had you seen him the night before?

A. Yes, for about thirty minutes after I got home from work. I walked over and saw him at his house.

Q. Tell us what happened the night of August 1, 1990.

A. I got off work at 11 :30 at night. Gary met me at the hospital. We had talked on the phone that day, and he came to the hospital. I told him when I got off, and he said he'd come back. I went to a rental house lawn and he followed me there. I told him to leave his car there.

Q. Why did you tell him to do that?

A. I didn't know what Mike would do if he saw the car at the trailer.

Q. Why did you and Gary decide to go to your trailer?

A. To talk about the case. He worked first shift as a mechanic and I was on second shift at the hospital, and this was the only time we had to talk. The trailer was only a couple of minutes away. We didn't talk about the case on the way. He wasn't feeling well.

Q. What time was this?

A. About quarter to twelve. I offered him a Coke, and he told me my mother was at the door.

Q. Did you discuss the case?

A. We never got a chance. Mother came and said Mike had called her and wanted to know who I was seeing and threatened to blow his brains out and she tried to calm him down.

Q. Did your mother come in?

A. No.

Q. Did you and Gary then discuss the case?

A. No. Just a few seconds later--I had just closed and locked the door--Mike was banging on it. I told him to go away. I was tired. He busted my door in.

Q. How many doors do you have? Is there a storm door?

A. Yes.

Q. Can you see through the door?

A. Yes. It's glass, but it's also a regular door. It has a glass pane about like that (holding her fingers up to indicate around twelve inches) that you can see through. But it's not regular glass. You can't see through it well, just a fuzzy view.

Q. Then how could you tell it was Mike?

A. I knew it was. I recognized his voice.

Q. Where was Gary?

A. I told him to go to the back bedroom and stay there.

Q. Did you see him go back there?

A. Yes.

Q. As the door flew open, what did you do?

A..I started screaming and ran towards Gary.

Q. Did you see a weapon?

A. I didn't look.

Q. Did you see the expression on Mike's face?

A. I stopped half way there and looked at him. He was enraged. His eyes were wild. He didn't say anything, just started chasing me. All three of us ended up together in the hallway. Then he turned his attention from me to Gary.

This last sentence was rather oddly stilted. The jury would later learn through the SBI agent's testimony that this was exactly his wording from his report when he had questioned her. It was obvious that she had recently read the report and repeated it word for word.

Q. When did he notice Gary?

A. Immediately. He said, "You're a dead son of a bitch." He was screaming and lunged toward Gary. That's when I saw the pistol in Mike's hand.

Q. Did Gary say anything to Mike?

A. Yes. He said, "No, Bud, you're going to jail." They started fighting, and I left the trailer.

Q. Why?

A. To go to a telephone to call the police. I went to Grace's mobile home right up the hill. It's about a quarter of a mile at the most. I ran up the dirt road and pounded on her door and she let me in and I called 911 .

Q. Did you hear anything from your trailer?

A. Yes. Gunshots. It wasn't very long. I only heard two. I was screaming. I told Grace that Mike was down there. He had broke in. I was in hysterics. Grace called the dispatcher.

Q. Had you and Mike talked about getting married?

A. He discussed it--when we dated the first time.

Q. Were you interested in getting married to Mike?

A. No.

Q. Had you made any plans?

A. No.

Q. Had he asked you to let him live there?

A. Yes.

Q. What did you reply?

A. No.

Q. After you called the police, what did you do?

A. When I saw the Sheriff's car, I ran down there.

Q. Tell the jury what you saw.

A. They were bringing Gary out on a stretcher. Mike was standing there un-handcuffed making all sorts of gestures. He said, "Now go kiss the dead son of a bitch."

Q. To whom?

A. Me. Then I said--*Her voice had cracked, and the tears came. Alecia stopped long enough to fight for composure before she continued.* I said, "Do you not realize who you just shot? The investigator from South Carolina." And then I walked off.

It was the defense lawyer's turn.

Mr. Burwell, who had a record from the telephone company in his hand, questioned Alecia about the different dates and times that Gary had called her.

From July 29 to August 1st, the day of the shooting, Gary had called her more than twenty times, some of the calls lasting thirty and forty minutes.

Mr. Burwell asked a series of questions with different dates and times: "Is it true that Gary called you at such and such a date and at such and such a time?" Some she claimed she did not recall, and most she answered with a simple, "He could have." On August 1st he had called her and talked for 31 minutes at 4:51 A.M. She didn't recall that. She testified that in twenty-one calls in three days, the two of them did not have time to discuss his investigation of her husband.

Mr. Burwell also tried to present quite a different picture of the relationship between Alecia and Mike.

Q. Sometime in late May of 1990, you commenced a relationship with the defendant?

A. Yes.

Q. In fact, from late May, 1990 until July 31, you spent every night together?

A. Not every night.

Q What nights did you miss?

A. I didn't keep a calendar. I spent the night of the 31st at my mother's residence.

Q. But you spent every other night in June with Mike?

A. Not every night. I told you, I didn't keep a calendar.

Q. Well, out of sixty nights, would you say fifty-five were together?

A. I don't think so.

Q. Did you spend the night with Mike in his house where his son Daniel also lived?

A. Yes.

Q. And you slept in the same bed?

A. Yes, sir.

Q. And you had sexual intercourse?

A. Not that often.

Q. You did not have sexual intercourse every night you slept with him?

A. Absolutely not.

Q. How many nights didn't you?

A. Several.

Q. Define several.

A. Maybe half the time.

Q. And the other half, you just slept together?

A. Yes.

Q. Did you give a statement to Detective Pruitt of the SBI?

A. Yes.

Q. But you didn't tell him about your relationship?

A. I don't think the question was asked.

Q. In fact, didn't you tell him you and Mike were just friends, that you had told Mike repeatedly that you just wanted to be friends?

A. Yes.

Q. But you were, in fact, sleeping with him?

A. Sometimes.

Q. But you told Detective Pruitt that you were strictly friends?

A. I would have liked it that way.

Q. You told him that Mike wanted to be more than friends, but you didn't?

A. I was afraid of him. He busted my mouth and threw me up against a wall.

Q. When did this happen?

A. That's when I broke it off in 1987, and I could see that violence coming back.

Mr. Burwell was clearly surprised at this information, and so was the Assistant District Attorney who seized upon it when it was his turn on redirect. It turned out that her mother was present at the time. It was clear that Mrs. Beam would be recalled to the stand. The only other new information Mr. Burwell brought out was that Mike's son Daniel had been with Alecia when she purchased her trailer and had picked out what would be his room when they moved in.

Alecia's neighbor Grace Stafford, who took the stand next, rented her trailer from Mrs. Beam. She testified that she had gone to bed around 11:30 that night and that Alecia had awakened her by banging on the door and explaining that Mike and Gary were fighting, they had a gun, and someone was going to get hurt. She described Alecia's demeanor as "pure terror."

Alecia, now seated in the courtroom, started crying and left.

Grace continued:

A. I heard the gunshots one to two minutes after she got there.

Q. How long was there between shots?

A. At the most, fifteen seconds.

Q. Could it have been shorter?

A. Yes. I was on hold with the dispatcher when I heard the shots. Lecia was so hysterical that I tried to dismiss it as some other noise. I accompanied her down to her trailer.

Several police cars and the ambulance were there. Mike was walking around in the front yard.

Q. Did you hear him say anything to her?

A. Yes. He said, "I don't give a damn who the son-of-a-bitch was. That's what you get for running around on me."

Q. Did she make any response?

A. No. She just started walking off with one of the deputies. She wanted to know if Gary was still alive.

Q. Did you hear Mike say anything else to her?

A. Yes. "You will be next."

Q. What was his tone when he said that?

A. He wasn't joking.

Mr. Burwell, on cross-examination, asked Grace what Mike's physical appearance was when she saw him that night.

A. His eyes were swollen.

Q. Swollen? One was more like almost gouged out, wasn't it?

A. No.

Q. Did he have a gash in his head or blood in his hair?

A. I don't know. I was not paying that much attention to his physical appearance. It was dark.

Officer Summers, currently with the Police Department, and formerly with the Sheriff's Department, was the first officer on the scene and accompanied by Deputy Ezelle. When he arrived, the trailer door was open and the lights were on.

"Yes," he knew Mike and had worked with him when Mike was a Sheriff's deputy.

"I recognized him, and I didn't know at the time who lived there. He handed me the gun and said, 'This is what I shot him with.' He was holding it like he was trying to preserve it without messing up fingerprints. I observed the wounds about his person and asked where the man was and he told me. I found a white male face-up on the floor in the back bedroom. He had a faint pulse and was unable to say anything. There was a large blood stain on his shirt. The furniture was in disarray, and I noticed a briefcase laying in the room."

And then the jury saw the gun. The officer was showing how the defendant had held it. It was black and cold and mean looking. They talked about it clinically, identifying make and model. His testimony droned on and some of the jurors looked sleepy. The courtroom was warm.

Cross-examination did not last long, but Mr. Burwell did establish that Mike had told Officer Summers that it was not his gun.

Q. Was there evidence of a struggle?

A. Yes. It looked like there had been a fight. There were a lot of blood stains, mostly on the carpet.

Q. Did Mike Wallace look like he had been pistol whipped?

A. I don't know about that, but he had a bad looking eye. It looked like his head needed four or five stitches. He was very excited and emotional.

The second officer corroborated the story of the first, as did the testimony of the rescue personnel.

The forensic witness, Detective Campbell, introduced a new twist. He explained how they could take handwipings while looking for components of gunshot residue that would show up upon chemical analysis. This was done by using previously prepared Q-tips, moistening them with nitric acid and then swabbing the hands of the parties. The Q-tips were then sealed in plastic bags until they were analyzed. The hand-wipings from the deceased, Gary Quinn, showed that he had handled the gun. The hand-wipings from the defendant, Mike Wallace, however, were inconclusive.

By this time, we knew Gary Quinn was dead. We knew that Mike Wallace had pulled the trigger. We knew the gun wasn't his, though, and we knew there had been a struggle. That was being driven home by the defense every time they got a chance. But what had to be bothering the jury was that the defendant had not even known whom he shot. It sounded like a jealous rage. Shoot now, questions later. This was Alecia's trailer. There was a man there. It didn't matter if he was her long lost brother or an encyclopedia salesman or a messenger telling her she had won the sweepstakes. This is what the prosecution wanted them to think. But that was too simple. Here we had a former Sheriff's deputy, and if he had gone there really suspecting that she was seeing someone else, as Mrs. Beam testified, and ready to "blow his head off," why had he not brought a weapon with him?

I needed a break. I headed to the only refuge I had found, the small law library behind the judge's chamber. The courthouse in Rutherfordton was old and massive with a long expanse of stairs to huge marble pillars. Inside, it was high-ceilinged and marble floored, but the rooms were small by today's standards. It housed the usual county offices and the District Attorney's office. The judge's chamber was barely large enough for the oversized vintage desk and two wooden chairs, and only one person could move about at a time. The law library was not much bigger, but it at least had a window and didn't feel like a closet. I walked to the window for some fresh air. When I turned around, Mrs. Beam, Alecia's mother, had come in and sat at the small conference table. She began making small talk, but I had no way of knowing what would come next. There was no way she could have known who I was. I had sat in the audience and maintained a low profile.

"I'm sorry, Mrs. Beam, but I don't know whether we should be talking. I'm Judge Thompson's wife."

"Oh. Well, I guess it would be all right if we just didn't discuss the case, wouldn't it?"

"Yes. I just didn't want you to say anything about it before I told you who I was."

"Well, we'll just talk about the weather. Isn't it beautiful outside?"

She was right. There was nothing inappropriate about our talking about other things. I just did not want her to tell me anything that conflicted with the testimony that I would feel compelled to tell Jack, would struggle with, decide not to tell him until the verdict was in, and would therefore be generally miserable about. She was also right about the weather. It was unseasonably warm for March in the mountains, and we were having a preview of Spring. In fact, if I hadn't been shopping the first week I was here, I would have had nothing but wool clothes. Good old North Carolina. If you don't like the weather, hang around a few days. It had been freezing last week, we had snow on the weekend, and now it was in the upper seventies.

When we had exhausted the subject of the weather, she told me about her past.

"I'll be so glad when this is over. It's been a hard two years. My husband died last year, and now this. I worked all my life at the Tanner industry, and then I had to retire to take care of him. He was sick for a year, and then he was dead." Her eyes welled with tears, and she held out her left hand.

"Look. I'm still wearing my wedding rings. I can't take them off. It still seems like he's just away somewhere and he'll come back. He was in and out of the hospital so much, that it still seems normal for him to be gone for a little while."

At that point, a younger woman whom I had seen sitting with the Beam family entered the room crying.

"Is it all right if I sit in here?" she asked.

"Of course," I said, "and I'm going back to the courtroom. Would you like me to close the door?"

Mrs. Beam nodded.

Court broke for lunch.

Over lunch, I asked Jack about Mrs. Beam's testimony regarding the telephone conversation she had with Mike. She said Mike had told her he was sure Alecia was dating someone else and he "wanted to blow his brains out," meaning Gary's brains. Yet, in later testimony, something indicated that he could have meant his own brains. Jack had heard it that way, that she meant Mike wanted to blow out his own brains.

The lawyers, so familiar with their own case and what they understand, forget the jury is hearing it for the first time. We decided this was a point we would have to listen for in other testimony or in closing arguments. I wondered which way the jury had interpreted Mike's statement.

Jack wanted to get back to his cubicle of a chamber and work on the charge that he would give the jury when both sides rested their case. I decided to walk around and check out the main street of old-fashioned, picturesque Rutherfordton.

Window shopping didn't take long, because there weren't that many windows, but the few shops that fronted the street had been well maintained, and the seasoned buildings and large trees created a restful and homey atmosphere.

I browsed a while in a sizable antique store, finding wonderful ancient chests and trunks that looked like treasure chests out of sailing ships, silver, jewelry, curious small appliances, quilts, and figurines of all descriptions. Most of the items were truly old, and the prices seemed quite reasonable. They had several things I would have loved to buy, including a mahogany music cabinet that would have made a great bar and a brass backed, three-way, stand-up dresser mirror that I would have absolutely no place to put.

My only purchase was what looked to be a first edition of Charles Dickens' <u>Child's History of England</u> that had been given to "Gerald H. Winchester, Xmas 1900, From Mabel." On the inside front cover, the original price of $.23 had been stamped in purple ink. I paid $10.00.

Chapter 1, 'Ancient England and the Romans' begins:

> "If you look at a Map of the World, you will see, in the left-hand upper corner of the Eastern Hemisphere, two Islands lying in the sea. They are England and Scotland, and Ireland. England and Scotland form the greater part of these islands. Ireland is the next in size. The little neighboring islands, which are so small upon the Map as to be mere dots, are chiefly little bits of Scotland--broken off, I dare say, in the course of a great length of time, by the power of the restless water. In the old days, a long, long while ago, before Our Saviour was born on earth and lay asleep in a manger, these Islands were in the same place, and the stormy sea roared around them, just as it roars now. But the sea was not alive, then, with great ships and brave sailors, sailing to and from all parts of the world. It was very lonely. The Islands lay solitary, in the great expanse of water. The foaming waves dashed against their cliffs, and the bleak winds blew over their forests; but the winds and waves brought no adventurers to land upon the Islands, and the savage Islanders knew nothing of the rest of the world, and the rest of the world knew nothing of them."

History was never my best subject. Math makes sense. History is history. Logic is not required. I thought, "Here is a history book that I might actually enjoy because it is so beautifully written, and most importantly, it is on a child's level, and maybe I can understand it." There was no publishing date, and flipping to the last page, I read the last few lines:

> "Queen Victoria...came to the throne on the twentieth of June, one thousand eight hundred and thirty seven...She is very good, and much beloved. So I end, like the crier, with
>
> "GOD SAVE THE QUEEN!"

Carrying my new treasure, I stepped into a drugstore to buy a news-paper, mainly to check the coverage on the case, and found myself carried back in time. In the back was a genuine soda fountain with stools bolted to the floor. The highly polished floor was made up of large blue tiles with a pat-tern that set the counter apart. Behind the counter was an older woman who had gray hair fashioned in a bun on top of her head, and she was talking, or rather, listening to a young girl at the counter expounding on the wonderful deviled eggs and how she could never have gotten through the day without one. I ordered a fountain Coke and sat on a stool at the counter to read the trial article just so I could eavesdrop.

The newspaper reporter had quoted Mrs. Beam on Mike "blowing out his brains," and had understood it the same way I had. This didn't mean I was right; the issue was simply confused.

The girl at the counter left, and I tried to start a conversation with the woman. But she was either shy or wary of newcomers, so I exchanged pleasantries and left to walk to the courthouse. Two doors down was another drugstore, a large chain franchise, looking like any other drugstore anywhere, and I hoped the family-owned one could stay in competition.

Lingering at the drugstore had caused me to miss the beginning of the defense evidence.

The defendant, Mike Wallace, was on the stand, and he told a differ-ent tale.

"Yes," he and Alecia had slept together every night until the night of the shooting, and "yes," they had sexual relations most of those nights. On the day in question, he had talked to her, and she told him she was coming to his place right after work. He had cooked supper for her, and when she didn't come, he wondered what was wrong and had called her mother. Her mother had asked, "Isn't she with you?," and that's when he became worried.

"She didn't always come straight home, but even if she had stopped at the convenience store, she would have been there by now. I rode out to the trailer and saw lights on, and then one light went out. Just her car was there. I banged on the door, and it suddenly opened. This man was standing there with a gun and hit me in the head. I never saw Alecia, but heard her voice once during the scuffle. "

He described the struggle in great detail, saying he had escaped from the man one time and lunged for the back door, but Gary had caught him and dragged him back.

In the bedroom, Mike's head got stuck in the bottom part of the nightstand, and Gary had plunged the gun into his eye. While they were struggling, he had heard the gun go off twice, but his opponent was still fighting. Gary suddenly went limp on top of him. Mike rolled him off and ran for the front door. The pathologist would later confirm that Gary could have kept fighting for a while, the wounds being where they were.

His story was quite a departure from Alecia's, and credible to a point. The jury was listening intently to his testimony and they were with him, believing him, until the part about the door. They had seen the pictures of the door, and it had been practically destroyed. Most of them also knew that trailer doors don't just open, especially new trailer doors.

You could see the jurors' faces change at that point. His voice was strong now, and the defendant was feeling brave. He further testified that he did not even know the victim had been actually shot until the emergency team got there.

This statement was in direct conflict with evidence presented by too many other witnesses. An officer had said Mike had handed him the gun, demonstrating that he handled it like a law enforcement officer, and quoted, "Here's the gun I shot him with."

Mrs. Beam had testified that Mike had come to her house and told her "I shot that man."

One witness could have remembered it incorrectly, but two independent ones made Mike's version questionable. He also denied making the statements on the phone to Mrs. Beam, the assault on Alecia in front of her mother during their previous relationship and the statements he had made at the scene of being glad he "shot the son-of-a-bitch," although several witnesses had testified to hearing him. This denial was the most critical.

It's true Alecia's testimony had been flawed. The jury knew she was hedging about her relationship with Mike, but the neighbor's testimony and the officers' testimonies corroborated most of the rest of her story. The whole truth was not what the jury was getting, and they knew it.

The discrepancies in Mike's account were brought out on cross- examination. He had done so well at first while his lawyer had the floor that he had become too self-assured and had denied too many critical points that had been testified to by too many people.

But the D. A. wasn't finished with him yet. He saw that Mike was slipping up and kept after him about the fatal shots.

When were the shots fired? He didn't know. What room? He didn't know. Did he hear the shots?

"Yes. The first two shots I fired--I mean--the first two shots that were fired --"

It was too late. A hush had fallen on the courtroom. Even the judge was leaning forward.

The D. A. would say in his final argument, "and the truth came out and from his own lips."

In a surprise move, Mr. Burwell, the defense lawyer, called Alecia back to the stand. He had already questioned her about her relationship with Gary, and she had insisted that theirs was purely a business relationship, despite the fact that she had lengthy phone conversations with him in the middle of the night and had taken him to her trailer to talk about the case.

> Q. Ms. Horton, did you turn out any lights in the trailer after you and Gary got there?"
>
> A. I believe I turned off the living room light.

Q. And why did you do that?

A. I really don't remember.

Q. Ms. Horton, isn't it true that you told someone in the District Attorney's office that the reason Mike was so mad was that he may have seen you kissing Gary through the glass in the trailer door?"

A. Yes.

Q. No further questions.

The jury was clearly disgusted. They were supposed to find the truth, and it was obvious that in order to do this, they would have to sift through everyone's lies. They were already upset with the defendant, and now they felt the same disgust with the main witness against him. They knew Alecia had hedged on how many times they had slept together. Maybe that could have been excused. But the point was that now all her testimony was tainted. The defense attorney had now proved Alecia was lying, but in the process, he could have hurt the defendant more.

The prosecution had tried to paint a picture of an enraged, jealous man, and this testimony would strengthen that. When all was said and done, Mike's fatal mistake, whether he had seen them kissing or not, had been to break in the trailer door. This act alone showed his mood and capacity for violence. The defense put on a few more witnesses to confirm what Mike had portrayed as a firm relationship with Alecia.

The defense rested.

The judge's charge to the jury is confusing at best. He explains the law and the elements of all the offenses they will have to consider: second degree murder, voluntary manslaughter, involuntary manslaughter, and not guilty. The line between voluntary and involuntary manslaughter is a thin one, and one that lawyers struggle with. To ask a jury to do this in strict accordance with the way the law is written after hearing it only one time is usually more than they can handle. Jurors understand it as best they can, and then base their decision on instinct and common sense, supposedly.

We all hung around for approximately three hours to hear the verdict. This wait is the hardest part of a trial for the lawyers on both sides; they ponder what they should have done or not done, wish they had not asked that one question that they didn't know the answer to, or think of another question they wish they had asked.

The jury finally knocked on the jury room door, and everyone assembled.

"Mr. Foreman of the jury, will you please stand and give us your name," his Honor started. After the foreman complied, the Judge continued:

"Please answer the following questions yes or no. Have you reached a verdict?"

"Yes, your Honor."

"Is the jury unanimous in their verdict?"

"Yes, your Honor."

"Would you please pass the verdict sheet to the bailiff."

There is a pause in time as the bailiff takes the sheet and hands it to the Judge. What looks like an ordinary piece of paper contains the fate of the defendant decided by twelve people he has never met and will most likely never see again.

The Judge read it in silence with no change of expression and passed it to the Clerk to be read aloud.

"You the jury find J. Michael Wallace guilty of Voluntary Manslaughter."

The defendant sat stolidly still.

His attorney asked that the jury be polled. This is a slow process. One by one, each juror stands and is asked in three different ways if this was his individual verdict. All answered that it was. After all had their turn, they were asked to stand and answer the same questions as a group. Again, they agreed that this was their verdict.

His Honor thanked the jury for their time and effort and excused them from their duty. He told them they could stay in the courtroom for sentencing if they wished, and some chose to do so, sitting quietly in the back.

The presumptive sentence for voluntary manslaughter is six years in North Carolina, but the Judge has the discretion to add or subtract due to aggravating or mitigating circumstances. The prosecution presented no aggravating factors, but he found the mitigating factor of no prior criminal record to be worth one year off the sentence.

Before he passed sentence, the Judge warned that there were to be no outcries or emotional displays in the courtroom. What they didn't know was that he had requested extra bailiffs to be present in the courtroom, just in case.

Michael Wallace was then sentenced to five years in prison.

The chill always comes when the sentencing by the Judge concludes with the final reality, "He is in custody."

The defense attorney asked that Mike Wallace be allowed a moment to spend with his family, all of whom had been present in the courtroom from the beginning of the case. When permission was granted, he turned to greet them, and his face was a mask of determination and control. But as arms reached out for him, his mask began to break. The deputy decided these farewells could better take place in the hall, and he took Mike's arm to lead him there, his family following.

Mr. Burwell walked halfway to the Judge's bench to ask if something could be done concerning his client's imprisonment conditions. He was worried that as a former law enforcement officer, Mike would be subject to abuse by other inmates. What everyone knew, and no one was saying, was that if he were thrown directly into the prison system, after helping to convict some of the prisoners, he might be in danger. The Judge turned to the Clerk and instructed her to make it a part of the record that it was the recommendation of the Court that the defendant be segregated from the rest of the prison population, and turning to Mr. Burwell, said, "That's all I can do."

The bailiff accompanied us down the darkened halls and stairs of the courthouse and out to the parking lot. We were looking forward to a restaurant we had discovered on top of a mountain overlooking Lake Lure. The defendant's family was standing across the street watching us, probably not knowing how they felt just yet. Those emotions would change with the passage of time and could range from being grateful that he hadn't received twenty years for second degree murder to wondering why he wasn't put on probation. In any case, they would worry about him. I was on my way to a glass of wine and a good dinner. I doubted if any of them were hungry. We would drive home in the morning. Jack's time in Rutherfordton was over.

The next morning, we stopped to turn in some keys to the Clerk. Entering the courthouse, we noticed a woman who had been one of the jurors. She was talking animatedly with her female companion. It was obvious that she had been crying and she appeared agitated. Several people told Jack that Mr. Burwell had been trying to get in touch with him.

We found Mr. Burwell upstairs, an open statute book on his lap. He told us that one of the jurors, a woman, had telephoned him last night and wanted to see him this morning. She told him that she was having a difficult time with the verdict. She said that one of the male jurors had bullied her into voting the way she had. The man had presented his own theory and convinced the others that there had to have been a second gun, and it had to have been Mike's.

"Second gun?" I heard myself asking. "What second gun?"

"Who knows?" Mr. Burwell shrugged.

We were astonished. However, knowing the jury had been fully instructed, had deliberated without interference, and had been polled individually regarding their verdict, there was nothing to be done. Mr. Burwell had reached the same conclusion. Try as he might, he could find nothing in the North Carolina General Statutes that applied to warranting a new trial in this circumstance. The verdict must stand.

We said our goodbyes and left.

"Where in the world did that come from?" I asked Jack.

"You've got me," he replied. "There was no evidence at all to support it. They pulled that one out of thin air."

There was nothing more to say. We were trying to comprehend how a juror could take it upon himself to make up facts that didn't exist and then convince eleven others.

As we found our way to the Interstate, I was thinking of a series of novels I had read a long time ago. Throughout his political sagas, Allen Drury consistently employs the same theme: America usually winds up doing the right thing, but for the wrong reasons.

Whether he is wrong or right, I often feel the same way about juries. Although I believe in the theory of the jury system, the reality can be frightening.

Given a choice, if I were guilty as charged, I would want a jury. Whereas a judge would weigh only the evidence, anything can happen in a jury room.

If I were innocent or a constitutional question was involved, I would opt for a judge any day.

The verdict in this case, however, was probably as it should have been, but based on the evidence, not on wild conjecture.

Lost in our own thoughts, we rode in silence on this clear Spring day, drinking in the hills and valleys lined up on the horizon, so unlike the flatlands we call home.

CHAPTER TWO

───────

April: State v. Medlin

Jack's next assignment was a three-month-stint in Raleigh, the State Capitol. Having one base of operation would be easier to handle for both of us.

Besides housing the Legislature, other appropriate government buildings, and North Carolina State University, Raleigh makes up one third of what is known as the Research Triangle. Another side of the triangle is the city of Durham, home of the Bulls, Duke University, and Duke Medical Center. The third side is Chapel Hill, home of the University of North Carolina, "blue heaven" to its alumni, and known to the rest of the nation as the Country Club of the South. Located in the middle of the triangle is the Research Park, corporate headquarters for many household-name conglomerates. Of course, the Park attracts people from all parts of the United States, and consequently, lures a large population of young professionals, our oldest son Allen included.

As you can gather, this area is pretty much "uptown," or at least as uptown as it gets in these parts, and we are proud of it. The new people from "the North," however, are still adjusting to our ways. At one time, they looked down their noses at us Southerners, and despite the increased migration, some still do. It's not as bad as it used to be, though. When my parents were married, my father's family in Boston were most surprised when they discovered we wore shoes down here. Let me try to clear the air. Historically a genteel people, we welcome strangers, but we do have a few conditions. One is that we don't want a dense population, massive industrialization and the pollution that goes with it. Secondly, we will continue to take time for the amenities, to enjoy life and each other. And finally, our most common complaint is summed up by a popular bumper sticker: "We don't care how they do it in Buffalo." As for the shoes, we don't go barefoot until the first of May or wear white until after Easter.

Raleigh is only sixty miles away, and Jack could commute each day, or so we thought at first. During his assignment, two capital cases would fall to his Court, and by mid-week of the first week, he realized he did not need the two hours and twenty minutes commute on Interstate 40 added to his day.

I had stayed home for two weeks to catch up on household maintenance and wait for something other than guilty pleas, and *in the third week that happened, a first degree murder case.*

Thursday morning we left for Raleigh together.

One topic of conversation as we drove up there was my new "image." As His Honor's wife, immediately after introduction to any member of the courthouse staff, man or woman, I am always told where the nearest stores are to be found. Presumably, it is my job to shop while my husband attends to important matters. In all fairness, I suppose this is a natural attitude, especially in the South, and the fact that I have time to accompany him would seem to indicate that I have nothing else to do. That doesn't make it any less annoying.

During the drive from Fayetteville to Raleigh, Jack told me about the lawyers and clerks he had already met and how much he liked them. His clerk's name was Maggie, and he thought she was special.

"She's one of those people that just does whatever has to be done, like the old-fashioned secretary that really takes care of you," he expounded.

That's, great," I said, "but if she says one word about shopping......

He laughed. He knew that since my "early retirement," I still felt like a lone swallow at Capistrano in the dead of winter who had missed the signal to fly South.

We entered the courthouse, a virtual maze, and found our way to his office.

"Maggie, let me introduce you to my wife," Jack said.

"How are you?" Maggie said enthusiastically. "It's so nice that you come to be with him. And we're in a great location. Belks is right across the street, and if it were not for their basement, I'd go naked."

Jack smiled and hurriedly walked on into his chambers and left me to fumble, Maggie smiling broadly.

"Well, I'm not much of a shopper," I said, "but I may just have to check that out." There was no use venting my hang-ups on Maggie, and as it turned out, she knew me better than I did. Jack's morning was spent in the final throes of jury selection, and I decided that Belks might not be so bad. Having been on campus for a while, I did need some new grown-up clothes. I came back with two suits for court-wear and a red silk dinner dress and ingratiated myself to all by behaving appropriately. Now, I could sit in the courtroom.

First Degree Murder is the only capital offense in North Carolina and the only occasion in which a jury, rather than a judge, also determines the sentence, either life in prison or death by gas chamber or lethal injection--not much of a choice when you come down to it.

Selecting a jury in a capital case is a slow, laborious process. The several different ways to proceed are all tedious. Even though Mr. Medlin had pled guilty to first degree murder, a full trial had to be presented. The jury, out of necessity, had to hear all the evidence in order to decide the sentence. In addition to the evidence, per se, the sentencing phase would also include factors that could not have been presented in the guilt/innocence phase. The State could present aggravating circumstances, such as prior criminal record or the fact that the murder was committed for pecuniary gain, which would make this murder case more deserving of the death penalty than other murder cases.

The defense, in turn, could present mitigating circumstances, which could be anything at all they thought spoke well of their client or provided some insight to his behavior, thus showing that he exhibited some redeeming value to society and should receive life imprisonment instead.

Three groups of twelve people were selected and told to return at staggered times during the week. Then each member of a twelve-person panel was brought into the courtroom one by one and questioned. For many of them, it was their first time in a courtroom, and here they were alone in the jury box with no one in the room except the prosecutor, defense attorneys, defendant, clerk, His Honor, and a court reporter taking down every word he or she said.

The Judge informed each that this was a sentencing hearing for murder. The defendant had also pled guilty to armed robbery, but this would not be their concern. That sentence was up to him.

For the attorneys, the most pertinent question was how each person felt about the death penalty. Anyone who felt strongly against the death penalty in any instance, regardless of what the evidence showed, was obviously not desirable to the State.

Karen, a fresh-faced, all-American, barely-out-of-college attractive blonde, who looked more as if she wanted to be out playing tennis, sat in the jury box alone. She lived at home with her parents; her father was a retired pastor, her mother, a caterer. She stated that "yes," she did believe in the death penalty in certain cases, but did not know what those circumstances would be--right on target--she could find for the State if she thought this case warranted it or for the defense if it didn't.

"But" she also added, "I feel a little bit uncomfortable with it. I don't feel comfortable being someone who judges whether somebody lives or dies."

It is not uncommon for people to feel this way. But the alternative of having one person decide, perhaps a judge, instead of twelve people, would be far worse. Drawing from my Ayn Rand phase twenty years ago, I remembered a quote from Atlas Shrugged *that I still believe today: "Your mind is the only judge of truth, reality the final court of appeals." The first part, before the comma, is what I consider to be a good definition of "beyond a reasonable doubt." The second part, after the comma-well, reality can be another story. At any rate, reason is all any of us have to work with, and that includes jurors. It's easy to believe in the death penalty if you're not the one to decide, but at Karen's age, I might have had the same misgivings.*

Karen's mind-set could give the State a problem, but by itself is not enough to ask the judge to excuse for cause, so the lawyer will try to "rehabilitate" the juror by a series of other questions. If the juror doesn't make a major blunder, but the State still doesn't want her and cause has not been shown to the Judge, the prosecutor can remove her by using one of his limited preemptory challenges.

The State wants to avoid this, of course, because the next person called may be even less desirable for this case, and at some point, his challenges will run out. The prosecutor continues:

> Q. Feeling uncomfortable is not unusual. Is there anything about you that would prevent you from hearing the evidence and following the judge's instructions?
>
> A. No.
>
> Q. Your decision would not be based on feelings, but on facts and on the law. Could you do that?
>
> A. Yes.

Q. If the aggravating circumstances outweigh the mitigating circumstances, it would be your duty under the law to sentence Mr. Medlin to death. Could you do that?

A. Yes.

All eyes in the courtroom turn and wait for this answer. It is a heavy burden for any citizen to bear. A juror had no idea when called for jury duty what type of case he or she might hear, and a capital case is the worst possible scenario.

Q. You understand this is not an academic question, but an actual decision of whether the man sitting across from you at that table lives or dies?

A. Yes.

Q. Is there any reason, known only to yourself, that you could not serve?

A. No.

She had given all the right answers, but the wavering of the first reply had bothered the prosecutor, and Karen was excused.

Mr. Garrett, I shall call him, was good looking, gray-haired, worked with computers and had two grown children. His son was a police officer, a fact not usually desirable to the defense, assuming that he might favor law enforcement and therefore, the State. He had no problem with the death penalty:

"There are certain crimes or certain acts committed that call for it when a person has no remorse and would not benefit from the prison system."

Q. How do you feel about life imprisonment?

A. Personally, I would find it harder, but a person could still contribute something to society.

Q. In other words, you believe both sentences are appropriate, depending on the facts?

A. Yes.

Q. However, if you are told that remorse is not something a jury should consider--the judge will instruct you on what you can consider--could you decide solely on what the law says?

A. Yes.

Mr. Garrett seemed intelligent and open-minded, and he was also accepted by the defense, despite the fact that his son was in law enforcement.

The last of the jurors and alternate jurors were chosen, and the Court took a break.

Evelyn Hill, the Assistant District Attorney assigned to try the case, came into Jack's outer office and asked if she could see "Simon."

"Yes. Judge Legree is free," laughed Maggie, and introduced me to Evelyn, who told me my husband had been a task-master all week, starting court early, ending late, and taking a shortened lunch break so that it wouldn't take longer than a week to pick a jury.

"But it worked," she admitted. "I think picking a jury in a capital case in four days is a new record for me."

Evelyn was known to be one of the best prosecutors in North Carolina, I had been told, and I was soon to be impressed from my own observation.

Representing the State, Ms. Hill gave her opening statement, telling the jury why this man was a candidate for the gas chamber. She informed them the evidence would show that Jeff Medlin, with premeditation and deliberation, planned to rob the place of his former employment, and had told his friend that he would have to kill whoever happened to be working that shift so they couldn't identify him. She then described how he had carried on a conversation with Darla Cline, waited until she turned her back to start mopping the floor, and had brutally killed her while she begged for her life. She had been repeatedly hit with brass knuckles, and when that didn't work, he had slashed her sixteen times with his pocketknife.

Looking at the boyish, slightly built nineteen-year-old defendant, sitting so casually at the defense table, it was hard to believe she was talking about him. He ought to have horns or something to mark what surely didn't show on the outside. He looked perfectly normal, like one of our children's friends that come in and out my door at will.

The defense gave a brief opening statement, saying that Jeff had admitted his guilt to this terrible crime. He is pleading only that he be allowed to live and be productive, even though that would be limited to the inside of a prison.

Ms. Hill called her first witness.

Janet Davis was a Quick Mart employee in Wilson County. One day when she was on the telephone, "a white man came in and put a gun in my face, and said, 'Put the phone down.'" Cocking the gun, he said, "Give me your money."

The gun was a .45, the amount was one hundred dollars, and the man was Jeff Medlin. Two more witnesses established the following: another customer had come in, and upon hearing what had happened, followed Mr. Medlin's car and obtained the license number, which was broadcast by the police, and he had been quickly picked up. Instead of being sentenced for armed robbery, however, Jeff Medlin had pled guilty to common law robbery, received a lighter sentence, and had served his time.

Some of the jurors looked confused--what did this have to do with the murder of Darla Cline? But Ms. Hill was making a point she had told them about in her opening argument: Prior conviction: aggravating circumstance. The jury would hear it often enough to become familiar with the terms and the significance.

Jeff Medlin had not learned his lesson. Shortly after being released from prison, he killed Darla Cline. If he had been convicted of Armed Robbery in the previous case instead of pleading to Common Law Robbery, he would not have been free to do so.

Plea bargains have become a necessary part of our system. Because the courts are so backlogged, it is virtually impossible to try every case. Although we don't know all the factors that resulted in this former plea, it had turned out to be a fatal decision for Darla Cline.

Betty Hawley took the stand. She was a waitress and cook at Johnson's Restaurant, also known as "the Forks," an open- twenty-four-hours establishment located in the small community of Zebulon, where the homicide had taken place. On the day of the murder on September 10, 1990, she had worked the 2:00 P.M. to 10:00 P. M. shift and left around 10:30. She checked out the cash register and counted the money with Darla, who was relieving her. This was not to have been Darla's normal shift--someone else was supposed to work that night--and she had been a last minute substitute.

She put the money in an envelope and stored it in the office. There was also a metal box under the cash register containing petty cash. A separate plastic box contained money "for cigarettes." Fifty dollars was left in the cash register to start Darla's shift.

When Betty left, two customers were drinking coffee, and Darla was working by herself.

"Yes," she knew that Darla and her husband lived above the restaurant, and the entrance to their apartment was by steps on the outside of the building.

The defense, on cross-examination, focused on the metal petty cash box and how much money was kept in it. They tried to show that most of that money was from poker machines, and that on that night it contained about a thousand dollars.

From now on, it would be dubbed the "poker box."

Upon taking the stand Mr. Louis Bagwell told Ms. Hill "Everybody calls me Pete." Pete had a newspaper route for The News and Observer, affectionately and unaffectionately, depending on your politics, dubbed the N & O across the State. His first stop each morning was at Johnson's Restaurant at 4:10 A.M. He had talked to Darla that morning, and she had given him a Mountain Dew in exchange for a paper.

"She had the mop and the bucket out and was gettin' ready to mop the floor, but I don't believe she'd done any mopping yet." He left five minutes later by the unlocked front door. "A car was pulled around to the back, but I didn't pay no mind to that."

Thomas Hobbs was next up on the witness stand. He and his son Ronald were out early that morning on business and saw a sign indicating a Truck Stop. At 4:30 A. M., they had pulled off the freeway to get some coffee. Johnson's was well-lit, but no one was there. He and his son took turns going to the Men's Room. Mr. Hobbs sat down at a booth. No one came, so, seeing a coffee pot, he poured two cups himself. Still no one came.

"I thought they might be angry, seeing as I had helped myself, so I stuck my head in the kitchen door and saw a leg and blood on the floor. I didn't go any further. I went to the restroom and got my son. My son saw an outside phone booth through the front window and called 911 from there and told them he thought there had been foul play. They told us not to go back in, so we stayed in our truck and waited."

Ola Keohene, a waitress and cook at Johnson's, testified next that she had worked at the restaurant four years and knew Jeff. He had worked there in the past.

The defense asked Ola if "Mrs. Johnson ever asked you not to make the pay-offs on the poker machines in the public part of the restaurant?"

"No."

She seemed puzzled, as if it had never occurred to her that there had been anything wrong. The defense was trying to establish that besides the poker machines, there were side bets, and that for "forty credits" people were paid $10.00. (Gambling is illegal in North Carolina, but common, nonetheless.)

Rosa Pulley, a Deputy Sheriff and the first officer on the scene, took the stand. She testified that two men in a truck told her what they had found. She went into the kitchen and found a body lying in an extreme amount of blood. The woman's eyes were open and she was obviously dead. She called in, requesting a supervisor, an investigator, and the rescue squad, the latter arriving at 5:05. She advised them that the woman was dead and not to disturb anything in the kitchen.

Darla's husband, Terry Cline, came downstairs from his apartment above Johnson's at 5:25 and identified himself. He said he had been upstairs since ten o'clock the previous night. He was put into a police car until he could be questioned.

Garland Tant, rescue squad volunteer, described what he found when he arrived. He examined the body: the pupils were set and she was a grayish-ash color and not breathing. He was not allowed to officially declare anyone dead, but there was no sign of life, so he did not disturb anything.

I had not realized until Ms. Hill called him to the stand that the man sitting to my left was the husband of Darla Cline. He was slightly built, and his shoulders slumped. He looked as if he hadn't had a good night's sleep in a long time, and had listened to the previous testimony as if in a trance. The courtroom was painfully silent.

Terry Cline testified that on the evening of September tenth, he had arrived home around seven o'clock, and Darla was there. She went to work at ten o'clock, but her usual schedule was three to eleven. It was hot outside, and he was running the air conditioner, a noisy window unit that must have prevented him from hearing the death screams of his wife. He woke up at 5:00 M. and got dressed for work.

Going down the stairs to the restaurant, he found it swarming with police.

When he told them who he was, he was held until they could question him. He sat in a police car about thirty minutes and stood outside it for an hour to an hour-and-a-half before they had time for him. He gave a detective permission to search his apartment, but still no one would tell him what had happened or why they were there.

"It wasn't until lunchtime that someone finally told me what was going on. He told me there had been a robbery--"

He hesitated, tried to compose himself, but broke down as he finished.

"--and then they told me she had been murdered."

He tearfully identified Darla in a photograph of them together that had been taken earlier that summer. The photograph was admitted into evidence, and now the jury knew what Darla looked like alive. She appeared to be in her early thirties, slightly built and slim, with long brown hair that touched past her shoulders. Her eyes were laughing. They would soon see her photographed image dead often enough.

Throughout Terry Cline's testimony, Jeff had hung his head, finding it painful to face Darla's husband. Jack Hall, one of his attorneys, had put his hand on Jeff's arm several times, a small gesture, one of support, and it was good to show the jury that his client was someone he could touch.

Jean Johnson, the manager of the out-of-state owned restaurant, testified next. Darla was working Shirley's shift. The amount of money in the poker box in the kitchen was usually around $800.00 on a weekday and $1500.00 on a weekend. She also knew the defendant. He had been coming into Johnson's since he was thirteen years old. While he was still in high school, he had cooked and waited on tables for a year or more.

"Yes," he knew where the money was kept. All the employees did. She had last seen him three or four weeks before when he had filled in as a short order cook for a month.

"But he couldn't be around any of the money. I told him so."

Q. Why was that?

A. Because of the robbery he had done.

Q. Was he working for you at the time Darla was killed?

A. No.

Q. Why not?

A. He hadn't shown up. He came in, wanted his pay ahead of time, and didn't never show up again.

Q. Was it your policy to pay employees in advance?

A. No. But whatever was the reason, I just went ahead and did it.

Jeff, and the other employees were allowed to charge their meals. When he did not show up, there were several tickets that had not been paid.

"The next Friday, there was a new one, so I instructed the girls not to let him charge any more food, because he no longer worked there."

The defense was more interested in the poker box. The poker machines were making money, not from the quarters that were inserted into the machines themselves, but from gambling on the side. Each employee was responsible to make the pay-offs, write them in a book, and account for the money separately. In addition to bills, the box contained rolls of coin stamped with the name of the business.

Q. For that reason, a greater amount of cash was kept in that box?" the defense queried.

A. Yes. That and cashing company checks for truck drivers and making change for big bills.

It was almost lunchtime, and I left the courtroom a little early to stretch my legs. On breaks, I spent part of the time looking out the high window in the Judge's Chambers, overlooking the mall, the bricked streets on which the Courthouse and the Federal Building fronted. In nice weather employees who had brought their lunch sat on the planters and steps and talked. Vendors hawked their wares to those who had not brought their lunch. During our stay, "Alive after Five" included a band that was periodically scheduled on the mall, and the young professionals flocked around enthusiastically after their work day. The food and drink stands included everything from soft pretzels to Greek pita sandwiches to fudge sundaes. The longest lines were for beer.

Today, upon reaching chambers, I heard someone singing, and glancing out the window, I found the source. A guitarist had set up and was singing "Native Son."

At lunch recess, we would cross that mall and walk a couple of blocks to the Capitol City Club, where Jack had maintained his membership after leaving his Fayetteville law firm. The food, atmosphere, and service were all excellent, and we took advantage of its being close to the courthouse and within walking distance; also, we were less likely to run into jurors there.

Judge Pou Bailey came into chambers to find Jack, and learning where we were headed for lunch, called ahead to see if they were going to object to his failure to wear a tie. He was a charter member, and I got the impression that the club would willingly bend the rules for him.

Pou and Jack went back a long way. Their first encounter was in January of 1970, when Jack, as the newly elected District Attorney, first had to deal with the renowned character he had heard horror stories about. Judge Bailey, was rumored to eat for breakfast District Attorneys who didn't have their courtrooms in order. Jack's assistants had been alerted to be prepared. If the first case scheduled for trial resulted in a plea, the next case would be ready to try on a moment's notice, witnesses on stand-by. Court was not to break down.

Judge Bailey was impressed after he had been worked long hours during his six months in Fayetteville, and Jack and he became good friends. He was to step in and out of our lives for many years.

One of the most significant occasions had occurred two years after their first encounter. Jack was still District Attorney and was responsible for uncovering and exposing the case-fixing practices of the local political machine. During the investigation, the "other side" got dirty. They tapped our telephone, and I became so distrustful--previously, I never locked my doors in the daytime--that I called the telephone company and asked them to describe their employee at my door before I would let him "untap" it. In addition, someone called on a Saturday morning to tell me a bomb would go off under our house at eleven o'clock. Prepared by the SBI, who had become part of the investigation, I left the phone off the hook, took my two toddlers who were watching cartoons in their footie pajamas (the older two were at basketball practice) next door and dialed a special number to trace the call. I walked back to our house to find one SBI agent in our carport, gun drawn, and another in our den.

The investigation completed, Judge Bailey had presided at the ensuing hearing which was the springboard for obtaining sufficient information to force the resignation of our Clerk of Court who had been at the heart of the corruption. Without Judge Bailey's trust and insight, this could not have been accomplished. There was no precedent to follow, but he had never tried to avoid new ground.

We had not seen the Judge for a few years, not since he had retired, although he still was what they called an Emergency Judge and periodically heard extremely complicated civil cases which took months or years of preparation and trial. His current case was still in the pretrial stages and had three

thousand plaintiffs complaining about the noise in their neighborhoods ema-
nating from the Raleigh\Durham airport. We were delighted to see him and
catch up on his news. Listening to his colorful courtroom "war stories" at
lunch would be one of the highlights of our stay in Raleigh.

After a nice lunch, and good conversation, we headed back to the
courtroom where the drama continued to unfold.

The first witness was a crime scene investigator, who had finger-
printed the victim's body. He explained that her fingerprints could be used
for comparison to other prints at the crime scene to distinguish them
from other fingerprints. Her clothing had been tested for blood, fiber,
and hair samples. A substance called lumenal was sprayed in the kitchen
area. Lumenal chemically reacts with blood that is no longer visible to the
human eye to become evident, even blood that has been washed or wiped
away. The chemical makes the blood appear fluorescent.

A reaction revealed blood on the concrete floor inside and on the
concrete outside. A shoe track in the sand was exposed, and a plaster cast
was made to compare to the shoes of anyone suspected of the crime.

Subsequently, when searching Jeff's friend Rick's residence in
Wilson, the investigator found some Reebok tennis shoes with blood on
them in the closet. On analysis, they discovered head hair stuck to the bottom of the Reeboks. In addition, he had found rolled coins with the restaurant's stamp in a drawer, a pair of blue work pants that were retrieved from
a trash can in Rick's residence, two pocketknives in a desk drawer, and
Jeff's checkbook, which were now all presented into evidence. In his custody were more items an agent in Atlantic Beach had turned over to him:
a blood sample from the driver's side front seat of a Nissan Sentra; a navy
blue T-shirt; First Federal Bank canvas bags, the kind used for depositing
checks and cash for businesses; and a black-handled pocketknife. These
had all been turned over to the SBI laboratory for chemical analysis. Of the
twenty-three latent prints lifted, some were not of good value, and none

matched. The plaster cast of the shoe print had an "insufficient amount of detail for a conclusive identification."

Sometimes, a witness like this one is out of chronological order, mainly to accommodate the witness' schedule. Why Jeff and why Rick's residence had been searched had yet to be established.

The next witnesses revealed why. They would explain to the jury how the defendant had been caught. Later in the same morning of the murder, Jeff had driven to Atlantic Beach with his roommate Dana, and Cari, using Cari's car, and as is so often the case, fate had played a hand--fate and an alert officer. A police car just happened to be behind them, and the three were stopped for driving too slowly, 20 in a 40 mile per hour zone, and for having an expired license tag. For some reason, Officer Harris asked permission to search their car, and Jeff gave his consent. Finding the rolled coins, the officer asked Jeff about them. Jeff replied that he owned a vending machine business in Zebulon. He had taken this money out for a vacation, and needed to exchange the ones and fives for larger bills. Officer Harris gave Jeff directions to the bank, and sent the three on their way, but he had a hunch something was wrong, and he thought he would do some checking.

Rick Baker, who had been Jeff's friend and short-term roommate, took the stand to testify. He was baby-faced, with a full head of wavy dark brown hair, a lock falling on his forehead. He told the jury that Jeff came to see him and wanted him to help him rob a place; he also told him that they would have to kill the waitress who was working that shift. He helped Jeff put a rope and cinder block into the trunk of his car to weigh down the body after they threw it in the nearby river. Jeff drew a map of the layout of the restaurant on a vacuum cleaner bag. Rick told Jeff he would help him, but they would have to do it before 2:30 A.M. because he had to get some sleep before going to work. When they arrived, they found cars at the restaurant, so they kept riding around. One of the places they would ride by was the Radio Shack to check the time on the big clock in the window, because neither of them had worn a watch and Rick was concerned about the time. There were still cars at the restaurant at 2:30 A.M., Rick's deadline, so Jeff took him home and went back alone.

Rick had seen Jeff again at 4:45 A.M. He had come to his back door "with blood all over," wearing blue jeans and Reeboks. He told Rick he had killed the waitress. Rick opened the metal box with a screwdriver, and Jeff gave him a hundred dollars. Jeff then washed the blood off in the bathroom, changed into some shorts, leaving his jeans on the floor, at the same time informing Rick that he had stabbed her with his pocketknife, hit her with brass knuckles, and left her bleeding to death.

"It was the perfect crime," Jeff told Rick, "there were no witnesses. It was the best get-away."

He put some of the rolled coins in a desk drawer and the rest of the money into a Crown Royal bag and left, telling Rick he would be back in a few days to get his clothes.

Rick was arrested later for accessory after the fact of armed robbery and murder and, after waiving his rights, he first told detectives he didn't know anything about it.

"I didn't want to get myself in trouble," he stated simply. Upon further questioning, he told Detective Duckworth his story and signed a statement he had written himself. Although this was the first time he had been arrested, he had also taken part in a robbery in Zebulon with Jeff's brother. Subsequently, charged with common law robbery, he had agreed to testify in this case in exchange for a plea bargain for three years for the common law robbery charge. He was presently serving this sentence.

On cross examination by the defense, Rick said he had spent the day with Jeff from lunchtime to 2:30 A.M. They had some beers and had smoked marijuana several times that day, including after midnight. At some point, he said, Jeff appeared to lose control of his car, making a 360 degree turn. Apparently, the defense was trying to mitigate Jeff's act with a claim that he was under the influence.

When Ms. Hill questioned him again, however, Rick said that he had told the detective he did not think Jeff was drunk that night.

Detective K. E. Duckworth came to the stand. Looking quite official, he had a high forehead and wire rimmed glasses, and presented a competent and no-nonsense presence. He described the crime scene as he had observed it. There were cigarettes and cigarette butts on the table along with the morning News and Observer. Then he found the body in the kitchen, "face down on her left side in a tremendous amount of blood."

Suspecting robbery, he checked the cash register, which was closed, but there was thirty-five dollars and change in the register and a plastic container that held some small amount of currency. This, he explained, is why Terry, Darla Cline's husband, was not told right away about her death. The money was still there, so domestic violence was a possibility. Duckworth's team searched the upstairs apartment, looking for weapons and money from the cash box. "Yes," he had noticed the noisy window air conditioning unit. A thorough search was conducted, but nothing implicated Mr. Cline in his wife's death. After talking to the manager of the restaurant and knowing the poker box was missing, robbery again appeared to be the motive, and he finally revealed the bad news to Terry Cline. Terry fainted.

After receiving a call at 11:50 A.M. on September eleventh from the Atlantic Beach police, Duckworth ran a PIN (Police Information Network) check on Jeffrey Brian Medlin and obtained a Zebulon address. At 11:54 he requested a criminal history that gave him Jeff's description: six feet and a hundred and fifty-five pounds, as well as a history of his previous charges and convictions.

When interviewing Ms. Johnson, the manager of the restaurant, Duckworth learned that Jeff was a past employee who had failed to show up for work and that as an employee he would know where the money was kept, even though he had not been allowed to handle it because of his criminal record. The shelf over the Pepsi cooler from which the cash box was taken was "neat and tidy," and she said that the box should have had eight to nine hundred dollars in it in the following denominations: $280.00 in rolled quarters, ten dollars in a roll; $100.00 in one dollar bills, and the balance in five dollar bills.

While Duckworth was obtaining this information, Officer Harris in Atlantic Beach had told Officer Casassa to call and check out Jeff's story about the vending machine business and the rolled coins; he learned that Jeff was a suspect in a robbery and murder. Harris left a message for Detective Duckworth.

When Duckworth called back he talked to Officer Galizia and asked her to locate the vehicle and hold its occupants for questioning.

Galizia asked for a written request to that effect, stating that it was "reference to a homicide this A.M." and on Duckworth's authority.

Telephoning back and forth, the police at Atlantic Beach filled Duckworth in on developments. The red Nissan had been located, and its passengers were known to be staying in Room 222 of the Iron Steamer Motel at Pine Knoll Shores. Duckworth received a computer message at 4:39 P.M on September 11 from Chief Duke in Atlantic Beach that the subjects had been apprehended and were being held. "Please FAX copies of the search warrant" to him.

"I immediately called Chief Duke and told him that I did not have a warrant on file at that time," Detective Duckworth testified.

Chief Duke called his District Attorney for advice and called Duckworth back, stating that it was his intention to release the suspects. He had been under the impression that Wake County authorities already had warrants--in fact, his own dispatcher had told him there were warrants, something he had apparently assumed from the conversations. Chief Duke knew that if he detained them without the proper documents, any case against them would be in legal jeopardy.

Amazingly, when Chief Duke told Jeff, Cari, and Dana that they were free to go, they chose to stay and wait for the Wake County deputies that Duke had told them were coming to talk to them.

Still in Raleigh, Detective Duckworth and Detective Pearce went to the home of Judge Stephens for a search warrant and warrants for arrest for robbery with a dangerous weapon, based on the information from Chief Duke in Atlantic Beach and information they had gathered themselves.

While the Wake County detectives were on their way, Jeff kept remarking to the Atlantic Beach officers that he knew what they wanted and he wanted to talk to them. He acted as if he couldn't wait and wanted to talk to the officers immediately where he was.

Detective Tolar of Atlantic Beach obliged him, and Jeff was still talking when Duckworth and Pierce got there at midnight.

Duckworth was not able to talk to Jeff until 4:45 A.M., and by then, Jeff had already told his story. He was brought back to Wake County, booked, and put into a cell.

During the early morning hours of September 12th, and after obtaining a new warrant for murder, Duckworth went home for some overdue sleep. At 9:30 that same morning, he received a call that Rick was under arrest and Duckworth left his bed to talk to the second suspect.

On September 13th, Duckworth's first normal shift in several days, he received a call at 10:55 A.M. from the jailer that Jeff Medlin wanted to see him. Asking another detective to accompany him as a witness, he went to the jail. After signing a waiver of his rights (that Ms. Hill now read to the jury), Jeff started talking to Duckworth.

"He wanted me to know that he and Rick had planned the robbery, but it was Rick that had planned to murder the waitress because 'he had placed a cinder block and rope in my trunk.'"

They were going to put the body in the trunk and attach the cinder block to it there. Jeff asked the detective if his fingerprints would show up on the cinder block and he was told they might, although Duckworth knew that lifting fingerprints from cinder block would have been "very unlikely."

Jeff described the knife, as having a three-to-four inch blade, a cork-screw attachment, and a black handle, and he also told where he had disposed of it.

Duckworth then talked to Rick who told him that Jeff was the one that planned the robbery and murder, drawing a map of the restaurant for him in his bedroom. Asked about the cinder block and rope, Rick said Jeff had intended to use them to throw the body in the river.

Q. Which river?

A. The river near Bisset's crossroads.

Q. Who tied the rope to the cinder block?

A. We both did. We had to knock the mortar out of one of the holes to put the rope through.

The rope and cinder block were located exactly where Rick told Duckworth they would be, but the map was never found.

Captain Pickett, an eighteen-year veteran of the Wake County's Sheriff's Department, had searched the off-ramp where Jeff said he threw the knife on September the 12th. He had asked the Highway Department to delay mowing the grass. On foot, the area was a fifteen mile stretch. On September the 19th, he tried again, and he was there only fifteen minutes when he found a knife fitting Jeff's description sticking up in the ground.

Detective Tolar, blonde and athletic looking, testified next. He was the one that Jeff had wanted to talk to before Duckworth arrived in Atlantic Beach. He explained that on a routine check in the murder investigation, he interviewed local merchants, asking if any rolled coin with the stamp of the restaurant had been exchanged for bills.

"No," was the answer he had received, but one of the merchants told him about Jeff Medlin, a former employee who had robbed before.

> Q. Until Mr. Strickland gave you Jeff Medlin's name, was he a suspect in the case?
>
> A. No. He was not.
>
> Q. Did you even know he existed at that point?
>
> A. No. I did not.

This was how Jeff's name had entered the picture, setting the stage for the call from the Atlantic Beach police inquiring had he had a business there that involved rolled coin.

It was the same day of the murder and at ten o'clock that night that Jeff told Tolar the first story after signing a waiver of his rights. Jeff said he had been drinking that day, smoking pot, and using cocaine. He had started doing drugs when he was sixteen. He said he had also smoked a couple of joints that morning with Darla (*although there was never to be any evidence presented that Darla smoked marijuana*).

The first version of his story went like this:

On the morning of the tenth, he had gotten up to go to work but had gone to Wilson instead to fill out a job application for Pizza Inn. He had gotten the job and was supposed to start on the morning of the eleventh. He spent the day "riding around and getting high." Late that night, he went to a "drug buddy's" house because he had run out of joints, but there was no answer to his knock on the door. At three or four in the morning, he went to the restaurant, spoke to Darla, told her he was going to the bathroom, and then asked her if she had any marijuana.

"I have some homegrown. We'll smoke some if you want to," Darla had told him.

"She told me to hide when some headlights came up, because no one was supposed to be in that part of the store that time of night. I saw the newspaper man hand her a paper and her hand him a Mountain Dew."

The rest, though, was Rick's doing. He described how he had run out to the car and said they had to get out of there. Rick had the cash box, and using a screwdriver and crowbar to open it, had given Jeff his share and told him not to spend more than one hundred dollars.

At that point in this "confession," they took a break. When Jeff came back, he told about the activities at the beach and how they had been stopped by the police.

"Rick told me it was a perfect crime. No witnesses."

At that time, Tolar told Jeff he didn't believe him. He thought Jeff had killed Darla, but Jeff denied it. Tolar left.

Detective Pearce took over. Tolar tried to return to the interview room later, but Jeff wouldn't talk in front of him, so he left.

Detective Pearce followed Tolar on the witness stand. He had bushy, reddish-brown hair and a mustache to match. He had taken up with Jeff where Tolar left off. Armed with Tolar's notes, Pearce had read them to Jeff, but Jeff would not look him in the eye. He told Jeff it was "time to get to the bottom of this matter." Jeff asked him if he was with the District Attorney's office, and Pearce told him, no, he was with the Wake County Sheriff's Department.

"At that point, Jeff stood up, stared down at the floor, and said, 'I killed the waitress.'"

Jeff changed his story. The plan was to knock her (*whoever was there*) out with brass knuckles but not to kill her. He and Rick went there twice, but cars were there. At 2:30, Rick had to go home, so he took him. Jeff went back alone and there was only one car there now, and an old man was sleeping in it. He had the brass knuckles on his hand when he went in, but Darla turned and saw him, so he slipped them off his hand and into his pocket, and they talked. Darla told him that she was thinking of quitting her job because of the night hours, and she began mopping the floor. When she turned her back, he struck her in the head. She started screaming. He hit her ten to fifteen times, and she continued to scream. She told him, "Just take the money." Pulling out his pocketknife, he began stabbing her repeatedly.

Jeff's parents were sitting in the courtroom. They were openly crying and clinging to each other, not wanting to hear what they were hearing. Jeff hung his head.

Detective Pearce said Jeff finished by telling him where he had thrown the knife and the cash box and then about his trip to the beach.

The only thing Jeff wanted to change in his statement as written by Detective Pearce was that he wanted it specifically stated that neither his girlfriend nor his friend who had been arrested with him had any knowledge of the robbery or the killing.

In addition, Jeff had sketched three drawings, and now Detective Pearce came down from the stand to show them to the jury. Map Number One depicted where he drove and parked between the restaurant and Highway 87, and a path showing where he had walked until he saw Darla. Map Two was of the kitchen area and where Darla stood--a small dot indicating her existence--and where he had sneaked up behind her. The third map showed where he had thrown the T-shirt, metal box, and money bags from the highway into a creek, and also locating the trailer park where he lived.

At a later date, following the map and actually wading in the creek, Pearce had pulled a blue T-shirt from the bottom along with a vinyl money bag, later identified by Jean Johnson. Jeff had disposed of the items only one-tenth of a mile from his home.

Pearce ended his testimony by stating that when he talked to Jeff, the defendant did not appear to be under the influence of anything.

It was after five o'clock, and Court was recessed for the day. The jury had a lot of information to digest. So far, they had heard plenty of evidence against Jeff, none for.

The prosecution presents all of its evidence first, and with a guilty plea, there is little cross-examination by the defense. The evidence at this point definitely appeared one-sided.

Jack and I had come prepared to spend the night if the day was too draining, rather than making the hour and a half trip back to Fayetteville, and we decided to do just that. We were somewhat stunned by the evidence so far. Our talk at dinner centered on the case. The testimony had presented a chilling mental picture of two young men knocking the mortar out of the hole in the cinder block so they could tie a rope to it to weigh down a body. Despite their horrific plan, they had driven around watching the time so one of them would not be late for work. Their intended victim was random.

In the morning, we returned to the courthouse, still somber and heavy-hearted.

Doctor LeGrand, a pathologist with Wake Medical Center, was the next witness.

He was slight, and his neat haircut and glasses gave him a studious appearance. He informed the jury that whenever there is a violent or unnatural death, the law requires that an autopsy be performed to determine the cause of death. He tried to tell the jury how Darla had appeared when he examined her, but his descriptions appeared clinical and cold: she had "lacerations on the forehead and bridge of the nose...."the nose was displaced to the right side...." Instead of saying that her throat was cut, he said, the "left lobe of the thyroid gland was lacerated." I doubt if many on the jury understood, but, despite the terminology, they would soon see for themselves in color eight-by- ten's.

After lunch, the pathologist continued. Judge Thompson, at the request of Ms. Hill, warned against emotional displays by anyone in the courtroom. The autopsy photographs were about to be introduced, and the audience, especially any members of the decedent's family or the defendant's family, were told that if they were afraid they could not maintain their composure, they might want to leave the courtroom during this testimony.

The prosecutor was merciful in several ways. First of all, she had waited until after lunch to introduce the pictures. Secondly, she narrowed her exhibits down to thirteen of the fifty photographs taken during the autopsy. These were all taken after the victim was "washed of the profusion of blood for the purpose of a closer examination of the wounds." A pocket-knife could do an extensive amount of damage. The "wounds" were gaping holes, revealing muscle and connecting tissues.

"None were inflicted post-mortem," said the pathologist.

Q. Does that mean she was in pain?

A. She would have felt each one."

Standing in front of the jurors, the good doctor continued, marking on a poster drawing of a female body the location of the wounds seen in the photographs. The poster seemed a bit unnecessary. The photographs said it all.

I watched the jury as each picture was passed, and their reactions varied. The young woman with long black hair on the back row looked pale and kept her hand to her mouth, while the young man in the black and gold T-shirt in front of her paused momentarily in his gum chewing as each picture was introduced. All of the jurors were effected, but I noticed that the women passed the graphic photos on to the next person faster than the men.

The wounds on Darla's arms, between her thumb and elbow and on the back of her left hand, indicated she had tried to shield herself from her attacker. According to Dr. LeGrand, she was still conscious for a while before she died. He concluded that the fatal wound was to the jugular vein, "due to the high rate of blood flow and connection to the central nervous system," and it would have taken fifteen to twenty minutes to drain.

She had slowly bled to death. It was the doctor's opinion that if not for that jugular wound, she possibly could have lived. She would have been able to talk and "could have been physically able to apply compression to her deepest wounds and summon help."

At the time these gruesome photographs were taken, this woman no longer felt anything, but the pain and terror she must have endured, desperately gasping for breath while her life blood emptied onto the cold kitchen tiles, was nauseous to think about.

Q. How many wounds were there as a result of a knife?

A. Sixteen.

Q. How many wounds were caused as a result of brass knuckles?

A. Six.

Despite the judge's caution, Jeff's parents were visibly shaken, huddling together, arms around each other, and sobbing. While most of the jury were directing their eyes to the witness, the young blonde, athletic, male juror on the front row kept glancing at them. Jeff's mother could bear no more and left the courtroom, but his father stayed, white handkerchief covering his eyes.

The State rested.

Up to this point, there had not been much activity by the defense team. There had not been a lot to say. Their client had pled guilty, therefore eliminating most of the objections to the evidence presented by the State.

Thus, their defense had appeared exceedingly low-key. This did not mean, however, that they didn't know what they were doing.

Stephen Smith and Jack Hall were well-known defense attorneys and regarded by their peers as experienced and competent. I was conscious of their quiet efforts throughout the prosecution's presentation to keep their presence known to the jury.

Steve Smith was tall, slim, and handsome, with a boyish face and softly wavy, brown hair. He was on his feet promptly, but unobtrusively, whenever he could assist the female prosecutor carry a box of exhibits or set up an easel in front of the jury, as if to say, "This evidence is appropriate, and we are not opposed. Ms. Hill is just doing her job. No problem."

Jack Hall, a sometime actor in the local theater group, used his talent admirably in the courtroom as well as on stage. Full-figured and bearded, he appeared to be a cross between Raymond Burr and Orson Wells. His dignified, scholarly manner exuded confidence and congeniality. Instead of the clipped "No questions" that one usually heard from opposing counsel, he played the role differently.

"Good morning, Detective Duckworth," he intoned slowly in deep sonorous tones. "I have no questions for you this morning."

The two defense lawyers were perfect Southern gentlemen, and their manners sat well with the jury. Their time had arrived, and it would be their burden to place before the jury a portrait of the other Jeff Medlin by introducing mitigating circumstances in favor of life imprisonment.

While the Court in a capital case cannot consider any aggravating circumstances other than the ones listed by statute, mitigating circumstances are practically open-ended, including everything from being a boy scout to playing little league soccer to loving one's mother. This personal history is not presented to excuse what the defendant did, but to show some redeeming qualities that make him more human and deserving of life. While this information is clearly irrelevant in the guilt/innocent phase, the sentencing phase is wide open. Knowing the case would be automatically appealed, most judges, out of an abundance of caution, would allow anything within reason that the defense presented.

The State had depicted the defendant as mean as a pit bull, but the defense would say that he licked his master's face and fetched his newspaper on Sunday mornings.

Although it is repeated to the jury by the attorneys and by the judge in his charge that sympathy is not an issue and should not affect their decision, the reality is that sympathy is exactly what mitigating factors are designed to evoke. For the most part, the factors are emotional, not intellectual. "He is human." But what is allowed is a cry for sympathy. For what other possible reason could loving his mother have anything to do with stabbing someone sixteen times for six-hundred dollars? Who cares if he played soccer?

It would be interesting to see what they would say about Jeff that could offset, even remotely, his cold crime.

Mr. Brantley, the Program Director of the Granville Correction Center had known the defendant when he was serving his time for the previous robbery. At first he was reluctant to answer Jeff's lawyers' questions because he was concerned about the privacy regarding an inmate's records, but he was soon reassured that since it was the inmate's attorney who was questioning him, Jeff had obviously waived that right.

> Q. Did he show any violent tendencies to staff or other inmates?
>
> A. Not as I recall.
>
> Q. He was assigned to the kitchen. Is that a job that is a reward for good conduct?
>
> A. Generally, it is because of the inmates' skills, but they do want people who will not cause problems.

He described Jeff's attitude as polite and as one who carried himself well, created no problems, and participated in substance abuse programs.

Brenda (Medlin) Driver, took the stand. Tall, slim, and blonde, she looked too young to be Jeff's mother. She testified to a bad marriage in which her husband picked out her clothes and forbade her to wear make-up. He was the jealous type and didn't trust her. As a father, his conduct was abusive. Nathan had come home drunk as often as not and had disciplined the two boys physically with little or no provocation.

"This would happen two to three times a week when Jeff was three or four years old. He would get whipped for things like spilling his milk-- eight to ten licks."

However, on cross-examination by Ms. Hill, she conceded that Jeff's father's "good old-fashioned whippings," as she had called them, could also be called "normal spankings" using his hand or his belt on the buttocks area. "No," he had never beaten his sons or abused them in an obsessive manner.

In fact, the jury learned that when she had finally separated from Jeff's father, she had agreed that her estranged husband could have custody of both eleven year old Jeff and his older brother, while she retained custody of the much younger daughter.

When her son's attorney Steve Smith asked her about a tape of a local television program that Jeff had appeared on two years ago, everything stopped. The prosecutor objected and wanted to be heard.

When a question of law is to be heard, the jury is sent to the jury room until the judge rules one way or another. Although the jurors probably welcome such occasions as an added restroom break or a time to stretch their legs, they may feel cheated of information that could make a difference in the way they view the case. They are told not to speculate on what is being ruled on, but they are human.

The judge had to view the eight-to-ten minute video in order to make his decision as to whether it was admissible as showing prior conduct or good acts.

The prosecutor claimed that the tape was hearsay and objected to the jury's being able to hear the defendant speak on the tape. On the tape, Jeff would not be subject to her cross-examination, as he would be if he took the stand in person.

Everyone but the jury watched the television. The local Durham program had been aired two years ago on WTVD, Channel 11. A seventeen-year-old Jeff was on the screen declaring himself, in the hopes of reaching other teen-agers, an alcoholic and drug addict--beer and pot-- and explaining how his life had taken a downhill turn.

It was an impressive interview and especially jolting when Jeff said twice that he wanted to stop taking drugs and stop "drinking because I don't want to die." The defense wanted the jury to hear this plea for life and apply it to the current situation.

But the irony was apparent, and this strategy could possibly work against him. Obviously, since the time of this tape, his behavior had gone from bad to worse--Darla Cline was dead. The jury could decide that his rehabilitation did not seem more, but less likely.

The Supreme Court is liberal as to what constitutes a mitigating circumstance. They would probably consider this baring of soul as substantial and say that the jury should have been allowed to see this side of the defendant.

His Honor agreed. The jury was brought in to view the tape.

Jeff's father, Nathan Medlin, was the next witness for the defense. He tearfully testified in his son's behalf, admitting his own drunkenness and bad temper and the times he had vented his anger on his son. Though he had completed the ninth grade, he could neither read nor write. "Yes," he had been jealous of his wife and had used profanity toward her and in front of the children. He was apologetic about "all the hurt years I put her through," and he thought she had been a good mother--although she had not visited the boys as often as he thought she should after the separation.

He testified that Jeff had played midget football and had earned enough money at Pizza Inn to buy a car. Suspecting his son of drug use, he had found Jeff at his brother's house "high." Jeff told his father he needed help, and he had agreed to send him to CHAPS, a drug rehabilitation center. Later, he had talked with his son about joining the Army.

Jeff had signed up for active duty upon completion of high school, but he never made it. Instead, he had been sentenced to jail for the Quick Mart robbery.

"Yes," he was familiar with Johnson's Restaurant. The manager had called him into the back room one time to talk to him concerning Jeff's problems. And he had also known Darla Cline. "Yes," Jeff had played football in junior high and was on the Student Council in the tenth grade.

When Ms. Hill, the prosecutor, cross-examined, she asked Nathan Medlin if he too, as a child, had been on the receiving end of "whippings" by his parents. "Yes, ma'am," he replied "with a tobacco stick or switch, depending on which one got ahold of me."

> Q. Well, I'm just guessing, but would your father use the tobacco stick and your mother the switch?"
>
> A. Yes, ma'am.
>
> Q. Do you remember Jeff being involved in a fight?
>
> A. Yes, because I went up to the courthouse with him.

Jeff had been in CHAPS not once, but twice. After he was released the first time, he had a contract with his father and certain rules he promised to follow, but Jeff did not uphold his part. He had to reenter CHAPS.

> Q. After he got out, did you have a new contract?
>
> A. He was to do like he was supposed to. There won't no contract. That was just me telling the young 'un that.

When Mrs. Pope, the younger sister of Jeff's mother, took the stand, I noticed that Jeff's mother was not present, and it soon became apparent why. Mrs. Pope testified that her sister Brenda had married at age fourteen, at a time when she was still wetting the bed and sucking her thumb and playing with baby dolls. Brenda's new husband had kept her sisters from seeing his wife the entire time they were married.

"We snuck to see her anyway when he was at work and had to be careful not to mention it around him. He would not let Brenda attend my wedding."

She added that her sister had a "quick temper," was "quick to hit," and used abusive language.

"She continues to use it, even to me."

Her attitude was haughty and indignant. She would never use "such filthy language" herself and found it "deplorable." Certainly, his mother's constant curses had effected Jeff as a child.

But she could only have been offended skin deep. She admitted during cross-examination that "yes," in the past she had let Brenda baby-sit for her one-year-old child on a daily basis while she went to work.

Mrs. Farmer, Brenda's older sister, painted a similar picture of Jeff's parents, but she displayed more tolerance. She did not enjoy her role of having to defame her sister to help Jeff, her nephew and a good friend of her daughter. She described her sister's marriage to Nathan, Jeff's father: "Brenda did *what* he said *when* he said. She liked chocolate covered dough-nuts, but we would have to take the box and drink cups with us when we left so he didn't know we'd been there. She was so young. I don't think she knew any better."

After Jeff's family, the counselor from the drug rehabilitation center had a few good things to say about Jeff, and Mr. Moose from the Polk Youth Center said he had used Jeff as a tutor and grader in the heating and air conditioning class during the last six months of his incarceration. Jeff had been helpful to the other students.

What may have turned the case was the testimony of Jeff's high school teachers. They were educated, articulate, and openly disturbed to be in this courtroom, as if they fervently wished they could have done something--anything--to have influenced Jeff's later decisions.

Virginia Lowery had taught Jeff twelfth grade English, and she candidly told the jury that she had dreaded having him as a student. She knew him from the halls. He had long hair and hung around with the drug crowd. When her turn came to have him in her class, she assigned him a front-row, center seat to keep an eye on him. But she found her assessment of Jeff had been wrong, and he was a pleasant surprise. When he was absent for seven to eight weeks while a patient at CHAPS, she had made out lesson plans that were taken to him by his parents.

"He very sincerely wanted to graduate from high school. He was always very polite and respectful. I even had some 'yes, ma'ams.'"

Q. How would you describe his attitude?

A. He wanted to get off drugs and stay off drugs—drugs and alcohol. His companions made it harder, and because ours is a small town, it was difficult to get away from them.

After Jeff's arrest, he wrote her two letters requesting her help so that he could graduate. She honored his request with assignments, and he did, in fact, graduate.

"I'd do anything I could to help him. I was very fond of Jeff. I like him very much. He was very well-behaved."

Ms. Lanier taught eleventh grade U. S. History at Zebulon High School, but she knew of Jeff peripherally from the ninth grade.

"My first impression was that he was loud, possibly hardheaded. I thought he was obnoxious. In the tenth grade, he was always putting his arm around a girl or putting his feet on the furniture. When he got into my advanced class, I was shocked and angry. I thought he would ruin my class because he would not live up to my expectations of an advanced student, and I obtained permission to remove him if necessary. I put him on the front row directly in front of me. I thought he would be intimidated by me and by the class." *Ms. Lanier's voice cracked, and she had to pause to regain her composure. We all waited patiently until she continued.* "But to my surprise, he lived up to all my expectations in that class. He was very enthusiastic and wanted to keep up. He became my teacher's assistant. The next year, when the Principal needed to put him somewhere for an extra period, Jeff volunteered to be my assistant again.

Q. How would you describe his attitude?

A. He was honest, humble and respectful and said, 'Yes, ma'am.'

It was obvious to the jury as well as to everyone else in this court-room that Jeff's former teachers were visibly shaken by the setting and the occasion at which they were asked to give their sincere accolades. They had recognized his potential, but not for murder.

It always seems to happen in a long trial. Toward the end of the second week, somehow, the people involved start feeling like old buddies.

As soon as court resumed after the luncheon recess, Jack Hall, defense attorney, made His Honor aware of what had happened shortly before. While he was sitting on a bench on the mall enjoying the Spring weather, someone sat down beside him. The man's face was familiar, but Mr. Hall could not place him. The two discussed the refreshing breezes that would soon turn stifling, if there was a breeze at all, as the summer progressed. He did not have on his "juror" badge, but Mr. Hall realized who he was when he asked, "About how much longer do you think this trial will go?" Another juror, a lady in a purple dress, had called to him across the mall and had told him he would not have too much longer to enjoy the sunshine (*meaning that court would soon resume*).

Then it was Ms. Hill's turn. She informed the Court that she too had been approached by the lady in the purple dress, who told her she had beautiful fingernails. Ms. Hill told her she could not talk to her until the trial ended.

His Honor smiled and said he didn't believe any harm had been done, but he would again make it clear to the jury that they were not to talk to *any* parties of the case, about *anything*, weather included, and he would instruct them to wear their juror badges even during recesses.

No matter how many times they are instructed, jurors assume they are supposed to refrain from discussing the case only, but not to suspend their naturally friendly personalities.

I was reminded of a conversation we had with a couple we met at a bed and breakfast in St. Augustine when we were on our way back from Key West the year before. He was from North Carolina, and his girlfriend was from Switzerland. We met them late one night on the upstairs porch, all of us chatting away like old friends. She was charming, smiling often, but, never having met us before, she had little to say. He told us that she wasn't really that shy, just not in tune yet with our customs. He made his point by telling us that this morning, after they had taken a long walk on the beach, she had told him how impressed she was with him.

"What do you mean?" he asked.

"Well, all the people that you know here."

"But I don't know anyone here besides you."

"What about all those people who smiled and said hello to you?"

We all laughed. She did not understand yet that was just good southern manners.

When the jury was brought in later, I looked for the woman in the purple dress. She wore a matching scarf in her hair.

Now, with the illicit but innocent encounters with jury members properly noted on the court record, the attorney returned to the serious business ahead. The defense declared its intention to rest. For rebuttal evidence, Evelyn Hill wanted to call Dana, who had been arrested in Atlantic Beach with Jeff, to the stand. The defense was opposed. The jury was still waiting in their special room that adjoined the courtroom while Ms. Hill addressed the judge.

She argued to the Court that Jeff's statement on the tape, "At thirteen, I became hooked on drugs," and the testimony of subsequent witnesses had given the jury the impression that Jeff was helplessly addicted, and she wanted to show that he wasn't and was therefore a liar. She also wanted to combat his "honest and humble" image as portrayed by the counselors and teachers. Ms. Hill told His Honor that in keeping with her "open-file" policy, she had summarized this evidence for the defense attorneys yesterday and had also given them copies of written statements Dana had made to law enforcement officials.

The defense, however, maintained that there was nothing in those written statements that showed the defendant's behavior on drugs or his inconsistent use of them, which she had claimed she wanted to show.

Ms. Hill countered the defense argument with some clever strategy. In addition to the written statements Dana had given the police, he had also been interviewed by Ms. Hill. Unlike the divulged written statements, she had not revealed the contents of the interview to the defense, but would do so now in support of her argument to allow him to testify. She then read aloud the handwritten notes jotted on the front of her file, and even apologized for not having these notes typed for the defense. She read Dana's answers to her questions word for word while the defense team listened intently, nodded, and thanked her for this voluntary disclosure.

During this discourse, Dana, who was seated in the courtroom audience, also listened intently. If he had forgotten precisely what he had told her, he had just been reminded, and in his exact words. She had reviewed his

testimony with him at a crucial point, immediately before he took the stand,
and in open court.

Judge Thompson ruled for the State. The jury was brought in, and
Dana was called to the stand. His testimony would be revealing.

Q. How long have you known Jeff Medlin?

A. He was my roommate since July of 1990 in Zebulon.

Q. Until September of 1990?

A. Yes.

Q. Did you see the defendant use drugs?

A. Yes.

Q. What type of drugs?

A. Marijuana, alcohol, and cocaine.

Q. How many times did you see him use cocaine?

A. One time.

Q. Did he use drugs every day?

A. No.

Q. Did he work?

A. Yes.

Q. Were you with the defendant when he used marijuana?

A. Yes.

Q. What effect did it have on him?

A. It would make him talkative and happy-go-lucky.

The defense was not pleased. They had tried to portray Jeff as a victim, controlled by the abusive substances he put in his body. But now they could see the "Aha" look on the jurors' faces.

Q. Did you see the defendant on the tenth of September?

A. Yes. About eleven o'clock at night.

Q. Was there anything unusual about his behavior?

A. No, ma'am.

Q. When did you next see him?

A. At six o'clock in the morning in the hallway.

Q. What hallway?

A. The trailer.

Q. What was he doing?

A. Talking to Lori and me.

Q. What was he talking about?

A. He asked if I wanted to go the beach with them. I asked him how he could pay for it.

Q. What did he say?

A. He said not to worry about it.

Q. What happened next?

A. We put on our clothes and got in the car together.

Q. Whose car?

A. Cari's car.

Q. Who was driving?

A. Jeff.

Q. Was there anything unusual about his behavior?

A. No.

Q. Did you ask him any questions?

A. Yes. I asked him how blood got on his seat.

Q. What did he say?

A. He said he cut his knuckles and must have wiped them on the seat.

Q. Did you look at his knuckles?

A. Yes. They were cut.

Q. What happened next?

A. We stopped to eat breakfast and we switched drivers.

Q. Why did you do that?

A. Jeff said he was tired, and he fell asleep in the passenger seat.

Q. Who drove?

A. I did.

Q. What did you do next?

A. When we got to the beach, we stopped at a convenience store. Jeff got a soda and made a phone call. Then we went to the Iron Steamer and got a room. Jeff paid for the room, but told me to register.

Q. Why did he tell you to register?

A. Because I had a driver's license.

Q. What did you do then?

A. We went to the room and talked. Jeff decided we were going swimming, so we did, in the pool and in the ocean. We went on the boardwalk and got something to drink and played a couple of video games and went back to the room.

Q. What happened next?

A. The front desk called and said there was a problem. They had overcharged us.

Q. Previous to the front desk calling, had you seen any money?

A. Yes. It was in bags.

Q. Where was it?

A. Jeff put it on the bed.

Q. Did you ask where he got the money?

A. Yes.

Q. What did he tell you?

A. The quarters were from a pinball machine, and he made a cocaine deal the night before, and that's where he got the rest of it.

Dana then explained that Jeff wanted him to go to the bank with him and exchange the cash for one hundred dollar bills and get paper rolls for the loose coins. They had already been stopped by the police for an expired license tag, and the police had found the money when they searched the car and had asked Jeff where it came from.

"Did he tell the police he got the money from a cocaine deal the night before?" the prosecutor quipped.

"No."

(A juror on the back row stifled a smile with his hand.)

Taking an alternate route back to the motel, Jeff and Dana lost their way. Back in the room, Dana gave Jeff the hundred dollar bills and started rolling loose quarters. It was at this time that the front office called their room, asking one of them to come to the desk because they had been mistakenly overcharged for the room. Jeff told him that he should be the one to go because the room was registered in his name.

Q. What happened when you went to the motel office?

A. I was picked up by the police, handcuffed, and taken to the station. The police told me that Jeff was a suspect in a murder case. They told me I was free to go, but the Wake County detectives would want to talk to me, and I volunteered to stay and talk to them.

Q. From the time you saw the defendant at six o'clock in the morning until you were picked up by the police, did you see the defendant use any drugs?

A. No.

Q. Did you see the defendant take any drugs with him?

A. No.

Q. Did the defendant make any effort to buy drugs at the beach?

A. No.

Dana left the stand, his facial expression conveying that he had not liked testifying against his friend. Although none of his testimony revealed any actual wrong-doing on Jeff's part, the information was still very damaging. He had portrayed Jeff as "talkative and happy-go-lucky" after indulging in marijuana and also indicated that buying drugs was not Jeff's first priority when he had money--not the behavior of a helpless addict. The jury wouldn't consider Jeff very humble or honest when he had easily lied not only to the police, but also to Dana about the blood on the seat and the money. More significantly, perhaps, was the cold indifference the defendant displayed just a few hours after Darla had been left to bleed to death. Dana had painted a picture of a normal, merry holiday at the beach, swimming in the ocean, taking a dip in the pool, and playing video games.

With no apparent remorse for what he had done, Jeff had used the blood money to entertain himself and his buddies, who had happily participated.

Dana, even if he believed the cocaine deal story, had no qualms about helping Jeff spend illegally obtained money.

The evidence in the case concluded, the jury had only final arguments to hear before deliberating. It was ten-thirty in the morning. The attorneys and judge needed time to conduct the charge conference and agree on the issues that the jury would decide upon. Because of the complexity and the length of time required, the jury was told they had the rest of this Thursday off and to return Friday morning at nine-thirty.

The remainder of the day was to be spent on administrative matters, so I decided to spend my afternoon at the hotel with my book. Charge conferences are not spectator inspiring. Jack returned about five o'clock, saying all matters had been accomplished, and he also had an interesting aside to relate: One of the defense attorneys, Mr. Hall, kept Jack company while they waited for Maggie to finish typing the agreed upon jury verdict form. Mr. Hall told Jack that Dana's attorney had related this information to him. Now it was my turn to hear.

"You remember Dana testifying that the same morning after the murder that they had stopped on the way to Atlantic Beach for breakfast?" Jack asked me.

"Yes."

"Guess what the defendant had for breakfast?"

"What?"

"Brains and eggs."

"Good God. I don't think I wanted to know that."

I could picture the jurors' faces turning green. I mentioned this tidbit to Evelyn Hill after the trial and asked if she had known about it.

"I knew it." she said, "I just thought it was too disgusting to bring out, so I didn't ask him."

I agreed. The information, in and of itself, was meaningless as evidence; the jury might have transferred their disgust to the prosecution even asking the question simply for its repugnant effect. Then again, their disgust could have been for Jeff.

Friday morning, the courtroom was filled with spectators, many of them other attorneys who admired these three colleagues and knew that their closing arguments would be especially well executed. They were not disappointed.

The judge instructed the jury that final arguments are *not* evidence, but are given to help them evaluate the evidence as each party saw it. The attorneys were not witnesses, and the jurors were to be guided by their *own* recollections of what the witnesses' testimony had been. He also explained that they would first hear from the defendant himself. In a capital case, the defendant had the right of allocution: he could stand before the jury and say whatever he wished.

Jeff Medlin slowly came to his feet, looking small and as if he was hoping that the gods from Mount Olympus would shroud him with a heavy fog and render him invisible. But no gods came, and, in a barely audible and quivering voice, he spoke.

"Good morning."

"Good morning," some of the jurors replied.

"I'm sorry for all this. It may sound hypocritical to you, but I am sorry for all the pain I caused to Mr. Cline, the family, and everyone involved," Jeff said softly, turning to the spectators.

Terry Cline bowed his head and let his tears flow. A young girl in her teens, who was sitting beside him, was also crying.

Jeff's voice failed him, and it was apparent he could not remember all those things he had planned to say.

"For that, I'm truly sorry," he finally managed, before resuming his seat at the defense table, sandwiched between the two lawyers who were trying to save his life.

The courtroom was hushed.

Ms. Hill would give her closing argument first.

"You've probably wondered, since the defendant pled guilty, why the State brought in all the bloody evidence? Darla Cline lived and breathed and had dreams just like you and me, and that's her blood--her blood on those clothes and tennis shoes ... "

"This murder was planned, intentional, premeditated. Jeff Medlin had quit his job two weeks earlier and had begun planning ... "

"That night, he drives to the restaurant between one and three o'clock in the morning, based on his knowledge that there would not be many people there ... he and Rick ride by twice. There are too many cars, too many witnesses. He takes Rick home, and the defendant goes back at three-thirty and he sees an old man sleeping in a car, watches for a minute, and walks in. The brass knuckles are already on his hand, and murder is already in his mind, and she turns around and sees him. He could have left then. "All the time he's looking her in the eye, he knows he's going to kill her. Darla gets up, lights a cigarette--you saw the freshly lit cigarette in the picture--and starts mopping the floor. He sneaks up behind her ..."

Terry Cline looked dazed, like nothing was really getting through. The young woman with him had to leave the room. Jeff's father was sobbing.

Ms. Hill continued: He pulls her hair to bring her head back and plunges the knife in her throat all the way to her backbone ... there were sixteen slashes from his knife. The knife blade went through her arm as she held her arms up and fought for her life. Darla Cline did not want to die. She pleaded with him to 'just take the money.' Even then, he could have left and she would be alive today, but that's not what he chose. The defendant wants you to believe that he had horrible parents, a horrible childhood, a horrible home life, and that he was horribly addicted. But I tell you that he has manipulated every person, every system he has come in contact with.

Ms. Hill attacked the mitigating circumstances which had been presented by the defense, turning them inside-out to give another perspective of the same evidence. She contended that Jeff Medlin had had second chances more than once. He had entered the drug rehabilitation program twice at a cost of fifteen thousand dollars to his parents, but he had continued to take drugs. She sarcastically told the jurors that she knew they were delighted that Jeff had shown that he could adjust to prison life.

"He said himself on the video tape that he didn't want to die or go to jail, but he was the one that chose armed robbery and murder. Jeff had chance after chance, break after break. It has been shown that he can follow the rules, he's not retarded, and he's not emotionally handicapped. He's had far less problems than a lot of kids on the street, but they're not in here--he is."

Five of the mitigating circumstances concerned Jeff's family. "But," Ms. Hill argued, "they want it both ways. They want you to believe that he had a horrible father, a horrible mother, a horrible childhood. So how was he so polite and honest and humble? This 'horrible' family supported him, bringing his lessons to the prison, putting him in drug programs. 'Facts is facts.' Truth can't bend and sway both ways. Jeff Medlin has had more breaks than many folks. His family had a three-bedroom home, food and clothes, and he didn't lack for anything. What Jeff Medlin did not have was inner strength and inner conviction."

Ms. Hill sat down after an hour and forty-five minutes.

It was Defense Attorney Steve Smith's turn next. His job was a challenge.

Mr. Smith told the jury he felt humble; it was difficult to stand up and argue life and death. He also wanted them to consider that the basis of our law stems from our Christian tradition, and that their decision was an individual and personal one.

"You're the one responsible for that decision. You have to sleep with it, and it will be a part of your being from now on. I apologize for the awesome decision you have to make. Neither you nor I wrote that law, but you now bear the brunt of it ... "Your decision should not be based on revenge, retaliation or outrage ... even if you find all the aggravating circumstances, you can't stop thinking at that point. The law says that's not enough. The second thing you must consider are the mitigating circumstances ... you are not limited to factors dealing with the offense itself. You can consider any aspect of the defendant's background and character if *you* deem it a sufficient reason to support a sentence of life in prison."

"Three of the most influential men in history were murderers. Moses struck down an Egyptian overseer, an instant capital offense under their law .... King David put Bathsheba's husband on the front row of battle, knowing he had little chance of survival, yet David is the symbol of peace and love and justice ... Paul, when he was still called Saul, participated in or stood by, according to which version you read, while Stephen was stoned to death ... "

"Jeff Medlin is at peace with his Maker and with himself in prison ... he has the potential of becoming an 'old lifer' who helps young cons ...

Jesus was called upon to speak on the death penalty once. The Scribes and Pharisees wanted to get him to say something in opposition to the law and get rid of Him ... adultery was a capital offense at that time, but when the adulteress was brought before Him, He said, 'Let him who is without sin cast the first stone.' He rejected anger, vengeance, and retaliation ... "

"Much later in our history, Abraham Lincoln said, 'listen to the better angels of your nature.' Choose hope. Choose life."

Steve Smith resumed his seat and yielded the floor to his co-counsel, Jack Hall, who took his place at the podium, methodically arranged his notes, and began in his authoritative baritone voice.

"How? Why? and What? These are three questions I want to explore with you and I want you to explore. How did we get here? Why are we here? What can you do about it? Under the law, the death penalty is not always the most appropriate punishment for murder. The State has presented thirty-five witnesses and one hundred and twenty-seven items of evidence to tell you that Jeff Medlin intentionally, premeditatively, and deliberately committed murder while in the course of a felony, and that's what the evidence adds up to. However, if you take away one part, the part of what *he* said--all *his* statements, you are left with little or no evidence to tie him to the crime scene."

Mr. Hall recounted the evidence of the State, reminding the jury that no identifiable marker was found that could differentiate Jeff's blood from Darla's, that despite the latest technology and the large number of fingerprints gathered, that none were good enough for a match, that an expert had told them that he could not conclusively match the bloody shoe track to the known shoe of Jeff Medlin, and that the hair sample yielded no evidence that it had been transferred from Darla to Jeff. In other words, the scientific evidence was insufficient to place Jeff Medlin at the scene of Darla Cline's murder. Jeff had done that himself.

"The key to the State's case is Jeff's statements. Jeff stayed when he was told he was free to go and was anxious to make a statement. The tape of his first statement, although not the full truth, contained sufficient evidence to convict him. It was Jeff's statement that led to Rick, the maps and diagrams, and the subsequent wading in the stream by the detective to find the evidence. Don't you forget that's how we got here to this stage of the proceedings."

"Why are we here? We've seen people weep for Darla Cline and for Jeff Medlin ... But Gandhi said 'an eye for an eye will soon make the world blind' ... Keep an open mind to the possibility of life imprisonment ... was it a bad family life? He was not a brain in school. He abused marijuana and alcohol ... Some of your relatives have survived those things ... How did they survive it? What helped?"

"What can we do about it?"

Mr. Hall related a story of six people stranded on a desert island, all from different segments of society, and one was a young boy:

"Who would you save or why? In times of disaster, the tradition is to save the women and children first. The premise is to save the future, to save the potential to give our society the tools with which to save itself down the line ... consider the good that men do and where they do it ... Jeff's history in a structured environment tells us repeatedly that he functions well. His teachers call him productive and helpful ... The counselors from CHAPS say that he was able to do what he was told to do and do it well, politely and cooperatively ... Use him to influence others as a resource that may be valuable to us ... Youth is just half of the life God planned for this boy. You can see that he gets the future."

The arguments concluded, the jury was excused for lunch.

Jack and I walked to the old and recently renovated part of downtown known as "city market." We chose Greenshield's for lunch, mainly because we could sit outside on this perfect Spring day on a covered old brick patio beside cobblestone streets lined with small art shops. We were quiet and reflective, knowing the time for deciding Jeff Medlin's fate was at hand. After the lunch recess, Jack would charge the jury, explaining the choices open to them under the law. Then it would be up to them. We watched a mother bird feed her newborn in an eave overhead and one Mercedes after another roll by the fashionable shops. Either way the verdict was decided, we knew there was one nineteen-year- old who would never have the privilege of sitting where we sat now.

Predictably, the size of the audience was greatly reduced for Judge Thompson's charge to the jury. The lawyers in the case would not have been there if they had not been required to. Judges' charges are equally as boring as jury selections. One by one, the aggravating circumstances are listed, and then the jury is told that if they find them to be of greater weight than the thirty-two mitigating circumstances offered by the defense, they must find the death penalty; if not, they must recommend life in prison. Each circumstance had to be decided individually. The jury had to be unanimous to find that an *aggravating* factor existed, but the law (recently decided by the U.S. Supreme Court in State v. McKoy) required only *one* juror to believe a *mitigating* factor was valid.

The charge was necessarily long, intricate, and arduous, and the jury was left with only an hour to deliberate on this Friday afternoon. Shortly after five o'clock, they were dismissed until Monday morning at ten. The spectators remained seated as the jury filed out, and it was obvious from their faces that they were in strong disagreement at this point. Having the weekend to dwell on the issues could be bad or could be good. Some could become convinced of their position--perhaps adamant, and close their minds to differing views on Monday. Some could become confused, not sure of their understanding of the Judge's charge, and they would need frank and open debate from their fellow jurors to guide them.

We drove home to Fayetteville Friday night and spent a good part of the weekend preparing for a long week ahead, slipping some golf time in between unpacking, laundry, and repacking. The attorneys had told us they were convinced the jury would be out several days.

They were wrong.

The first news that greeted us Monday morning was that Darla Cline's husband, Terry, had been arrested over the weekend for DWI. He was in jail, and the State asked that he be released to hear the verdict when it was returned. The jury, safely secured behind closed doors by ten o'clock, continued their deliberations from Friday.

Even though trying to outguess a jury is an exercise in futility, Evelyn Hill, Jack Hall, Steve Smith, Jack, and I stood around in Jack's outer office discussing what we thought would carry the most weight with the jury. It gave us something to do. Maggie, bless her, kept the coffee pot refilled.

Under the law, Jeff was an adult, but some of us felt his age would be the most significant mitigating factor.

That the jury had not been in agreement had been obvious when they had left the courtroom Friday. One could only imagine their debate.

"His teachers were very complimentary--and he was only nineteen."

"But he committed murder."

"His counselors said he does well in a structured environment like prison--and he was nineteen."

"You'd do well in prison too if all the guards had guns. You wouldn't have a whole lot of choice."

"He was addicted to marijuana and alcohol. Look, he was nineteen."

"A lot of kids smoke pot and drink beer. They don't go around killing people for money."

"His family is supportive. They were in the courtroom every day. Besides, he was nineteen."

"They were supportive before. It didn't do much good."

"But, he was nineteen."

An hour later, a juror knocked on the inside of the jury room door, the signal that they had reached a verdict or needed to speak to the Court. The bailiff relayed the message--they had a question. The judge relayed back that they were to write it down and hand it to the bailiff. Their question involved Issue Three: "Are the mitigating circumstances *insufficient* to outweigh the aggravating circumstances?" They wanted to know if their answer of "yes" or "no" had to be unanimous. Judge Thompson brought the jury into the courtroom and re-instructed on only this section of the nearly two-hour charge.

Lodged in all the verbiage somewhere, the answer essentially was "yes."

The second knock came less than ten minutes later. They thought they had figured it out, but, alas, they had not. Seated again in the courtroom jury box, they answered "no," they were not unanimous on Issue Three. They were told to retire to their juryroom to resume their deliberations.

I sympathized with them. The higher courts have all but insisted by their rulings--tantamount to the stone tablets dictated by God to Moses--that most of the trial judge's charge be given in specific language that has been packaged as "pattern jury instructions." (Additional suggestions from the attorneys can also be submitted for consideration by the judge, but the bulk of the charge as written has been labeled "approved" by the higher court.) Therefore, most judges are reluctant to deviate from the approved form to avoid reversal--no need to try the case again. The intent of the approved language is to ensure a precise explanation of the law, not leaving this task to the degree of articulate ability of any one judge, and to provide a uniformity in the trial courts. Seems fair, probably is fair, and countless hours over many years have honed these instructions to be fair. The problem is the language. Written by judges, it is, therefore, legalese. The average person does not know the vocabulary. Even if some of them understand the words, the issues are complex, having been decided through two hundred years of changes, and the jurors hear the elements governing these issues one time.

This jury was intelligent in their own fields of endeavor and had been more than adequately educated by able attorneys on both sides of this case. From jury selection on, the process was explained, with the key phrases used repeatedly, so that by the time the judge gave them the law, they knew more than most juries. The fact that this particular jury still did not comprehend what they were supposed to do confirmed that there was a communication problem.

At 12:30 P. M., the bailiff stuck his head into the Judge's chambers.

"They say they're ready this time."

Jeff Medlin was brought from the holding cell, the attorneys were collected, spectators gathered, the jury summoned.

The jurors took their respective seats, all heads down, all looking solemn, but not grave.

This time they were unanimous.

Jeff Medlin could live. Jeff turned to his family, and gave them a thumbs up.

Brenda Medlin Driver did not see her son's gesture. She was clinging to her sister and her estranged husband Nathan, sobbing openly.

The jury was dismissed, Jeff stood, and the sentence was pronounced. After imposing the life sentence as recommended by the jury for the murder of Darla Cline, His Honor added the maximum of forty years for the armed robbery of Johnson's Restaurant to begin at the expiration of the life sentence. Translated, "life plus forty" in North Carolina at that time meant that it would be approximately thirty years before Jeff Medlin would be eligible for parole consideration.

He would be forty-nine years of age chronologically, but old and worn and experienced well beyond that number, never celebrating the aspects of life most of us take for granted. And his family was happy.

Evelyn Hill was not. This crime clearly warranted the death penalty, in her view. She knew that the death penalty existed because the legislature knew the people of North Carolina demanded that it exist, and it was her duty to prosecute what the law dictated. Darla Cline's murder was unprovoked, brutal, cold, and unforgivable. The aggravating circumstances of "prior conviction," "murder committed for the purpose of preventing arrest," and "pecuniary gain" had all been proved. Only the aggravating circumstance of "especially heinous, atrocious or cruel" was subjective. These factors were balanced against the mitigating factors of "impaired capacity" (drug addiction), "age of the defendant," "adjusting well to structured environment," "participating in drug rehabilitation programs," "favorable impression on teachers," "father who abused alcohol," "quick-tempered mother," and "supportive family."

None but "age" had seemed that pivotal in our discussion around the coffee pot. Glancing at the verdict sheet, however, we had proved, once again, the uselessness of predicting a jury's reasoning. Answering the issue of whether or not they considered Jeff's age a mitigating factor, the jury foreman had written "no."

Strictly following the guidelines of the law, thereby discussing and making a decision on each issue, the jury should have taken a longer time than a total of three hours to reach this verdict.

Perhaps Paul Simon said it best in his song THE BOXER: "A man hears what he wants to hear and disregards the rest."

Maybe the death penalty is a good concept until it becomes personal, and that's where it collapses. There exists some redeeming quality in every human being.

The jury had spoken: We value *life*, Darla Cline's *and* Jeff Medlin's.

Evelyn blamed the blonde, athletic juror on the front row, having watched him closely during the trial and having nicknamed him "the surfer." Steve Smith and Jack Hall confirmed her suspicions. Talking with the jury afterwards, they had learned that at the very beginning of their deliberations, "the surfer" had walked into the jury room, taken a seat, and announced: "I don't care what the rest of you do. I'm not going to vote for death."

Jeff's attorneys were grateful, but they admitted they had been lucky to have him. They had wanted to excuse this particular juror, but Jeff had wanted him left on the jury because he was close to his age and was someone he could identify with. Wisely, the defense team had listened to their client.

Jeff had saved his own life early in his trial.

CHAPTER THREE

May-June: State v. Davis

The Medlin case behind us on Monday, and an unexpected, four free days in front of us, we headed for the beach. I was having an "ocean attack" brought on by the beautiful weather and my never- ending call to the sea. I've always found it reassuring that even when I'm not there to see them, the waves continue to swoosh and crash on the shore. In a world where all you can count on is change, the ocean, at least, is constant.

This weekend we would start our scheduled week of vacation at Key West, one of our favorite places, for many reasons: turquoise water, tennis shoes and shorts, folk music, lunch at Louie's Backyard, sailing with Dan (our favorite minstrel), the Pigeon House Restaurant, the bartender Nancy at the Pigeon House who introduces us to the colorful locals, or "conchs," as they call themselves, and the most resplendent sunsets ever unfurled by God and beheld by man. Locals and tourists alike gather each day to witness, as if for the first time, the giant crimson ball slip slowly, silently from the watercolor sky into the emerald sea. As the final moments arrive, a hush falls--all conversation ceases as if someone has given a signal--and awestruck beings pay homage to this daily miracle. On Mallory Square, the locals show off their talents--fire-eaters, jugglers, fortune tellers, Uncle Sam on stilts, dogs climbing ladders--and hawkers sell their wares. Key lime pie, of course, is the favored dish.

Refreshed, relaxed and happy, we returned from our Elysian Fields to the real world. The temperatures at home were also prematurely high--in the high nineties, and the humidity made you feel as if you were breathing water.

Arriving home late Saturday afternoon, we unpacked only to repack immediately for the next two days. This time the shorts and tennis shoes were left behind. We would have to dress like parents. This would be the third college graduation we would attend in the last few months; mine, this past December; Craig's, a few weeks ago; and now this one. Tomorrow morning we would drive to Winston-Salem for a two-day ceremony. Our daughter Kathy was graduating with honors from Wake Forest Law School.

Jack commuted to Raleigh the next two weeks to handle dockets filled with guilty pleas. But during the last week in May, jury selection began for another capital case in his courtroom.

In one way, the Davis case was similar to the Medlin case, Medlin had pled guilty, and the jury had determined the sentence. But Eugene Davis had not pled guilty. Davis had been found guilty by a previous jury, and their sentence had been death. That had been six years ago. However, the N.C. Court of Appeals had overturned that decision--not the guilt or innocent phase, only the sentencing phase, and a new jury would decide on life or death. The conviction stood. As in Medlin, the jury would be told they would not consider his innocence; he was guilty, but they would have to hear the case in its entirety to determine the sentence.

This process is unique only to capital cases, in which the jury instead of the judge decides the sentence.

The error made, according to the appellate court, was that the aggravating circumstances murder "committed in the process of a common law robbery" and murder "committed for pecuniary gain" were redundant.

True. What was also redundant was trying this case again. The evidence had not changed.

The trial would take three weeks, and the taxpayers would foot the bill for the Judge, prosecutor, two defense attorneys, court reporter, clerk, bailiffs, and the jury. Only money versus a man's life, one could argue. But was the cost of the death penalty, which more times than not resulted in a second trial, becoming exorbitant and prohibitive? If the taxpayers were paying attention, the public would know this case was being tried for the second time. The newspaper would tell them that much. What most wouldn't know was that because this was a "capital" case, two lawyers instead of one would be paid by the State, plus the expenses of any witnesses, regardless of their geographic location, whatever investigator, psychiatrist and/or psychologist the defense chose to employ, etcetera--a defense someone who was considered by law "financially able" to hire his own attorney couldn't possibly afford. Then, if death was the outcome again, the same case would mandatorily be appealed again; therefore, again, subject to reversal and retrial.

Having the option of the death penalty, as was the will of "the people," compelled not just "careful" justice, but bending- over-backwards-standing-on-your-head-whistling-Dixie justice.

I accompanied Jack to Raleigh on June 3rd for the first day of evidence.

Maggie had the coffee hot and the Belks sales ad on prominent display for my benefit when we walked in. Jack said that if she kept aiding and abetting me to shop, he would have to hold her in contempt. Don Holland, the court reporter in the Medlin case, would be transcribing this trial also. Seemed like old home week.

The jury, comprised of eight women and four men, with three alternates (two men and one woman) had been chosen last week. The Clerk empaneled them: "Sit together, hear the evidence, and render your verdict accordingly." After these words, the clerk sent the jury immediately to their special room adjoining the courtroom.

Before the evidence could commence, a matter of law had to be settled.

The defendant had been convicted of first degree murder in his first trial, but that jury had answered "no" on their verdict form to finding "second degree rape" and "sexual offense" as aggravating circumstances. The State had not charged Mr. Davis with those crimes originally, because it was not until the first trial was underway that the prosecution had learned quite accidentally from a witness on the stand that the victim had sexual intercourse shortly before her death, either voluntarily or involuntarily. The State had blamed Eugene Davis because of the time factor stated by the pathologist--twelve to twenty-four hours before death--and had added rape and sexual assault to the aggravating circumstances.

Now, in the second trial, the defense was claiming double jeopardy if these two aggravating circumstances were again presented by the State. One jury had not believed the evidence supported these factors, so a second jury should not be allowed to consider them, the defense argued.

The Assistant District Attorney, Jacquie Lambert, asked His Honor to defer ruling on the double jeopardy question until she had more time for research--her staff was working on it and she did not intend to spell out the aggravating circumstances in her opening argument anyway. His Honor agreed to allow her some time to prepare her argument if no reference was made or evidence presented regarding these two offenses before his ruling. She promised not to broach the subject.

The defendant, Eugene Davis, had been brought into the courtroom in shackles, but the bailiff had removed the chains before the jury entered. He was now seated at the defense table between his two lawyers. He was black and tall, with a brush-top hair style, clipped closely on the sides, and he was wearing black- frame glasses. His blue and white plaid sports shirt stretched to cover his Herculean shoulders. His attorneys appeared slight by comparison.

The jurors, a distinguished looking panel, were brought back into the courtroom. This jury would not be privy to the previously decided death sentence. Instead, all they would know is what Judge Thompson told them:

"This case was tried in October and November of 1985 here in Wake County. Thereafter, as a result of certain legal proceedings, a sentencing hearing was ordered, which is the purpose of this proceeding and the reason it is here before you today. "

Jacquie Lambert was prosecutor for the State. In her early thirties, she was petite, attractive, and professional. Her straight blonde hair was pulled back and held by a white ribbon clasp at the nape of her neck.

She stood in front of the jury and began her opening argument, a forecast of what the evidence would show, a roadmap for them to follow:

"Since you are not the jury that convicted Mr. Davis in 1985, the State will present the same evidence of the prior trial to give you the basis for their decision of guilty.... However, some of the testimony will be read from the transcript because some of the original witnesses could not be here in person; one is deceased, others cannot be here due to illness or old age, and one witness, the State cannot find. But you will hear that Mr. Davis was convicted of brutally killing a seventy-year-old disabled woman."

The jury now learned that Vivian Whitaker was the victim. Having suffered a stroke, she had walked with a cane. She had lived in Apartment 405 at the Carriage House Apartments, a high- rise building for the elderly and handicapped. She had been a friend of Betty Davis, the mother of the defendant, living down the hall from her and on the same floor. The two had visited each other often, watched television together, and Vivian had shared Betty's telephone.

When Eugene Davis visited his mother, he had also frequented Mrs. Whitaker's apartment.

The evidence would further show that less than an hour after Vivian Whitaker's death, Eugene Davis was selling her property: a portable radio for two dollars and a ring that she wore on her left ring finger for one dollar.

His fingerprints had been lifted from the jewelry box found thrown on the bed and from a coffee can hidden in the closet, where the victim had stored some necklaces and cash. His palm prints had been left on a Raleigh newspaper, dated March 1, the day of the murder, which had been found under the victim's left arm. Mrs. Whitaker had been severely beaten--nine ribs were broken, one lung was punctured, and her liver had been severed in two pieces--all prior to her death. She had also been strangled.

Concluding her synopsis of the case, Ms. Lambert took her seat.

Duncan McMillan, one of the attorneys for the defense, gave a brief opening statement. He was tall and thin, around thirty-five, with a full head of slightly wavy brown hair, a dimple when he smiled, and no tan. His white pallor confirmed that he had been too busy in the preparation of this case to enjoy any time outside this summer. His co-counsel, Mike Dodd, was also slim, with closely cropped black/brown hair and a natural dark complexion. He had not enjoyed his summer either. We would hear from him later.

Mr. McMillan stood and told the jury that Eugene Davis, his client, had been convicted of common law robbery and the first degree murder of Vivian Whitaker.

"Now, seven years and three months after her death, you must decide between his life and death. You will decide what the evidence shows. Please do three things. First, go by the rules in weighing the evidence. That is what keeps us civilized.... These rules have developed over two hundred years. Second, it is vitally important to keep an open mind until all the evidence has been presented. Third, examine the evidence from all angles and examine it again.... Each of you needs to be sure."

Mr. McMillan sat down, and Ms. Lambert, representing the State, called her first witness.

On March 1, 1984, Officer Jeffrey Karpovich had been on routine patrol, assigned to respond to citizen complaints and to make the initial investigation of crimes. He testified that he had received a communication at 8:05 P.M. to go to Carriage House Apartments, a "five or six story building of limited access to its residents," on St. Mary's Street. Arriving at 8:08 by himself, he could not get into the building. The doors were locked daily at 8:00 P.M.

Two emergency rescue personnel arrived, but they could not get into the building either.

Officer Karpovich called to have someone come to unlock the doors, but Betty Davis had been on the look-out for the police. Mrs. Davis opened the door from the inside and led them to Vivian Whitaker's apartment. The three men entered Apartment 405.

"The first thing I saw was the victim on the floor," Karpovich told the jury. "The second thing was the condition of the apartment."

The woman lying on the floor was "face-up and motionless." He could see one bruise on her neck, but the emergency team was leaning over her and obstructing his view. When one of the rescue workers was searching for a pulse, he unbuttoned her jeans to get to her artery.

"I saw part of her abdomen exposed and touched it to see if the body was still warm," Karpovich stated.

"And was it?" Ms. Lambert asked.

"Yes, it was."

He testified that he had not touched or moved anything in the apartment. Three firemen had arrived just as the rescue squad determined that the woman was deceased, and they were told to leave. Karpovich then asked the rescue team to leave, secured the scene, and contacted his superiors by portable radio.

He had taken these actions to preserve physical evidence and "not let it be contaminated."

"I was sure this was a crime scene due to the mark on the neck and the condition of the apartment. It was a shambles. It had been ransacked--nothing was left untouched." When Officer Karpovich had first arrived, he had searched the hallway, and finding no one, he had ordered the area sealed off. A Patrolman was assigned to check around the neighborhood. Karpovich stayed for approximately two hours, while other detectives came and went. The crime scene was turned over to Patrolman Wheeler at 12:35 A.M.

The prosecutor, Ms. Lambert, rummaged in a sizeable box searching for her first exhibit. Setting aside the bulkiest of the exhibits, she leaned a poster-sized board against her counsel table. The large, blown-up color photograph showed the victim lying on the floor of her disarrayed apartment.

The defendant, Eugene Davis, seeing the poster, sprang to his feet and tried to leave the courtroom, violently shaking his head. Both bailiffs responded immediately, as did the two defense attorneys. The defendant was crying while the bailiffs restrained him, and his counsel requested they be allowed to talk with their client.

Judge Thompson allowed the bailiffs to escort Eugene from the courtroom, and the defense lawyers followed. The jury was sent to their room. The Judge requested that the spectators remain seated and not leave the courtroom unless it was absolutely necessary. The heavy entrance doors were loud and disruptive, and there was enough confusion for the moment.

Ten minutes later, Eugene and his attorneys, accompanied by the bailiffs, came into the courtroom and resumed their seats. The jury was summoned, and Officer Karpovich continued his testimony.

"Yes," he had been present when the medical examiner had officially proclaimed Mrs. Whitaker dead. Some things, he did remember now, had been touched at the scene. The TV had been blaring when he and the rescue personnel had arrived. One of them had turned it either down or off- -he didn't remember which. Also, the phone was ringing.

Ms. Lambert now asked him to identify what would become State's Exhibits, and an easel was positioned in front of the jury- box.

In this age of computer technology, nothing had yet replaced poster board on an easel in the courtroom.

Ms. Lambert showed the jury the following: a drawing of the floor plan of the apartment, an oversized color photograph of the victim on the floor of her apartment, and thirteen eight-by-ten color photographs of the victim and the crime scene, shot from different angles. The large picture of the victim showed a frail, elderly, black woman in blue jeans and a red-print shirt, her body lying amidst overturned flower pots. A newspaper was pinned under her left arm. Other eight-by-tens showed white sheets of paper, pocket books, the telephone on a chair, a jewelry box on the bed, drawers partially open with clothing hanging out, and bread and butter on the kitchen counter. The television was also shown; it was off. Several photographs were close-ups of the victim. Number fifteen showed just her face and neck. Pointing, Officer Karpovich continued:

"That was the injury that I recall most vividly from that night."

"To what part of her body?"

"Her neck."

Her body had been removed to the Wake Medical Center for an autopsy by order of the medical examiner.

Fred Hutchins, a blond, lanky, tall man took the stand. He was one of the paramedics who had arrived first at Apartment 405 that night and had to wait until Mrs. Davis, the defendant's mother, let them in the building. He had found no signs of life when he examined Mrs. Whitaker, so, in his opinion, she was deceased when they arrived. He had noticed "a horizontal mark to her left neck."

"Yes, he had been the one that unsnapped her jeans "to check for a femoral pulse."

The third witness, Lucy Scarborough, was seventy-two years old. She was a short, ample, black woman wearing a black, white, and red print dress, topped with a purple and blue flowered jacket. She had lived in Apartment 406 across the hall from Vivian Whitaker for eleven years.

"I was not a good friend, myself, but, yeah, I knew her."

Q. "Did you know Eugene?

A. "Yeah. I seen him go around there with his mama and I seen him go there to get his mama.

Q. Did you see Vivian Whitaker on that day, on March 1, 1984?

A. Yes, I did. It was around 5:30 when she went in her apartment. When we parted, I said to her, 'You've got on a beautiful dress.' And that's all I said to her, and she went in her apartment, and I went in mine. The next thing I knew, I heard a loud knock--just like that--" (*Ms. Scarborough demonstrated by pounding her fist in front of the microphone on the witness stand. The knock reverberated in the courtroom.*) I looked around like this, *demonstrating by looking over her right shoulder*) and saw my door was locked, so I didn't even move. I knew it wasn't at my door.

Q. Did you hear this knock about 6:30?

A. No. It was before that--a hard knock.

Q. Did you also know Mrs. Betty Davis, the defendant's mother?

A. Yes. She lived three doors up.

Beatrice Randolph walked slowly with her cane to the witness stand. Her hair was totally white, and she was wearing a dark flowered print dress over her small frame and a single-strand pearl choker. She had lived in Apartment 413 for eleven years. She described the complex as a building for "certain-age people-- not young folks--my category."

Q. Do you mind telling us how old you are?

A. No. I'm eighty-two.

Q. Did you know Vivian Whitaker?

A. I saw her going and coming in the elevator, maybe at the launderette, but we did not visit.

Q. Did you know Betty Davis?

A. I lived two doors from Mrs. Davis, but I never did see her. She was going and coming all the time.

Q. Do you recall that night, between seven and eight o'clock?

A. Yeah. Sure, I do. I heard somebody running down the hall and slam the Exit door. So I decided to look out the window and maybe I could see him when he hit the laundry--whoever it was- -and I saw the back of him.

Q. Could you tell if it was a man or woman?

A. It was a man--I could tell that much. I couldn't see his face.

Q. Could you tell if he was a black man or white?

A. Yes.

Q. Which one? Was it a black man or a white man?

A. A black man.

Mrs. Sears would testify next. Her bearing was almost regal as she used her cane to climb to the witness box. She also had white hair and was wearing a blue and white print blouse with a navy skirt and a white cardigan. She was eighty-one years old, had lived in Apartment 410 for eleven years, and had known Vivian Whitaker.

"I knew her when I saw her, mostly in the laundry room. I saw her dragging her foot."

She also knew Betty Davis, the defendant's mother. Mrs. Davis lived in 411.

"Christmas of 1983, she come to my apartment to use the telephone. I could not refuse her because it was Christmas Day. Then she used it one more time."

Q. Did you know her son?

A. I had seen him there--coming to visit his mother.

Q. Do you recall seeing or hearing anything on March 1, 1984?

A. I heard voices--very fast. I looked through the peephole, but I couldn't see anyone. I recognized Betty Davis' voice, but I did not know the man's voice. It was a very few seconds. God has given me good hearing, but I wouldn't open my door to see. I heard the exit door close unusually hard, and I heard another door close and the chain go on. I called Mr. Brown because it was so unusual to hear all this talking and the fire door closing so hard, but he didn't do a thing about it.

Q. Would you say this happened around 6:30?

A. I did not look at a clock, but my husband and I usually eat our evening meal around 6:00, and I had already washed the dishes and settled in my recliner.

Ms. Deborah Sanders was next to testify. In March of 1984, she had lived with her mother in Walnut Terrace, located behind the Memorial Auditorium.

Q. Do you know the defendant?

A. Yes.

Q. Had you known him prior to March of 1984?

A. Yes.

Q. How did you know him?

A. He did chores for my mother. She called him 'son.'

Q. The day before Eugene Davis was arrested, did you see him at your mother's home?

A. Yes. He was there when I came in with a cousin and a friend, Cecil Smith and Ronald Thorp.

Q. Isn't Ronald Thorp the grandson of Vivian Whitaker, the deceased?

A. Yes.

Eugene Davis had brought a ring and a radio, which the witness now identified, to Mrs. Primous's house. Ms. Sanders had bought the ring for one dollar--"that's what he asked"--and her mother had bought the radio for two dollars.

Someone in the courtroom groaned.

Q. Was Mr. Thorp present when you bought the ring?

A. Yes.

But when a police officer came to the house later, Ms. Sanders gave him the ring and told him whom she had bought it from and how much she paid for it.

Deborah Sanders' mother, Mary Primous, took the stand next. She had heard the defendant had been arrested, but:

"I had seen him on TV before I heard what he'd done. He had a ring and this radio here."

"Did he tell you where the radio came from or why he was selling it?"

"No."

After hearing of the arrest, Mrs. Primous had called the police and told them to come get the radio. Officers Parker and Munday had picked it up.

The State called Peggy Graham, the victim's daughter. Vivian Whitaker had been the mother of a large family.

> Q. How many of you are there?
>
> A. It's nine of us.

Peggy had not seen her mother that day, but usually talked to her every day.

> A. I had a habit of calling after I got home from work. That day, I tried to call her about six.
>
> Q. Did you get an answer?
>
> A. No.
>
> Q. Did you make any further efforts?
>
> A. Several. Until nine-thirty or ten.

Peggy Graham was again asked to identify her mother's possessions, now marked with evidence tags, six years after she had done so in the first trial.

She recognized the radio, saying her mother had ordered it from a catalog. Peggy had borrowed it several times and had just returned the radio to her mother the Sunday before the murder when her mother had come to dinner.

Ms. Lambert showed her the ring.

> A. It's Mother's ring, which my brother had given her.
>
> Q. Which brother?
>
> A. Rufus. She always wore it on her left hand, ring finger.

Ms. Lambert also had the witness identify some of the photographs of her mother's apartment.

Exhibit Number Ten showed a brown paper bag near a chair. Ms. Graham identified the contents, now in the courtroom, as belonging to her brother Gene.

She said he had spent the night with his mother because he had an appointment downtown and had brought a change of clothes, leaving his work clothes behind. She explained that the boots in the bag had the name of her deceased brother-in-law written inside them, but Gene wore them now. Exhibit Eighteen A was a green cigarette case belonging to her mother, which "she kept in her purse most of the time," and Exhibit Eighteen B was the cigarette lighter Peggy had given her mother.

Ms. Lambert showed Ms. Graham Exhibit Thirty-three. They were her mother's eyeglasses, she said in a quivering voice.

There were no further questions.

The victim's son, James Whitaker, was next to testify.

"I did not see her that Thursday, but she called me and invited me to supper."

> Q. What time did she call you?
>
> A. Around 11:30 A. M. But I couldn't get in touch with her at five o'clock. I called about three times. Then a friend

whose father lived at the Carriage House called me and told me she thought something was wrong, and I'd better check on my mother.

James also identified the ring.

> A. My brother gave it to her one year for Mother's Day. She always showed it off and said, 'Look at what my son gave me.'
>
> Q. Did you ever see her that she did not have it on?
>
> A. No.

James had also borrowed the radio from time to time.

Melba Thorp, wearing a denim skirt and white blouse, took the stand. She was Vivian Whitaker's oldest daughter. "I talked with my mother every day. I wasn't working at the time, and I visited every other day. I was into cooking, and she was too. On that day, we talked and talked from 12:30 on until 3:00 when she realized her 'soap' was on. Most people thought we were sisters because we were friends."

Her mother had spent the night with Melba several nights before her life ended, and when she had taken her mother home, Melba had gone up to the apartment and had seen the radio there at that time. After identifying the ring, cigarette lighter, and case, Mrs. Thorp also identified a coffee can, telling the jury that her mother sometimes kept jewelry in it.

"Most of her jewelry was Avon." She had also been known to hide cash in the can. "She always kept it in the corner of her closet. We didn't have no business going into it."

Examining the picture taken the day of the murder of her mother's closet, Melba said her mother "never kept it that way."

Almost every woman possesses jewelry of some kind. Many possibly hide some pieces. Jean Auel, author of Clan of the Cavebear would call it "memory;" that through some ancient instinct a woman inherits a trait that compels her to adorn herself with precious metals, stones or shells or imitations thereof. For, regardless of her financial status, a woman will acquire at least some jewelry in her lifetime which she counts among her most prized possessions. And in some cultures, an urge to decorate your body extends to the man.

Vivian had been especially proud of her ring, and she had valued her Avon jewelry enough to hide it in a can and hide the can in her closet.

Looking at more photographs of her mother's apartment, Melba Thorp identified Vivian's black cane, saying her mother had been paralyzed on her left side after suffering a stroke and she had difficulty walking. She testified that not only were the jewelry box, clothes, pocketbook (normally also in the closet), and telephone out of place, but the bed and dresser had also been rearranged since she had last been in her mother's apartment.

Gene Whitaker, another son of Vivian Whitaker, took the stand and testified briefly. "Yes," he had spent the night at his mother's place two days before she was killed. He had left his work clothes in a brown bag in her apartment.

His brother, Rufus Whitaker, Jr., was the next witness.

He identified the radio he had seen in her apartment and the ring he had given his mother for Mother's Day.

"It's a 'mother's ring.' The gold band was set with seven birthstones, one for each child she had borne.

The Supreme Court's "redundant" decision had yielded yet another side effect. Mrs. Whitaker's large, close family, once again, had been forced to summon fresh, vivid images of that dreadful night. If time had started to heal their wounds, the scabs were now ripped off, their pain rekindled.

The District Attorney's Office had not been able to locate Mr. Cherry, so his testimony would be read from the transcript of the trial six years ago by a member of their staff.

In 1984, Mr. Cherry had been in the moving and storage business. His mother had lived in Carriage House Apartments on the third floor. Between six and seven o'clock on the night of March the first, he had been at his mother's apartment. She was handicapped, and he went there to cook supper every night. He had heard "noises and voices" and someone saying, 'Stop. Stop. Go on. Go on.'

"It was a lady's voice." Something was vibrating against the floor of the fourth floor apartment above.

Mr. Gilbert Brown and Mrs. Doris Brown were also unavailable as witnesses, so their testimony from the previous trial was also read by a stand-in. The Browns had not only been residents of the Carriage House Apartments at the time Vivian Whitaker was murdered, but they also were employed as night supervisors or caretakers for the building. They had seen Eugene Davis inside the building at six-thirty that night. While they were reading the bulletin board, the defendant entered the elevator. The light over the elevator doors indicated that he had gone to the fourth floor. "Yes," Mr. Brown recalled Mrs. Sears calling him shortly before eight o'clock.

"She told me that she heard quite a ruckus upstairs. I told her to stay in her apartment and lock the doors." He did not intend to check out her complaint.

"We had trouble before, and I wasn't going up there."

It appeared that not only were the residents of the building reluctant to venture outside their apartment doors, but so were the people who were employed to handle the problems.

Doctor Kassa, the Medical Examiner for Wake County, testified next. In cases of violent or unnatural deaths, he told the jury, he was authorized to order an autopsy if he thought one was warranted.

He had ordered an autopsy on Vivian Whitaker. When he arrived that night after eight o'clock, he found the victim lying on her back on the floor with her "arms stretched out...at angles approaching ninety degrees from her body." Upon placing his hand underneath her back, he observed "there was still body heat present." Therefore, he had estimated the time of death to have "occurred within a matter of a few hours or less."

Ronald Thorp, Vivian Whitaker's grandson, could not be located by the State, so his testimony was read from the previous trial transcript. He had testified that on March 1, 1984, he had been waiting for Deborah Sanders to take her to get her check cashed, and he had seen Eugene Davis for the first time.

"When we got back, he was there and he had, you know, some things he wanted to sell. See, he was kindly nervous, shaky, you know, and Deborah and Cecil, my friend--they had went into the kitchen. So I stayed in--I was looking at TV. So later on that night, Deborah had showed me that ring there that she had got from Eugene, and I didn't notice the ring until later on. I thought about it. When I found out she had got killed, that is when I thought about the ring, and I went and told the detective that there was a fellow in Walnut Terrace selling some stuff, that he might want to look into it or whatever... Then he [Eugene] wanted to use the telephone, but he was so shaky, like he had to get--I think it was the mother to dial the number for him."

When Ronald was shown some of the pictures taken of his grand-mother's apartment, he was asked if she usually left her home in this messy state.

"Naw," he replied "She kept it clean."

At ten o'clock that night, upon learning of his grandmother's death, Ronald realized that had been her ring he was looking at just an hour or two before.

All of this testimony had taken place in the space of a day. Judge Thompson had to drive the hour-plus trip home, and he had work to do when he got there.

He would have to rule first thing in the morning on the double jeopardy question raised early this morning by the defense: "Second degree rape" and "Sexual assault" had been submitted to the first jury six years ago, but as two of the aggravating circumstances on the jury sheet, not as charges. That jury found these two factors as not valid and had marked "no" beside these two circumstances. The defendant had not been charged the first time with these crimes because this evidence was a surprise and had surfaced in the first trial through a witness from the witness stand. In the present trial, the defendant was charged with these two crimes.

The defense was contending that this evidence should not be allowed to enter this trial. Their argument was that the previous jury had already decided these issues and it would be double jeopardy to allow this evidence again. The prosecution, of course, argued that the evidence should be included.

Jack started his thinking process in the car and we talked about the case during most of the ride home.

The defense had offered a North Carolina Supreme Court case (State v. Silhan) as precedent that the evidence should not be admitted.

However *(and there's always a "however")* a U.S. Supreme Court case offered by the prosecutor (Poland v. Arizona) had ruled the opposite.

Normally, a U.S. Supreme Court case will override a State Supreme Court case regarding constitutional rights when there is a conflict in State law, because the U.S. Supreme Court is "the supreme law of the land," unless the State is more lenient or gives its citizens more rights than the federal government, as they had in Silhan.

Suffice it to say that the issue raised was complex. Both cases were law, but only a talented gypsy with a genuine crystal ball would be able to predict which way either court would rule, given the particular circumstances in this case.

Jack knew he had to do two things first, though, before making his decision. The transcript from the previous trial might provide some answers as to just what the evidence would be and he would have to read that tonight; then he would consider the prosecutor's argument in the morning.

Sifting through the seven-hundred-and-fifty page transcript to find those portions relating to the sexual evidence was a substantial task.

Sitting on the floor of his study, surrounded by transcript pages, I searched for the pertinent witnesses' testimonies while Jack read the mounting pages I handed him.

That's when it really got crazy. The transcript revealed that it had been the defense who had brought up the sexual evidence--the defense attorney kept asking why the rape-kit was not sent to the SBI lab for analysis.

Why a rape-kit? According to the evidence today, the victim had been found fully clothed, jeans in place. But further reading revealed that when her jeans were removed in order to do the autopsy, the Medical Examiner discovered that both of her legs were inside the same hole of her underpants. Suspecting possible sexual activity, the pathologist had taken the appropriate smears and had preserved them, using a rape-kit. But he had never relayed this information to the investigating police. Consequently, the police, knowing nothing about her state of undress underneath her clothes, never ordered an analysis of the smears. It amounted to a simple breakdown in communication.

But it was still not clear why the defense would want to bring it up in the first trial when the prosecution still didn't know about it. Reading the transcript, it became obvious that the District Attorney and the presiding judge were also confused, but only for a while. The light finally dawned as to what the defense attorney was doing. He was "chasing a rabbit"--trying to shift suspicion to another person and away from his client to raise reasonable doubt, a Matlock or Perry Mason tactic.

It seems that Mrs. Whitaker had a male friend. He had eaten dinner with Vivian the night before the murder and had asked her "to cook me something the next day." He testified, however, that he had not kept this date on the day of the murder and didn't try to call her until three hours after his usual time of arrival; dialing her number around eight o'clock, he got no answer, and he didn't try again. He admitted that he had never before "not shown up" when she was expecting him for a meal. "Yes," that was the first time. Yet, he did not keep calling her or try to check on her. He said it had been at least a week before that day since he had had sexual relations with Vivian.

"But is he telling the truth? Could he have been the killer?" the defense was hinting.

Also, why had no one inked this male friend's hands for the purpose of eliminating his prints from the crime scene, a precaution that was taken with several other people? Why was he not a suspect?

As a result of the defense raising the issue, the D. A. had the vaginal samples tested during the course of the first trial. He discovered now, a year after the autopsy, that there was semen present--the problem was that the tests were inconclusive as to what blood-type person produced this semen. One reason given was that the enzymes break down after some time has passed. "Who knows what the test may have shown a year ago?" was the point the defense was trying to make.

The State did not agree. The test did show that the victim had engaged in sexual activity within twelve to twenty-four hours before her death, so the prosecutor decided the man must have been Eugene Davis, and sexual offenses were added as aggravating circumstances for the jury to consider.

But the victim was a sexually active woman, the defense would argue; therefore, it could have been anyone within that time frame before the murder. Also, they would point out that the defendant had no scratches or marks on his body indicating someone had struggled with him. The jury had agreed on this point: they were not convinced that Eugene Davis had sexually assaulted her.

The first jury had convicted Eugene Davis of the murder, though, so the defense counsel's "rabbit" had not worked. The District Attorney, however, *had not been successful in turning the unexpected sexual evidence to his advantage either. He couldn't kill the hare after the defense had chased it.*

After reviewing the transcript evidence, whether double jeopardy attached and which Supreme Court case controlled was less important. In Jack's opinion, there simply was not substantial evidence to classify these two allegations as aggravating circumstances. But he would wait to hear what the prosecutor had come up with overnight.

It was late when we ate dinner, later when we packed, and early when we left for the following morning. Jack had decided to spend the rest of the week in Raleigh.

Throughout this week, during breaks, Maggie talked to me from behind the stacks of papers and files piled high on her desk. She had worked within the court system for many years, so I asked her about the length of time it had taken for this case to be reversed and tried again--six years seemed unusual--but then the no-go case in Rutherfordton had been five years old. Maggie confirmed that five or six years were not exceptional. A few weeks ago they had retried one after seven years. And none of the cases we were discussing were being retried because of the recent McKoy ruling.

All those were yet to come.

"Wouldn't it be more effective to legislate 'life without parole' as the most serious offense instead of spending all this money twice for each person on death row?" I asked.

"There you go," Maggie laughed. "You're looking for logic. I've warned you about that."

"Right. Besides, it probably wouldn't work. If life without parole was for the most serious offense, they'd eventually review it the same way."

"Not necessarily," Maggie shrugged, "that would be logical."

I laughed. Maggie always made me feel better.

The jury was kept out of the courtroom the next morning long enough for Judge Thompson to hear Ms. Lambert's argument. When she concluded, he asked if the State had any additional evidence of sexual assault or rape than they had at the previous trial. The reply was "no." The judge then recounted the evidence as he had understood it from the first trial transcript and gave the State the chance to add whatever else they had. The prosecutor had nothing more. Judge Thompson made his decision.

The Court ruled that any evidence of rape or sexual assault or, for that matter, sexual intercourse, would not be admissible, thereby granting the defense team's motion.

Apparently, the prosecutor had not expected this turn of events, which would greatly alter both the content and the length of her witnesses' testimony. She had lost two aggravating circumstances and had gained scheduling problems. Karen, her witness coordinator, would work overtime tonight.

Ms. Lambert's next witness was deceased. Therefore, Detective Willard Parker's testimony would be read by the investigator for the D. A.'s office. Detective Parker had been assigned to the Major Task Force Unit with the Investigative Division of the Raleigh Police Department and had become the chief case agent for the Whitaker homicide. He received the call at nine that night and arrived at her apartment at nine-thirty, riding up on the elevator with Officer Bob Hallisey, the evidence technician with the City- County Bureau of Identification. Hallisey "immediately began to take video tapes of the crime scene," he told the jury.

"I had a tape recorder with a mini-cassette in it, and I taped the events and the places that took place. The crime scene was photographed and videoed prior to anything else being done. I went in initially and looked at the apartment, and then I went out and stood by the door. Detective Arnold, having a great deal of experience in the field of collection and preservation of evidence, assisted the CCBI in their work on the inside of the room, and he relayed what was going on to me, and I put it on the tape recorder; also, occasionally he would call me in to look at something and I would record that and go back out."

Parker had supervised the lifting of latent fingerprints from objects in the room and from the neck of Vivian Whitaker. Bags were placed over her hands to preserve fingernail scrapings which would be taken at the hospital. Thirty-seven items were taken from the apartment, bagged, marked and preserved.

Detective Parker had also talked to Eugene Davis after he was arrested and had taken the defendant's clothing as well as samples of blood and hair which would be tested at the lab. He also took the Bic lighter that Eugene had been using and had casually put on the interrogation room table during his questioning. It was the same lighter that had been identified by Mrs. Whitaker's children. He asked Eugene about the lighter. Eugene explained that he had previously loaned Vivian Whitaker some cigarettes and that he had knocked on her door that night to ask her for some. When she walked down the hall to get some, he had reached in the apartment to get the lighter, but had not actually entered the apartment.

Detective Arnold, who had been with the Raleigh police Department at the time of the crime, testified that he had investigated the crime scene and had sat in during the questioning of the suspect. After Detective Parker had asked all the questions, the interview was taped and typed. Eugene had estimated that it had been around six o'clock that night when he had seen Vivian. He asked her where his mother was, and she said she had not seen his mother that day.

"I always go down to Mrs. Whitaker's to see if Mama's there. That's where mama be at all the time. I don't never go in there when Mama ain't there. She was a nice lady. Every time I asked her for a cigarette, if she had some, she'd give me one."

Detective Arnold asked him why he had been looking for his mother.

"I ain't got no place to go. I usually go to the soup line. I don't want Mama to know."

He said he could not stay with his mother because of the rules of the apartment house. After he talked with Mrs. Whitaker, she had brought him some cigarettes, and he had then gone to his mother's apartment to look in the refrigerator and cabinet for food. He had found none.

"Did you ask your mama for money?"

"Yes."

"Did she give you any?"

"No."

Eugene told the detective that he had left his mother's apartment ten minutes after he arrived. He then went to work at Buckeyes, played pool, and picked up cans. The last time he was in Mrs. Whitaker's apartment had been a week before. He was, again, looking for his mother. He had moved the bed out from the wall for her. The detective didn't believe him.

> Q. Why are you lying to me? How did you think you could kill her and go through everything and not leave fingerprints? How do you think I got an arrest warrant for you? Do you know where we got your fingerprints? Yesterday's newspaper, the Raleigh Times.
>
> A. Where?
>
> Q. From the newspaper. Right beside the body.
>
> A. Man, you ain't got that shit.
>
> Q. What caused it? What set you off?
>
> A. I wouldn't hurt her. Man, as many times as I've been down there with my mother. I got a feeling what you're trying to say is that I killed her.
>
> Q. You did kill her. I've got a warrant, and I had to have evidence to get it.
>
> A. I'll tell you a hundred thousand damn times that I didn't.

Q. How did we get your palm print off the newspaper next to the body?

A. I ain't been there yesterday. I have been in there before. Man, I wouldn't hurt nobody. I'm not a mean type person.

Q. Did you and her get into an argument over that watch that you were supposed to have stolen from her?

A. No. She told my mama, and my mama asked me, and I told mama, no, I did not take Mrs. Whitaker's watch.

Q. Did Mrs. Whitaker ask you about that watch again yesterday?

A. No. She didn't ask me nothing about that watch. She never asked me nothing about that watch.

Q. Did you ask her for money?

A. No. But I had before and she gave me ten dollars.

Q. She was a nice lady. I think you regret what happened and may not remember what happened. Were you drunk?

A. No. I was decently high, but by the time I got there, it had damn near wore off.

Parker testified that he persisted in asking Eugene Davis why he had killed Vivian Whitaker, and Eugene kept denying that he had.

Q. Well, something happened in the apartment that we don't know about other than what we are looking at. I don't know whether that woman slapped you or tried to cut you. I don't know...

A. That woman ain't never done nothing to me.

Q. I don't believe you would go there and deliberately hurt a woman that hadn't done anything to you. Something caused it. Something set it off. Just like a spark and a stick of dynamite. It doesn't go off by itself. Something caused it to go off. Do you ever have fits of anger when you just want to hurt somebody?

A. No.

During the interview, the detectives began wondering if Eugene Davis was a mental case or had blacked out and didn't remember anything.

Detective Hallisey described his investigation of the crime scene. The first thing he did was to record it on video tape for "preservation of initial contact." The second thing was to "process the body" for potential latent fingerprints not necessarily visible to the naked eye. In addition to the objects in the room, Vivian Whitaker's neck was also examined for prints: "I did make some lifts, but nothing that was readable." He told the jury that it was not unusual to obtain fingerprints that were not sufficient to use in a comparison. Explaining to the jury, he gave the following example: A child leaves the best fingerprints on a doorknob because he grabs it with his fingertips; when an adult grabs a doorknob and turns it, he is actually smearing the latent prints.

In this case, the victim's hands had been "processed" later at Wake County Morgue for clippings--the nails were clipped and then scraped for anything underneath. No residue of skin tissue or blood was found.

It was one o'clock and court was recessed for lunch until 2:30. Judge Bailey had brought Judge Brewer with him this time, and they joined us for lunch in the cafeteria across the mall. The discussion at lunch centered around the rise in crime and the consequent overcrowding in the jails, which resulted in inmates being released too soon; thereby, free to commit more crimes. The "more crimes" were therefore being committed by the same people, who were picked up by the same police, housed by the same jailers, and released by the

*same parole board. Put them in, let them out, put them in again. In some
instances, the judges felt that the people they sentenced were released by the
time they drove home that night. They were frustrated and angry. While the
legislature found it popular to write longer mandatory sentences into the law,
thus giving the impression of cracking down on crime, they did not find it
popular to go one step further and provide the funds to house those receiving
the longer sentences--the house that Jack built syndrome. Thus with no prison
space to maintain humane conditions, the parole board had no choice but to
reduce sentences drastically, and the cycle began anew.*

*At this point, except for the most serious offenses, prisoners were serv-
ing an average of one month for each year of their sentence: ten years = ten
months. The problem was not that simple, and certainly not new, just worse,
and with no viable alternative in sight. Some judges had started giving the
absolute maximum.*

*Cynically, they decided it would be simpler to have a computer ter-
minal on the Judge's bench with a direct link to the parole board. The judge
could pass sentence, key it in on his terminal, the parole board could reply,
and the offender could walk free from the courtroom. Think of all those secretaries and clerks who would not be needed; the prison vans could save on gas,
no new handcuffs needed; just take them off the guy leaving and put them
on the one coming in--an efficient and economic system. The only problem
was justice.*

After the lunch break, Court resumed for the afternoon, and Officer
Hallisey returned to the stand. Describing Vivian Whitaker's body on the
night she was killed, he had observed blood coming out of her right nos-
tril and a clotted area of blood on the bruised area of her neck. "Yes," her
brass bed was pulled out from the wall. Looking for fingerprints, he had
processed walls, doors, the hallway, the exit door to the stairs, the elevator,
a broken mirror and saucer found on the floor, and the headboard of her
bed. Some prints were useable, but not identifiable. Better prints were lifted
from her jewelry box, the lid of a coffee can, the telephone and the Raleigh

Times dated March 1, 1984. The results were turned over to SBI Agent Marty Ludas, along with the defendant's shoes that had been taken from him at the jail. The red smudge on the door that appeared in the photographs turned out to be "ordinary ketchup." Hair samples were taken from an inside door handle and a chair in the living room. These were also sent to the SBI lab along with hair samples from the victim and the defendant.

At the conclusion of Detective Hallisey's testimony, the defense requested a *voir dire* hearing concerning the testimony of Dr. LaGrand, the next witness scheduled by the State. The jury was sent out, and the good doctor could ultimately testify twice; now, and then again, before the jury, depending on how the Judge ruled on the defense motion to not admit his testimony.

Representing the defense, Mr. McMillan claimed that the Doctor's "opinions were speculative," without underlying data to support the opinions. Their questions concerned the autopsy report and the amount of blood present in the pleural cavity. Dr. LeGrand had stated in the previous trial, that based on his findings, in his opinion, that both the amount of blood found in the lungs and the severance of the liver, the victim's injuries had been caused by as many as three blows. The liver, which was "akin to a sponge full of blood" had been literally torn in two.

The defense wanted to challenge him on that opinion, mainly to lessen the chances for the prosecution to list "especially heinous, atrocious, or cruel" as an aggravating circumstance. Mr. McMillan wanted to show that "multiple blows" was an erroneous guess on the part of the witness.

Dr. LeGrand took the stand and Mr. McMillan asked the questions.

Q. Does blood flow out of the liver upon death?

A. No, sir.

Q. If the liver was severed a few moments after death-- after the heart stopped beating--the blood would have flowed out into the peritoneal cavity, would it not?

A. Not very much--a few cc's, but these structures tend to collapse where they are severed, and you can see clotting. There are other factors that play a part, such as post-mortem blood clots.

Q. Did you notice any post-mortem blood clotting on Vivian Whitaker's liver?

A. No.

Q. If you had, would you have recorded it?

A. Probably not.

Q. Do you know how much blood leaked out of the liver?

A. No, sir. But sufficient blood had leaked out of the liver so that the liver was no longer congested.

Q. You have no way of knowing if the heart was still beating at the time the liver was severed?

A. No. Except that the liver would be more congested if ....

The doctor was basing his opinion on the fact that the lung was punctured by a broken rib. He stated that a hard blow would have broken the ribs so that they pointed *outward*. Once the ribs were broken, it would have taken another blow to push the ribs into the lung. He admitted that there were no exterior marks to indicate multiple blows, but not knowing the "blunt instrument" used, the doctor contended one blow would have required extensive force.

Q. The more times you hit someone, the more you would expect to leave a mark, would you not?

A. Yes, sir. I'm not a physicist, but a blow powerful enough, quick enough....

They went back and forth, resulting in the doctor's saying, "You could argue either way--speculating in the absence of anything being presented that was used to inflict the wound." and "It could have happened with either one or multiple blows. I lean to multiple, but you could lean either way. "

One of the problems with medicine and the law is that doctors and lawyers want it both ways. "A reasonable degree of medical certainty" depends on who wants to know--who wants to nail down, and who wants to cloud the issue.

The defense then called their own expert, Dr. Page Hudson, to counter the prosecution expert and confuse the issue further. His first testimony would also be given outside the presence of the jury.

Dr. Hudson, among his many qualifications, had studied at the Department of Legal Medicine at Harvard. He had served as the Chief Medical Examiner in Raleigh from 1968 to 1986, and had taught at East Carolina University School of Medicine as a Professor of Pathology since that time, retiring in March of this year. The District Attorney stipulated to his qualifications as an expert in the field of pathology--the doctor was well known and highly respected. In the sixties, he had been primarily responsible for replacing North Carolina's non-medically trained Coroners with Medical Examiners, who had to be physicians.

Dr. Hudson had read the autopsy report and the transcript of Dr. LaGrand's testimony from the first trial, and he had been present for today's testimony. At the time of Mrs. Whitaker's autopsy, he had still been serving as the Chief Medical Examiner. He disagreed that multiple blows had been inflicted. In his opinion, it was most likely that one blow had caused the extensive damage to her lung, liver, diaphragm, and ribs.

Dr. LaGrand, himself highly qualified, now sat in the courtroom audience and listened to his predecessor and esteemed colleague disagree with him on this point.

A. It is most likely that one blow caused the damage to the lung, liver, diaphragm and ribs.

Q. On what basis, Dr. Hudson, do you form this opinion?

A. Experience with other cases. The impact site that would be required would be small. The effected areas are close in proximity and overlap each other. The ribs are attached to the sternum, and, in my opinion, a broad, heavy blow ... These are symmetrical rib fractures ...

Q. Do you recall that Dr. LaGrand said it would have taken three blows to cause these injuries?

A. Yes, sir. I recall that.

Q. Do you concur with that opinion?

A. The greater the number of impacts, the greater potential for superficial injuries, and I'm really impressed with the symmetry of the injuries here. If there were multiple blows, it would be expected to find multiple superficial injuries.

Q. Do you have an opinion about whether the severance of the liver occurred prior to death or after death?

A. No, sir. I cannot determine if it was a short time before or short time after. The amount of blood is not sufficient to determine that.

Q. In about how many autopsies have you been the chief pathologist?

A. Four thousand. And I have taken part hands-on in another four thousand or so and reviewed records on multiple thousands.

On cross-examination, the prosecutor gained little ground.

Q. Doctor, are you saying that it is more likely that one blow caused all the injuries?

A. No. Not at all. I'm saying that it would take only one blow to cause the injuries to the ribs, liver, lung, and diaphragm.

Q. On what basis do you form that opinion?

A. When the insult comes to the lower sternum, it will deliver crushing injuries without bruises.

Q. Do you have an opinion on what amount of force it would take?

A. The force is hard to quantify--not the force of being kicked by a horse, not a fist--it's not broad enough--a head, a butt, someone sitting on that area--

Q. Could a foot have caused the injuries?

A. Yes. In my opinion, an unshod foot could have--but a shoe with a sole, no.

The defense concluded with one counter question.

Q. Would the age of the victim have anything to do with the force of the blow?

A. Yes. The ribs are more brittle with age, especially in older women, due to osteoporosis.

The *voir dire* took the rest of this Wednesday afternoon. The Court took the issue of whether or not the jury would hear this testimony from the two doctors under advisement. At the conclusion of the two doctors' testimony for today, Dr. Hudson waited for court to be adjourned and approached the bench to talk to the judge. He had remembered Judge Thompson from his days as District Attorney in Fayetteville.

We ate dinner in a quiet Italian restaurant, Est-Est-Est, featuring homemade pasta, and turned in early.

The prosecution had emphasized the fingerprint evidence in their opening argument to the jury. The next morning, the jury would hear it first-hand from Marty Ludas, the next witness.

Mr. Ludas had been with the CCBI (County/City Bureau of Identification) for nine years, and had previously worked in the SBI crime lab, where his main job was to examine forensic evidence. Eugene Davis's prints had been "lifted" from a number of objects in Vivian Whitaker's apartment: right index finger from the side of the jewelry box, right index finger from the lid of the coffee can, right and left middle fingers and three separate right palm prints from the *Raleigh Times* dated the day of the murder. The jury was shown an impressive enlargement of a right palm print taken from the newspaper.

Agent Ludas had marked twenty points of identification that he had compared with Eugene Davis' palm, and there were more.

One by one, the fascinated jury examined the comparison for themselves.

In addition to the fingerprints, a fragmentary shoe track had been examined by Agent Ludas. The track had parallel lines which appeared to wave and would have come from a common topsider or deck-type shoe with a hard rubber sole. Exhibit 32, the actual shoes of the defendant, had a wavy pattern with parallel lines. Both the shoe and print were consistent in size and wear, but "the impression was too fragmentary to identify." In other words, "this shoe cannot be eliminated from making that impression" was the most the witness could testify to.

James Johnson, who was employed as a security guard, was sworn to testify next.

Q. What was your relationship with Vivian Whitaker?

A. Boyfriend and girlfriend.

Q. When was the last time you saw her alive?

A. The day before she passed.

Q. Were you supposed to see her on the night of March first?

A. I was.

Q. What time?

A. No specific time, whenever I get off work. But I didn't make it there that night.

Q. Did you call her to tell her you would not be coming?

A. I called her around eight o'clock.

Q. Did you get an answer?

A. No.

Q. How long had you been dating?

A. Twelve to fifteen years.

Q. Did you ever give Mrs. Whitaker money?

A. Yes, I did. Her and I both were going to the doctor. We were supposed to have a stash. If I needed it, I could get it; if she needed it, she could get it.

Q. Did you know where she kept that cash?

A. No. I didn't.

In the last trial, Mr. Johnson had testified that they had not had intercourse for a week. However, since the sexual evidence had been ruled inadmissible, he was excused without having to answer any questions regarding their sex life.)

It was now time for the jury to hear Dr. Lagrand's testimony. The court had ruled after his first testimony (*without the jury*) that there was sufficient criteria on which to base an opinion of multiple blows, even though that would conflict with another expert's opinion. Opinions of experts are just that, opinions, which could, and often did, vary.

For her first question, Ms. Lambert, the prosecutor, showed him the sixteen-by-twenty-color photograph of the victim lying on the floor of her apartment and asked Dr. LaGrand if he recognized her. He replied that he did.

Ms. Lambert then placed the over-sized photograph on the floor and leaned it against the witness box face-out in full view of the jury. Throughout this technically oriented testimony given by this mild, soft-spoken man, his clinical account would be personalized by this gruesome reminder of her violent death.

LaGrand found "particularly noteworthy" the bruising and scraping about her neck. He had found a blood-tinged fluid in her mouth and a fluid on the lips that was pink which would indicate that it was tinged with blood. During autopsy, he had determined that both calf muscles in her legs were atrophied, smaller than normal, which could have been caused by an older--or not so recent--stroke, which would result in weakness in her legs. Ribs two through nine on both the right and left side were fractured; there was a puncture of the pleura of the lung--the membrane that covers the surface of the lung--and approximately 300 milliliters (about a cup) of blood in the left pleural cavity. This was a significant amount, he explained to the jury, because no blood was ordinarily present in this location--that is, if she had died of natural causes. He attributed the tear in the lung to a blow to the ribs that caused the rib to be bent into the lung. Her liver was torn in two, indicated by its irregular edges.

He was talking too fast and his voice too low, dropping at the end of sentences.

Ms. Lambert asked him to look at the pictures of the autopsy while he described her injuries.

The problem was that the jury could not see the photographs he was referring to, so it seemed strange that the prosecutor bothered to have him look at the pictures. Everything the witness was saying could have been read from the autopsy report.

A defense attorney would later say that she should have questioned him first without the photographs and then have him explain to the jury, showing them the photographs.

The concept was to "tell the jury what you want to tell them, and then show them what you told them."

During this dry but disturbing testimony, the defendant sat with his head down while Mr. McMillan rubbed his arm and patted him on the shoulder.

It would be interesting to see how many blows Dr. LaGrand would now say it took to cause the damage to Vivian Whitaker's body after he had listened to Dr. Hudson testify without the jury present.

This time, it was "one or more forceful blows to the upper chest or abdominal area," but, when pressed, he held to the opinion of "at least two blows." He added that her heart was in a weakened state--she was a potential heart-attack candidate and could have had high blood pressure. Her brain showed signs of a previous stroke, and she had not been able to move quickly as a result of her medical condition.

Most jurors are bored with medical testimony. By that time in a murder case, they already know the victim is dead, they already know she didn't die in an automobile accident or on an operating table. It has been drummed into them that the cause of death was the knife, the gun, or, as in this case, the strangulation and the beating. So unless there are surprises, and there seldom are, medical testimony is repetitious, confirming what is already known. But this particular testimony won the prize. The monotonous questions and answers droned on all morning, the prosecutor asking not only about the abnormal findings, but every microscopic examination that was normal and every organ examination he had found normal.

Everyone in the courtroom more than welcomed the lunch recess.

Jack and I chose to walk to Greenshields and eat on their patio. This Spring-like weather was a bonus. The weather had gone from cold straight to a sweltering summer. Now Spring had returned for what we knew would be an all too brief stay.

This morning's superfluous questions to the good doctor had been tedious--why were they even asked? Jack didn't have an answer.

"Were all your other findings normal?"

"Yes."

End of story--ten seconds of pertinent testimony is preferable to two hours of "so what" testimony any day.

When court resumed in the afternoon, the picture of the victim, which had been placed strategically in front of the jury, had been removed and covered. By whom, one could only speculate.

Cross-examination of Dr. LaGrand was much easier this second-go-round, because he had slightly revised his testimony to "one or more blows could have caused her injuries."

The defense had scored a few points, even though they had not yet won the game.

Upon further questioning, he agreed that while it could have been one blow, he still had problems with it being less than two.

All of this "number of blows" quest was to diminish or support "especially heinous, atrocious, or cruel" as an aggravating factor the prosecution felt was essential to obtain the death penalty. The more blows, the more brutal.

No one had yet focused on the strangulation. His hands had been around her neck while she struggled to draw air with every ounce of energy she could muster as he squeezed harder and harder as she watched him, knowing she was going to die--atrocious enough. One blow or three blows did not seem that crucial, but in a death case, everything is crucial.

Fifteen minutes into the afternoon session, Dr. LaGrand was excused. The jury was given the autopsy photographs around which his hours of testimony had centered. They studied the pictures carefully and deliberately, trying to recollect all he had said.

The State rested.

Dr. Hudson was supposed to be the first witness for the defense, but he was not in the courtroom and not available at this time, so the jury received the rest of the afternoon off.

Friday morning, outside the presence of the jury, the defense argued to the Court against the use of "especially heinous, atrocious, or cruel" by the State as an aggravating circumstance. There was no evidence of excessive brutality, no evidence of torture, they contended.

The State countered with the "totality of the circumstances;" the victim was "helpless, aware of pending death, but unable to prevent it. The proximity of her assailant adds to it." Both sides presented case law to back them up.

His Honor overruled the defense objection: "Excessive brutality has to be a judgment call. That is for the jury, who reflect the standards or norms of acceptable behavior and relativity of unacceptable behavior." The two aggravating circumstances would be: "while in the commission of common law robbery," and "especially heinous, atrocious, or cruel."

The jury was brought in by the bailiff.

They looked more worn than they had earlier in the week. Some had tell-tale bags under their eyes.

The defense now had their turn at bat, and Dr. Page Hudson was called as their first witness. The State stipulated to his qualifications as an expert in forensic pathology, but the defense wanted the jury to hear his background anyway: he was described as a pioneer in his field, and his credentials were most impressive. Everyone but the jury had heard his testimony, and he now reiterated his opinions that were so important to the defense.

The State had secured "especially heinous, atrocious, or cruel" being submitted to the jury on the jury sheet for deliberation, but the jury itself would decide if they considered it such.

Q. Do you have an opinion as to the number of blows?

A. In my opinion, one blow would cause these injuries quite sufficiently--a broad blow by a blunt object.

Q. Her lung was punctured by a rib. Could that have happened from the same blow?

A. Certainly, that can happen.

Dr. Hudson did agree with Dr. LaGrand that strangulation was the cause of death. What they did not agree on was the amount of time. Dr. LaGrand had stated that strangling someone would take one, two, or three minutes. Now, the defense asked Dr. Hudson the same question.

Q. How long, in your opinion, would strangulation take?

A. First unconsciousness can and often does occur in a matter of ten, fifteen, twenty seconds. There is not an exact time. One can survive a certain amount of strangulation. I cannot say the number of seconds, but it is not a process that goes on for minutes.

Q. Could age have reduced her physical strength?

A. Yes. She was a small person and had suffered from a stroke.

How long it took Vivian Whitaker to die had become quite a concern. Exactly how many seconds or how many blows was an intellectual exercise. Her children, who were sitting in the courtroom, didn't care. She was dead for a radio and a ring.

Caroline Pendziwater, who worked with the Wake County Department of Social Services, took the stand to testify. Her first contact with Eugene Davis's family had been in 1976, and she had maintained contact for three years until her work position changed. She told us that Eugene Davis was born on October 6, 1965 to a family of farm laborers in rural Wake County. His father worked as a laborer and his mother as a cook. As an infant, Eugene was most often left with his eight-year-old sister, who provided his primary care, because of his parent's jobs. Ms. Pendziwater testified that both his mother and father drank heavily, and that drinking bouts frequently resulted in domestic violence. On one occasion, his mother had shot his father in the hand. Eugene's father said that he "gave up" parenting of the children. During the time Eugene was eighteen months until the time he was seven-years-old, his mother was admitted to Dorethea Dix, a State mental institution, five or six times. She was diagnosed as having psychotic tendencies and as a paranoid schizophrenic. She would become hysterical and depressed and was generally emotionally unstable. On top of this, she had a problem with alcohol.

Eugene was just eight when he broke into a neighbor's apartment. He would not stay at home, and his mother said it was hard to keep him there; he was having nightmares. As a child, he dressed as a "pimp-type adult person." There were reports that he was abused by the women in the apartment complex where he lived and that he had been admitted for psychiatric help. The referral to the Department of Social Services had come from the school system. They reported that he had been exposing himself and peeping under girls' skirts. He had a poor peer relationship and was two grades behind.

"His mother was not cooperative with the school system and did not understand and could not accept the idea that he had emotional problems. Her ability or inability to understand seemed to correlate with her mental state at that time." But she blamed herself that he was in trouble. At the age of nine, Eugene was admitted to a mental hospital. His doctor diagnosed Eugene as having a negative self-concept, no identification with a masculine role, and regressive behavior. In January of 1975, his mother was sent to the hospital for overdosing on Thorazine. She and her husband were separated. His grandmother was living with them to supervise the children. Three days later, Eugene also took an overdose so he could be with his mother.

While his mother remained in the psychiatric ward, Eugene was discharged, but he was seen weekly as an out-patient to monitor his progress until a foster household could be found for him. It was not easy to find a foster home for Eugene because of his emotional problems, which the defense was referring to as his "handicap." Finally, he was placed with an older couple in Zebulon who had raised their own children, although one child, who was handicapped, was still at home. The couple was also keeping two other boys as foster children, and Eugene now had two "foster brothers."

"The change was good for him. He made a quick adjustment; he was overly compliant, but he fit into the routine, becoming a good family member." He continued his weekly trips to the hospital and child therapy at Dix, which included medication. While he was in the foster home, Eugene's hobbies were mainly musical, which included playing the piano and singing in a choir. He was also willing to work on the family farm. After four years in the foster home, without having spent a single night with his real family, Eugene felt angry, hurt, and rejected, and he wanted to go home. So he ran away, arriving in Raleigh to visit his mother. His foster parents believed that his brother Anthony had been calling him and telling him to come home. While in Raleigh, Eugene was placed in a class for the emotionally disturbed, and in 1980, he was sent to the juvenile detention center for auto larceny. A visit was scheduled with his mother twice a month.

"He didn't seem to handle it well; it was traumatic to leave."

In 1980, Eugene attended the Echo Wilderness Camp, participating in a program that teaches children to be confronted by their behavior and deal with problems as a peer group. When he went home for Christmas, Eugene refused to go back to Echo, so he was turned over again to the juvenile authorities.

At age sixteen, Eugene was diagnosed as "Willie M" and placed in a program reserved for children with severe emotional problems. Back home, Eugene had repeatedly stolen money from his mother, and she was encouraged by the people treating Eugene to press charges--he had to learn that his actions were seriously wrong.

When the officer had read to the jury Eugene's statement taken the day after the murder, the jurors may have known that something was terribly amiss because of his answers. "Willie M" is a classification some of them would be familiar with. These children have usually been abandoned early in life, and one of the subsequent results is that they are deemed incapable of emotion and therefore, devoid of conscience. Human feelings of love, loyalty, respect, and compassion are not a matter of degree, depending on their upbringing, but are null and void--they do not exist.

The jurors had been given a great deal to think about.

Ms. Lambert cross-examined for the State.

Ms. Pendziwater revealed other information from her file: After complaints from school authorities, Eugene was declared hyperactive at age eight and admitted to the North Carolina Memorial Hospital by the State. The complaints included that he urinated on a boy's feet and at a teacher's door, that he was sexually overstimulated, and that he was very manipulative of the people around him.

"But his neurological reports were within normal limits," Ms. Pendziwater added. His performance IQ score was 101, with ninety to one-hundred being average. The tests showed he had the ability to learn and to pick up on social cues.

"No," he was not mentally retarded, had no psychosis and no brain damage.

Observations made in the mental hospital were that he "set peers up to get them into trouble, expressed himself inappropriately with female peers and some male peers, and used much denial when involved in inappropriate behavior."

After four months at the hospital, he had made progress, and he was better able to control his thoughts and behavior. The report stated that his strength was his ability to learn new material when he was so motivated and that his "social cues" were above normal for his age. The assessments of several other social workers were in Eugene's file. One of them stated that Eugene had no conscience.

The jury's initial impression of hopelessness for learning and practicing acceptable behavior by Eugene Davis had been altered. The system had tried, and at times, he had tried. Whether the system had failed him or he had failed the system was not clear.

After all that had been said about Mrs. Davis, Eugene's mother, the startled jury now learned that Eugene himself had a child that was approximately eight-years-old whom the court had placed in his mother's care on the recommendation of the Department of Social Services, the very agency that knew her history, and whose representatives had testified that it was her mental illness, alcoholism, and lack of mothering that had highly attributed to Eugene's handicap.

The witness was again questioned by Mr. McMillan of the defense team. He wanted it pointed out that Eugene's sister had turned out all right; she was functioning well as an adult with three children of her own. Not every child in a family is effected the same way by alcoholic and abusive parents, he contended. Also in Ms. Pendziwater's file was a story Eugene had written when he was ten years old in which "he expressed his feelings."

"The story is about a vampire that kills a little boy. Nothing is safe. These things were on his mind."

She read Eugene's story to the jury:

> "The Wind blows down the house, and the builders come and build it back the next day. The little boy moved in with his Mom and the house squeaked. A vampire came and said, 'Don't be afraid, I just want your blood.' The mother found him the next morning dead and she cried and cried and called the police and an ambulance and when he got to the hospital, they found out who killed him and found the vampire and killed him."

Eugene's sister, Augusta, took the stand. Now, twenty-nine- years-old, she testified that she had been left in charge of Eugene when he was a baby and she was eight. She told the jury that her mother and father were drunk frequently and would fight. Her father physically abused her mother. When her parents would make-up after one of their domestic quarrels, they would "go off for two or three days" and leave her to keep the other children. Her father had once shot her mother. She and Eugene had witnessed a neighbor shoot their father as he stood in his own doorway. Shot between the eyes, her father had wandered down the street until the police picked him up and took him to the hospital. The hospital sent him home, thinking he had just fallen down, and later that night, he had a stroke.

"Yes," she had heard her father tell Eugene that he was not his son.

She believed her brother had changed since he had been in prison. She had taken his son to visit, and "he seemed to have become more loving and caring. He was concerned for the welfare of his son."

Myra Norwood, another social worker, testified briefly and told the jury that Eugene was classified as aggressive with impulsive behavior. He had had no appropriate or consistent role models, and he patterns behavior by what he sees. He has a low self-image, a confused sense of who he is, lacks motivation, and operates on a day-to-day basis.

Dr. Gerald Seabrook, a child psychiatrist who had worked with Eugene from 1974 to 1979, took the stand. He described his patient as highly disturbed, impulsive, extremely anxious, and menacing. Eugene "has an anti-social personality disorder," which translated to mean "he is extremely difficult and has no regard for the rules of society or normal values." He manipulates and exploits other people "to act out conflicts against the world" and has little value for life or property because of "little value" to himself. The condition is "very hard to change" and "requires a great amount of motivation on his part and patience on the part of people who are trying to help him, and a change in his environment." Eugene had been "terrorized by chaos," for instance, when his mother was sick: he "could not hold on to progress." "The defendant has been looking for a home and found one in prison."

On cross-examination, Ms. Lambert brought out, through her questions, that as a child, Eugene had carried a knife at times.

The doctor admitted that he was "menacing in general."

"You weren't too comfortable around Eugene."

Q. It wouldn't be unusual for people to be afraid of him?

A. No.

Q. Isn't it true that many of the people charged with crimes have anti-social personalities?

A. Yes.

The defense lawyers would not let it go. They wanted to establish that it was "not a matter of choice to have an antisocial personality disorder."

At this point in a trial, the victim tends to fade from the scene. Vivian Whitaker had been the focus of attention during the State's evidence. But now the focus had changed to Eugene Davis. She was no longer flesh and blood. She had become generic-- a name, a photograph, never as vivid or real as the very much alive person in front of us who had taken her life and now begged the jury for his. We knew as much as we would be allowed to know about Vivian. Now the jury was getting to know Eugene Davis. The dead were dead, and the living must be dealt with. Person after person had said that he was mentally disturbed and had been since childhood. In trying to help him, people had spent time, energy, and money, all to no avail. The defense wanted more time, energy, and money spent on his behalf. In theory, he needed help; but in reality, he had repeatedly received help, and he had flunked every test. The jury would decide which argument was most valid.

Court was adjourned for the weekend, and we drove home to Fayetteville.

We left for Raleigh again early Monday morning.

Monday's testimony included that of another psychiatrist, Dr. Selwyn Rose, employed by the State and considered an expert in forensic psychology. He had examined Eugene Davis in 1985 before his first trial, and now, again, in 1991. Like the other diagnoses, his had been "anti-social personality disorder," a serious emotional problem or illness. He had found Eugene to be impulsive with no social values, a condition stemming from his childhood. Since the first trial, however, Dr. Rose believed Eugene had matured, become more aware of the consequences of his behavior. He was less defensive and more responsive. In his opinion, the defendant's emotional condition would improve with age. He had acknowledged his guilt, felt remorse; his prison record was pretty good; he followed the rules and had not been in "any major trouble."

Dr. Rose also testified that Eugene had written some letters to a pen pal, a member of a Bible study group. Two of these letters were admitted into evidence as examples of Eugene's ability to care for other people. Karen, the recipient of his first letter, was pregnant, but in danger of losing her· second child. Eugene wrote, telling her to have faith in God and sending her four dollars. The second letter was addressed to Karen and John. At this point, Karen had lost the baby, and Eugene sympathized:

"I open this letter with a sad heart for you. I wish to convey my deepest sympathy with the upmost of sincerity.

When a woman looses a baby she had been carrying in her for some time, she feels an emptiness that compares to nothing she had ever known. A certain part of her has also died with the child she has lost. And it will take a long time for the hurt that is within the depths of her heart to heel.

Even though you will never know the child you have lost, you will certainly know that he or she is in the bosom of gods arms. I know what it is to loose a child because i have also lost a child and experience the pain and the anguish that also follow. But you must be strong for John and Erin because they are with you to share in the pain that you feel. you will be able to have more children in the future for God will not let your suffering go beyond what you can bare.

So you be strong sister Karen. My heart aches for you also and i can only bring you words of comfort, But God can comfort your soul.

I hope John is being strong with you. it hurts a farther as well, so you both cling to each other for comfort. And look at Erin and know you are blessed. I am doing okay praise God. you are in my prayers always."

love Brother Eugene

On cross-examination, Ms. Lambert asked Dr. Rose if someone with anti-social personality disorder was in the same category as sociopath or psychopath. His answer was "Yes."

Didn't this disorder mean that someone had the following traits: superficial charm, unreliability, untruthfulness and insincerity, lack of remorse, lack of motivation, poor judgment, failure to learn from experience, incapability of feeling empathy with others, placing little value on life or property?

"Yes."

"Was it true that the defendant had no neurological dysfunction, no organic brain damage, no psychosis, no mental retardation, and was shown to be manipulative?"

"Yes."

The defense concluded its evidence with several brief witnesses:

Sergeant Ted Earp from Central Prison testified to Eugene's behavior since he had been incarcerated: he was an average inmate and didn't cause problems.

Laura Winslow of the N. C. Division of Mental Health confirmed that Eugene had been certified as Willie M in 1981. She described the designation as an "impulse control problem--he could not control himself."

Martha Waters, the Director of Child and Family Services, had her Master's Degree in Social Work and eighteen years experience with the emotionally disturbed. She told the jury that the defendant was among the first in Wake County to be certified Willie M.

Karen testified about her correspondence with Eugene, saying that she had received fifteen to twenty letters from him in 1988.

Robert Daakas, a member of the Chapel Hill Bible Church, had visited the defendant eight times in 1988 and had received fifteen to twenty letters from him as well as religious drawings.

The defense attorneys rested.

The thrust of the defense evidence had been to "humanize" Eugene and to stress to the jury that he could not help his "disorder," by whatever name it was currently called.

Although this case had originally been overturned because the State had listed two aggravating circumstances that were deemed "redundant," the defense, offering thirty-three mitigating circumstances, was entitled to an abundance of repetition.

One through twenty concerned the defendant's mental and/or emotional problems, the fact that he was different because of his mental and/or emotional problems, and that his mother and father had caused his mental and/or emotional problems. The remaining mitigating circumstances concerned his progress or behavior in prison; he had developed meaningful relationships, he had sought to help others, he has matured; his maturity has diminished his severe emotional handicap; his life has great value to him, his family and his friends; he has acknowledged his responsibility for the crimes he committed; he has fully acknowledged his guilt for Vivian Whitaker's death; and he has expressed remorse for his actions.

Tuesday morning, the defendant was wearing a white knit golf shirt, a departure from his usual plaid sports shirt. The smooth material emphasized his broad shoulders and powerful arms.

His physique had been discussed during the course of the trial. He had not always been the muscular person he now was. At the age of eighteen, the time of the murder, he had weighed between one-sixty-five and one-seventy. By the time of his first trial at age twenty, he weighed two-forty-five. During those two years, he had been locked in a one man cell with no area to exercise.

The jurors took their seats, but not for long.

The State wished to present two police officers for rebuttal evidence, but the defense team objected and asked to approach the bench.

Judge Thompson listened intently and sent the jury out.

The evidence that the defense claimed was irrelevant concerned two officers who would testify, if allowed, to two unrelated incidents (one in 1982 or 1983, and one in 1985) that concerned Eugene's attitude toward law enforcement.

"The sheer passage of time makes it irrelevant," the defense argued.

The State claimed the evidence was relevant as to the defendant's conduct in custody and in prison, one of the mitigating circumstances the defense wanted to present to the jury.

The judge stated that he had not read this portion of the previous transcript, and he would have to hear what the witnesses were going to say before he could rule.

"Is there any aspect of Officer Campen's testimony that will indicate violence toward law enforcement?"

The State read Campen's previous testimony to the Court.

"A confrontation initiated by the defendant while he was in custody, your Honor."

The Court ruled that the testimony contained "inconclusive inferences that could be drawn. "I will allow the motion *in limine* to exclude it."

The second witness, McAllister, was to testify that in 1982 or 1983 while he was working as an undercover officer, there had been a disturbance at a nightclub in which "the defendant indicated his intention to do harm to McAllister and other officers."

"As to McAllister's testimony, because I do not quite grasp what it is going to be, I will have to rule on it at the time. If the defendant expressed threats to law enforcement officers..."

"Would you like to read from the previous transcript?" asked Ms. Lambert.

"Yes. I have not read that part,"

She handed her copy to the judge; Mr. McMillan read his copy as well. Several minutes later, Judge Thompson gave his ruling.

"The only relevant evidence I see is a statement made by the defendant, but I do not feel it is relevant to the rebuttal of mitigating circumstances. Officer Campen, you can come down. Is there any other evidence the State intends to offer?"

"No, sir."

"While the jury is out, are there any changes in the mitigating circumstances?"

"None, your Honor."

"Does the defendant want to make a statement?"

"Yes, he does, your Honor," the defense lawyer answered.

"I would expect that to happen before the State's argument. Ms. Lambert, I know you had expected to put on further evidence this morning. What is your position as to arguments?"

"The State is ready to argue, your Honor."

The defense made a motion to prevent the State from seeking the death penalty on this defendant because of his emotional state.

The motion was denied.

The jury again took their seats.

Eugene Davis stood and turned to them.

"I just want to tell the family I'm sorry..."

One of Vivian's daughters quickly left the courtroom. Eugene hesitated, watching her, and continued in a soft, low voice.

...I caused so much pain and suffering. If allowed to live, I will tell others to continue their education and not have anything to do with crime, because it will mess up your life."

Eugene sat down after saying the only thing we would hear from him in this trial.

The State would argue first, and Ms. Lambert calmly stood at the podium in front of the jury and began. She was wearing a fuchsia suit this morning, confident that women no longer felt compelled to wear the standard navy or gray to court every day.

"This is probably the most important decision you will make in your life--life or death. All twelve of you have to make it, both as a group and individually. I know for you this is not a natural decision to make. All of us would like to preserve life, but during jury selection, you agreed that the death penalty was necessary. I did not ask you if you believed in it. That's the same as asking if you believe in war. But both are justified under certain circumstances... We still don't know the whole story of exactly what happened that day, March 1, 1984. She argued that the State had proven "especially heinous, atrocious, or cruel," citing each stage of the killing of Vivian Whitaker and the pain and suffering she had endured.

"After he beat her, it was not over. As she lay there defenseless, with his hands, he strangled the last bit of life out of her. Why? He didn't have to lift a hand against her to take her property. He didn't have to beat her. She was not a physical threat to him. What does it feel like to have a man put his hands around your throat and squeeze while you gasp for air? What was going on in her mind? Why is this happening to me? What were her last thoughts? However long it took, even if it were seconds or minutes, it must have seemed like an eternity. And the last humiliation was to take her ring. The State has proven 'especially heinous, atrocious, or cruel.' What more would it take? How much more indignity would it take? How much more pain or suffering would it take? "

Then Ms. Lambert recounted each piece of evidence as it had come from the witness stand to refresh the minds of the twelve people who, alone, would have to decide and asked them to make their decision based on the facts, not on sympathy or mercy.

The defense team gave their argument, a passionate and compelling plea to save Eugene Davis's life based on the thirty- three mitigating circumstances they were submitting to the jury. Their argument reiterated the defendant's diagnosis as Willie M and maintained that his upbringing was deprived and traumatic and that his parents had caused his mental condition. However, he had shown progress in prison, and taken responsibility for his actions and expressed remorse for killing Mrs. Whitaker.

Court recessed for lunch.

Judge Pou Bailey accompanied us for lunch again--a bonus for being in Raleigh. The pressures of a difficult case weigh on any judge, and Pou, a gifted storyteller, provided the comic relief.

Today, he related an experience quite a few years ago when he was sent to preside in Southport, a quaint seaside town on the coast of North Carolina with the charm of a New England fishing village. Judge Bailey, a licensed pilot, decided to fly himself there. He found, however, in looking at the map, the small Southport airport was colored light green, which indicated that it was frequently wet. He called the Sheriff in that county and asked him about the runway. This was in January. The Sheriff responded that the last time he had been to that airport was after Labor Day of the previous year to assist in taking people to the hospital after a plane had flipped over. He did not know the airstrip's present condition. Judge Bailey decided to forgo this challenge and fly into Wilmington, the closest airport of any size, and he asked the sheriff to pick him up and drive him to the Southport courthouse.

When all this came about on Monday morning, he said that it must have unnerved the Sheriff to pick up a "flying judge," and the Sheriff, chattering away, missed his turn and they wound up in another city. After making the Sheriff stop and ask directions at a gas station, a definite embarrassment to the head of law enforcement in the county (especially since he knew the station attendant), they finally arrived in Southport. Because of the delay, it was almost time for court to begin, and they found a crowd waiting in front, the Southport Courthouse not being adequate to hold those scheduled for the Monday morning court docket. To avoid walking through the crowd of defendants, the Sheriff led Judge Bailey around the building, and they both climbed to the second floor by the outside fire escape, the judge with "robe trailing."

When Judge Bailey reached his chambers, a desk sat in front of a commode, which also served as the only chair. In his droll way, Judge Bailey asked the Sheriff if this were not an unusual arrangement, and the Sheriff explained: previously they had had a lady judge here holding court who had pitched a fit that they didn't have a ladies' room on the second floor of the courthouse. She had to stand in line with all the defendants to use the public restroom downstairs. She demanded that a facility be immediately added to the second floor. Honoring her request, they called a plumber, who decided that the quickest and easiest location was above the first floor restroom, where he could connect onto existing pipes. Thus, the new porcelain bowl was installed in the judge's chambers. Although the plan included a privacy screen, it was soon discovered that if such a screen was installed, the desk would no longer fit, and the door could not be closed.

"Well," Judge Bailey continued, "Some seat was better than none, but it was difficult to hold meetings in chambers when the attorneys were struggling to control their snickering while negotiating a plea."

Not giving us time to recover from the first story, Judge Bailey launched into another one.

"This was not my only 'incident' with the Sheriff in those parts. Having been commissioned to hold court in Southport again, I decided this time to take a commercial flight and rent a car."

He asked the Sheriff to take care of renting the car for him, so it would be available on his arrival. Sure enough, a car was there waiting for him. Judge Bailey, then a bachelor after his first wife had died and before he married Ann, called another Judge in Wilmington, a good friend of his (whom I shall call Joe Simpson), told him to have someone drive him to Southport at the end of his court day, and the two of them would head the few miles across the State border into South Carolina and have some fun. Judge Simpson said it sounded like a good idea to him, and the two friends drove to Myrtle Beach, treated themselves to a fresh seafood dinner, and visited a beach club or two before returning to Southport well after midnight.

Too tired to take his friend Joe back to Wilmington and, since his motel room contained two double beds, he suggested that Joe spend the night, take Bailey's rental car back to Wilmington in the morning and return to Southport the following evening to repeat their adventure. Judge Simpson agreed.

The next morning, Judge Simpson, on his way back to Wilmington, dropped Judge Bailey off at the Southport courthouse. After getting out of the car, Judge Bailey turned casually to watch his friend drive away and noticed the car's license tag was red and white and proclaimed "The Land of Lincoln." Upon entering the courthouse, he asked the Sheriff where he had rented a car bearing an Illinois license plate. "Oh, hell, Judge. There wasn't no sense in you having to pay for a car. That's a stolen one we're holding for evidence."

Thinking about their excursion the night before, Judge Bailey couldn't believe what he was hearing, and he promptly called Joe in Wilmington. Warning him about the car, he strongly suggested that Judge Simpson not drive it back to Southport that evening until he secured some North Carolina tags. Judge Simpson wanted to know just how he was supposed to do that. Judge Bailey said he didn't rightly know how you could legally get tags without a title. He was on his own.

Judge Simpson appeared that night around six, returning Judge Bailey's "rented" car which now bore a North Carolina license plate. Judge Bailey didn't ask.

Our hour-and-a-half lunch recess had seemed like twenty minutes when we headed back to the courtroom.

The jury resumed their places in the jury box just long enough to receive the sentence-recommendation form they would fill out and then filed into the jury room to begin their deliberations.

The waiting game began. The bailiffs and the Clerk agreed--the recommendation would be life imprisonment.

There was no issue of guilt. That had been determined. The only defense was that the defendant was not wholly responsible because of his childhood, resulting in "anti-personality disorder." Yet it was agreed by the same psychiatrists testifying in his behalf that this was the stuff that most criminal behavior was made of. If his motive was money, and not much of it at that, an elderly woman's life had been meaningless to him. Stealing is anti-social in and of itself, but senseless and brutal murder gave it a new definition. Vivian Whitaker had certainly not been a threat to him--maybe she had tried to stop him and the situation got out of hand. Whatever the scenario, she was a person he liked, someone who had been kind to him, his mother's best friend, and he had turned on her viciously for a ring, a radio, and a few Avon necklaces--temporary pocket change in the end.

Part of the system from the time he was eight, he had been given every chance. The minute he was eighteen and "the system" had no place for him, he had not only slipped from grace, he had fallen. Every chance he had, every time he wasn't locked up, he had reverted to primal behavior.

The verdict came more quickly than any of us expected.

At precisely five o'clock, the jury knocked on the door, not with a question, but with a verdict:

Life imprisonment.

But there was a hitch. When the judge asked if this was their verdict and if they so assented to raise their hands, one did not-- juror number seven, the young woman with waist-length, brown hair on the front row. The judge asked the jury to go to their room for a few minutes.

The defense attorneys were on their feet. They asked that the Court accept the verdict as delivered before His Honor's inquiry. Their motion was denied. Instead, the judge told the attorneys that he was going to send them out to deliberate until 5:30. If they had not reached a unanimous verdict by that time, they would be released to come back in the morning.

The eleven-hand-count didn't make any sense. If it had been opposite, it would have been understandable; if the vote had been eleven to one for death and she had acquiesced and then regretted it, okay. But eleven to one for the lesser sentence--hold out for death?

At 5:30, there was a knock on the door. The jurors had a question. The judge told the bailiff to have them write it, and upon receiving it, His Honor read it aloud to the attorneys: "Is a majority response in the negative enough, or does it have to be twelve jurors for issue Three?" he read.

"I can re-instruct them as to issue Three," he told the attorneys.

The defense team proposed a re-wording, and the prosecutor asked that he re-instruct on issue Three. The jury was brought back.

"Do you unanimously find beyond a reasonable doubt that the mitigating circumstances are insufficient to outweigh the aggravating circumstances? You must weigh the mitigating circumstances that are found to exist against the aggravating circumstances that are found to exist. If the mitigating circumstances are insufficient... you must answer "yes". If the answer is "no," it is your duty to find life."

The jury was again sent out.

Mr. Dodd maintained that the wording of the issue was a problem. Where it said if you do *not* find, the word "unanimously" did not appear. He had a point.

"Let's see if they understand now," His Honor responded. He realized also what the problem was, but the *approved* form had been used, and jurors had to be given a chance to figure it out. There were smiles at the defense table for the first time in two-and-a-half weeks. Either way, they had won. The jury would be given a chance, but even if they were permanently "hung" and could not reach a unanimous decision, the Judge would then declare the sentence to be life, a rule on hung juries that applied only to capital cases.

So, unless by some fluke from Mars--this one woman could convince eleven others to her side, Eugene Davis' life had been spared. He would sleep better tonight than he had for the last six years on death row.

Everyone remained in the courtroom, and although individual words were indistinguishable, the Jury could be heard arguing loudly.

Twenty minutes later at 5:50, the jury again knocked on the door. Juror number seven's face was red-splotched. Upon questioning this time, all twelve jurors raised their hands. The judge thanked them for their close attention and they were dismissed.

The defendant stood with his two attorneys to receive the sentence. His Honor instructed that his life sentence would begin at the expiration of the common law robbery sentence he was currently serving.

The State had spared no expense in the consideration of Eugene Davis's chance to live, and he, at least, did not mind the cost nor the process. But the jurors and those involved in the case might have something to ponder.

The trial over, we left for Fayetteville. Not surprised or upset by the verdict, I wasn't satisfied either. It was the process I questioned. There are no winners in a life and death case, and the problem seemed circular.

The financial burden of having the death penalty as a choice is high. The equality of how the death penalty is meted out is questionable. Did juries in one locale give the death penalty too easily? Would their fellow citizens in another part of the State have done the same thing? Nevertheless, it was the law. If not the death penalty for this murder, when? In the wild, the rule is "survival of the fittest." In our society, we execute "the defective," that prey on the rest of us. Or do we?

How many people are actually executed? After years of appellate legal paperwork, most are not. Have the complex procedures and broad accommodation of mitigating circumstances imposed by the Supreme Court reduced "life versus death" in the courtroom to a "word game?" If this jury had recommended death, this case would be reviewed again with "strict scrutiny" by the higher court. It had to be. A man's life was at stake. But even if the game were played correctly, by the present rules, the conclusion of the higher court would most likely be that somewhere, somehow, someone had said something that did not pass the "strict scrutiny" standard, even if the high court put the case on "hold" and waited five or six years for changes in the law to apply, they could then send it back to be tried again. The plan seemed to be "keep reversing this case until the verdict is life," and this strategy appeared to be working.

The Davis trial had been a perfect example--with missing or deceased witnesses, seven-year-old evidence, and testimony that the prisoner had "found his home in prison." The State had three strikes called before the umpire yelled, "play ball."

Did the higher court disagree with "the people" and render the law superfluous and the District Attorney's job impossible? Was deciding a sentence in a capital case an intellectual exercise in a system designed to stall until the law was repealed? The law may be on the books, but it had become meaningless, and the cost exorbitant.

Still on our way home, my thoughts had come full circle. No answers. Perhaps, juries prefer to save the death sentence, the ultimate punishment, for the most extreme cases--the Charles Mansons, Richard Specks, and Jeffrey Dahmers of this world. But then, Charles Manson was still in prison, Richard Speck had died in prison, and Jeffrey Dahmer's trial was in Wisconsin, where there is no death penalty. That posed another question.

"Would it have been equal justice to kill Jeff Medlin or Eugene Davis because they lived in North Carolina instead of Wisconsin?" I said out loud.

"Different state," a legal mind I knew well pointed out. "Has nothing to do with it."

"True. I know that's the way it's set up--each State deciding whether or not they want the death penalty. But this still is the *United* States, is it not? Don't we fall under a common constitution that proclaims "equal justice?"

No response. Just a look I had seen before.

"I know," I said. "I'm looking for logic."

I knew that if I was looking for logic, I had missed the point.

Maggie was right.

CHAPTER FOUR

Preface

It was just another hot day in July of 1990 when *Sherry Wells reported to work at Shoney's at three-thirty in the afternoon.

Blonde, beautiful, and a new college graduate, Sherry had recently moved to Durham to be with her fiancé. Life was good.

But shortly before eight o'clock tonight, Sherry would notice a run in her stockings, a minor nuisance, but one that would mark the beginning of a night of terror that would change her life forever.

One year later, almost to the day, on another hot day in July, Sherry would appear in a Durham Courtroom to testify against the man she claimed had raped her.

Roland Stevens had pled not guilty. A jury would decide who was telling the truth.

July: State v. Roland W. Stevens

Judge Thompson had concluded his Raleigh assignment and was to hold court in Robeson County in Lumberton from July to December, according to his schedule.

However, on the third Friday of July, he learned by happenstance that he was scheduled for a case in Durham on the following Monday. Apparently, everyone who was supposed to know, did know, except him. Ann, the Judges' secretary in Durham, had left a message on his answering machine late Friday afternoon directing him to the judges' parking slots underneath the courthouse. If it had not been for her courteous gesture, he would have been a no-show on Monday, having received nothing in the mail indicating this assignment. This same lack of communication had also occurred to a friend of ours, but he wasn't as lucky. Judge Johnson had not received a commission for a particular week, so he did not know to be in Brunswick County on that Monday morning. The local Brunswick newspaper had carried the following banner headline: "Judge Doesn't Show for Court." Embarrassing, to say the least.

We already had big plans for the weekend, and it was too late to change them. This Sunday, Jack was to play in a charity golf tournament in Pinehurst as a guest of Judge Jim Webb, and I was to ride in the beverage cart and assist Jo, Jim's wife. Sunday morning was beautiful and sunny, not yet oppressively humid like most of our days in July, when we left at seven-thirty to make the forty-five minute drive to Pinehurst. Jack and Jim were on the same team, and they both played well, while I rode around the course with Jo, exchanging stories about our families and selecting Cokes, Sprites and beer from an ice-laden cooler for the players. By the middle of the day, the temperature had soared to the high nineties and our supply of drinks had dwindled.

Jack and I arrived home around four-thirty, hastily packed for a week, and reached Durham at nine o'clock that night. Too tired to dine out, we ordered a salad from room service and slept soundly.

Our motel, the Guest Quarters, was one we had stayed in several times in the past, the suites no more expensive than a room at most places. This time our large windows overlooked a lake bordered on the far side by a thick pine forest. Interspersed between low benches, large planters overflowing with red and white impatiens enhanced the walkways. and graceful weeping willows flanked a man-made, multi-tiered waterfall. I could do this.

Thinking jury selection would last all day, I stayed in the room Monday morning to cancel by phone a few appointments I had made for this week and to make my plans for the day--walking around the lake and then reading my book by the pool seemed a fun way to start. We had brought our tennis racquets, and tonight we could find time to play before the trial actually started, which entailed "homework" for Jack. The court clerk called before noon, however, to give me two messages: Jack would pick me up for lunch at one o'clock, and the evidence would begin this afternoon. Flexibility is not necessarily my strong suit, but I took my shower and dressed for court.

At lunch, Jack told me he would never have found the assigned parking space if Ann had not called, and when we arrived at the courthouse, I understood why. A card-triggered, massive steel door under the courthouse rolled open, then closed immediately after we drove through.

Wall signs were posted as to who was to park where, and ours said simply "Superior Judge." Surely, the extra length in the metal plate for the word Court in between was not beyond the state budget.

The charges were First Degree Rape, Second Degree Kidnapping, and First Degree Sexual Offense (in this instance, anal rape).

Because of his previous record, if Roland Wesley Stevens were convicted of these charges, he could also achieve the status of Habitual Felon.

The jury, picked this morning, eight women and four men, took their places.

Mary Winstead, an attractive, tall, blonde wearing maternity clothes, was the prosecutor for the State. She called *Sherry Wells, the victim, to the stand as her first witness.

Sherry was now twenty-one years old. She was an exceptionally pretty young woman with lightly frosted blonde hair in a mid-length natural style, clear blue eyes and a petite figure. She appeared highly nervous.

Sherry testified in a soft, unsteady voice that she had moved to Durham to be close to her fiancé, *Ted, who worked at Shoney's on Hillandale Road three nights a week. At the time of the incident, she had lived here for two months, working at the same Shoney's as the dining room manager. Her voice grew stronger as she recounted background facts.

"I was in charge of the entire wait staff and salad bar people. I strived for the best and tried to be a strong leader. The restaurant was in bad shape, and I tried to improve it."

Roland Stevens, the defendant, who had worked at Shoney's as a dishwasher and bus boy, was also under her supervision. On July 18, 1990, Sherry told the jury that she had gone to work at three or three-thirty in the afternoon to get a head start on some paperwork before her shift started at four.

"I don't think it was that busy that night, but it was hectic because the computers were messing up."

"Was the defendant working that night?"

"I think so. I don't remember if I saw him that day, but he was always there when I got there in the afternoons."

She described her employee uniform as a green skirt and vest, white oxford cloth button-down blouse, a plaid tie, panty hose, and good working shoes.

"That evening I had a big run in my panty hose. I was strict on the staff about their appearance. I lived only ten minutes, if that much, from work, and I asked my immediate supervisor if I could go home and change. I gave Billy Hayes the register keys to take over for me. I also thought I might be starting my menstrual period and needed to check and to change my hose."

Q. Do you remember what time it was when you left?

A. To be honest with you, I don't remember exactly. But from what I understand, it was about eight o'clock. I left by the front door and went to the back parking lot where we were required to park as employees.

Q. What happened then?

Sherry had recovered from her initial nervousness, and her answers had come more easily, until now.

A. I got in my car--I got in my car—*She hesitated, faltering in her composure. Her voice was trembling.* At that time I saw Roland Stevens. He motioned me to come this way. I followed around in the back of the parking lot--where the parking lot is--there is--a Cricket Inn is right there—and I drove around it to where he was.

Mrs. Winstead held up a diagram of the area while Sherry tried to explain in detail, but her voice kept breaking.

A. I saw him motioning--he was going--he had his hand on the door--I need a minute--

Sherry couldn't talk. She put her head in her hands and searched for strength to say what she had to say.

A. It was Room 149, from what I know now. I turned my car off and rolled my windows up. And I always lock my car--it's a new car--and I got out. I locked the doors and got out.

Q. Did you know why the defendant was motioning to you?

A. No, ma'am.

Q. What happened then?

A. I went to the door--

She was openly sobbing now.

A. I can't be exact about how he grabbed me....All I know--as soon as I got to the door, next thing I know, I'm against the wall being choked with a knife at my neck, and I didn't know what was going on.

Q. At that point did he say anything to you?

A. Not that I recall.

Q. Do you remember what the knife looked like?

A. It was a steak knife, one from Shoney's, I would imagine.

Q. How was he choking you?

A. His hands were around my neck. He kept telling me to shut up and choking me. He grabbed this knife from his back pocket and said, 'Shut up, or I'll kill you.' I didn't know what was going on.

Q. What did you do next?

A. He took me to the far bed.

She was still crying, and the words were coming haltingly between sobs.

He wanted me to get undressed. I kept asking, "What do you want? What do you want?" I just kept begging, 'Don't do this. No. No'. He started to undress me. I kept begging, 'No, please don't, please don't.' I started to unbutton my dress. I was so scared that I knew he was going to do it, and I started unbuttoning. He kept screaming 'I'll kill you if you don't shut up' and bringing the knife back up. He told me he'd tie me up with the sheets. He got madder and madder, and I kept thinking that if I didn't do this, he'd kill me. I had my underwear off--the only thing-- and he started taking them off, and I was still begging, 'Don't do this.' He threw me on the bed. I guess he finished taking off his clothes and he started trying to kiss me. I was turning my head and begging. He kept choking me and kept the knife right there and threatening to kill me.

Sherry was almost hysterical, the veins in her neck straining against her skin. The prosecutor asked for a break, and the jury was sent to the jury room. Another young woman who looked like her, probably her sister, helped Sherry walk out of the courtroom. The courtroom was silent.

Ten minutes later Sherry resumed the stand and continued her story.

A. He kept telling me to lie down. I did, finally.

Q. Did you lie on your back or your stomach?

A. On my back.

Q. What happened next?

Sherry paused, taking deep breaths.

A. It's hard for me to say--please be patient. He got on top of me--and he started touching me.

Q. Where was he touching you?

A. My--breasts. And he kept--trying to kiss me--

Her recovery did not last long: she was crying again.

A. He kept turning my head and trying to get me to kiss him, and I wouldn't do it, just wouldn't do it, and I couldn't shut up. He kept saying, "Shut up. Shut up," and I couldn't do it. I kept telling myself, "You're going to die. Shut up," but I just couldn't do it. And that's when he entered himself.

Q. By 'entered himself,' do you mean he put his penis in your vagina? Is that what you're saying?

A. Yes, ma'am.

Q. What happened then?

A. I kept begging, and I just kept thinking, "I'm going to die. He's going to kill me." And I kept saying, "Please God, help me. Please God, help me." And I just kept begging him, "Please, please, stop."

Q. What was he doing at that time?

A. He was having intercourse. It seemed like an eternity. Then he got off and told me to turn around--and I knew what he wanted. I knew. I knew... I just kept begging him, "Please don't. Please don't do this." And he just kept threatening me. And he reached and got his pants that were laying on the other bed, and he got a condom from his back pocket. I am so scared. I know he is going to kill me. I kept thinking, "Turn around, turn around. Do you want to die?" And then he inserted himself anally, and I kept begging, "Please don't. Oh, God."

Q. Was that painful?

A. Yes, ma'am.

Q. At that time, Sherry, were you facing the entrance door or the wall?

A. The wall.

By this time, Sherry was sobbing uncontrollably. When she was shown a picture of the motel room interior by the prosecutor, she almost knocked the microphone off the witness stand. Mrs. Winstead asked her to step down and show the jury where the assaults took place. Sherry came down and responded to the prosecutor's brief questions, identifying on which bed she had suffered the first assault and the wall she was facing during the second assault. More composed, she resumed the stand.

Q. Can you tell us what happened next?

A. It's--it's really foggy in what exact order it came in, because, if you can imagine, I was pretty out of it. He got real calm and real weird like--and that's when I started thinking he was going to take me in the bathroom and kill me. But he was so calm. I didn't understand. And he started to get dressed. I said, "Can I get dressed?" And he said, "Yes, you can get dressed." And he lit a cigarette--I smoked one too--and he told me, "I'm sorry for what I done. It happened to me when I was young, too. Can I pay you? Just take me back to the camp, and we'll forget about it." I said, "Sure, whatever you want. Please, just go back to the camp. I won't tell. I promise, I won't tell." And he just stood there...like real dazed and confused...It was like he was trying to decide what he wanted to do. And I just kept talking, trying to convince him, "Please let me take you back to the camp. I won't tell." And finally, he said, "All right."

Q. What happened then?

A. Before we walked out of the room, he told me if I tried anything, he didn't mind killing me because it didn't matter anyway.

Q. At that point, did you know where the knife was?

A. He had had it the whole time. He had that knife the whole time. He kept bringing it up next to my neck. If he wasn't choking me, he had the knife there. He'd tell me he was going to kill me, and it didn't bother him at all. He'd tell me, "It don't bother me."

Q. You had mentioned some strips of cloth. Did you see those?

A. Yes, ma'am. He had torn up strips of sheets and kept asking me, "Is this what you want me to do? Tie you up? You better just cooperate." That was my worst fear, because I knew if he tied me up, I was dead then. I knew I had no chance in the world if he tied me up.

Q. Did he ever tie you up with the cloth?

A. No, ma'am.

Q. What did he do with the strips?

A. He told me to put them in my pocket. He might need them.

Q. Did you put them in your pocket?

A. Yes, ma'am.

Q. What happened then as you left the room?

A. Like I said, he warned me, and he still had the knife. I was thinking, "This is it. he could just take you and kill you there and take your car and--you know. He had the knife by my side, and my car was right there. He got in on the driver's [side and slid] through, so that I couldn't get away and that he wouldn't be left--so we'd both end up in my car.

Q. Were you on the driver's side?

A. Yes, ma'am.

Q. Did you see anyone?

A. Yes, ma'am. On the far backhand side, there were people there. I couldn't yell, and there was enough distance away that they didn't see anything funny, I guess.

Q. When you told him you would drive him back to camp, what camp are you talking about?

A. Prison camp, I guess you call it.

Q. Was he on work release?

A. Yes, ma'am.

Q. Had you taken him back before?

A. Yes. One time. If they don't go back on the bus, it's our responsibility to carry them back. I figured if he was safe enough to work at Shoney's, you know...

The defendant ordered her to go "a certain way, so that nobody at Shoney's could see me," a different way from her usual route. She was begging him to throw the knife out of the car, and he told her he wasn't going to hurt her anymore. Sherry told the prosecutor that she did not know which way they went, but she remembered seeing about six houses with six black mailboxes in a row near some bushes.

"I tried to speed up to draw attention, but he caught on. I got all the way to the driveway of the prison camp, and he turned the wheel. He had changed his mind. He kept saying, 'I know you're going to tell.' And I kept saying, 'No. I won't tell. I promise, I won't tell.' I knew if he wasn't going back to the camp, he was going to carry me off somewhere and kill me. I knew I was dead. He said, 'Take me to the bus station.' I had just moved here, and I didn't know where it was. He kept saying, 'Drive downtown. Drive downtown. I've got to find a way out of here.'"

Sherry had not lived in Durham long, and, confused by the one-way streets, she had passed the downtown area. In frustration, she went the wrong way on one of them, asking Roland over and over to "just get out" of the car.

"I stopped the car, and he slammed the door into this huge telephone pole kind of thing. He asked me for money. I don't carry money. All I had was a dollar. He opened the door and hit it on a pole. All I know then is that I stepped on it, and I was out of there. There was a black man on the side of the street, and I said, "Please help me find a police station." He goes, "Take a left. Take a right. Take a left. Take a right." Like, forget it. So I just kept speeding. I didn't know where I was. I ended up at a gas station and I just told the cashier, 'Call the police. I've been raped.'"

Q. What did you do after the police got there?

A. I don't remember. I couldn't really talk. I was scared that he would see my car, because he told me, if I told, he'd kill me, and I really believed him. I got enough out because they went looking for him. First, I called Ted at Shoney's. They wanted me to go to the scene.

Q. You called Ted?

A. They did. I gave them the number and told them to get Ted.

Initially, the police had driven to the wrong Shoney's, and Sherry kept trying to tell them it was the wrong one. Ultimately, as they arrived in the right parking lot, Sherry pointed out the room of the motel and the police took her to the hospital.

Sherry continued to testify, even though each memory brought fresh tears.

Q. What happened when you got to the hospital?

A. Everybody in the world wanted to know what was wrong with me. I had doctors and all kinds of nurses--poking and prodding and asking me questions. The rape-crisis people came, and everybody was there--people who were looking for him from the corrections department, asking me where he was--just everybody. Then a doctor examined me.

Q. Was that painful?

A. Yes, ma'am.

Q. Did you tell the people who questioned you what happened?

A. Probably not as well as I have here.

Q. How long were you at the hospital?

A. It seemed like forever. I don't know--but I know I had to go home in a green hospital uniform.

Sherry was having trouble talking through her sobbing. Her hospital visit had tallied further humiliations.

Q. Why was that?

A. Because they took my clothes. They took everything--
not just clothes.

Q. Did you talk to Detective Franklin and give him a
statement?

A. Yes, ma'am. I think it was the following day.

Again, the prosecutor asked that the witness be allowed to take
a break.

*Sherry left the courtroom, but the rest of us remained seated, including
the solemn-faced jurors. Two of them, one man and one woman, used this
time to look over the audience, trying to guess what role, if any, the spectators
played or why they were here.*

*The black woman sitting beside me was curious too. Several times, I
had noticed that she seemed to be watching me. People in the courtroom will
usually converse at some point during the lulls, and I enjoy listening to what
they think about the testimony. Unfortunately, they don't feel as free if they
know I'm married to the judge, so I don't volunteer that information unless
they specifically ask.*

*She tapped me on the arm to get my attention. Her face looked younger
than her age, which was evidenced by her silver- streaked shoulder-length
hair, and she was wearing a transparent blue "poker" visor that coordinated
with her blue flowered dress.*

"Are you a reporter?" she asked, smiling.

"No. I'm just observing," I replied.

"You must be his mother, then," she said, smile disappearing.

"Whose mother?" I asked, puzzled.

"His mother," she said, pointing to the defendant's back.

"No. No. I am not his mother." It was definitely time for me to come clean.

"I'm just here with my husband. I'm Judge Thompson's wife."

*"Go on," she laughed, brushing my arm with her hand. "Are you really
his wife?"*

"Yes. We're from Fayetteville, and I usually come with him when it's too far to commute."

"And you watch his trials?"

"Yes," I shrugged, "That's what I do."

"Well, it's nice to meet you. My name is Margaret."

It was my turn.

"Are you connected with this case?"

"No. I just come here to watch. It's kind of my hobby. What happens in real life is more interesting than anything you can see on TV, especially those afternoon soap operas, don't you think?"

"Yes, I do," I agreed.

"Last week, I seen a drug case. It was a black girl, and she slept the whole time during the trial," she said scornfully. "She'll be sentenced next week," Margaret added with a knowing wink, as if she felt the punishment should be steeper because the defendant didn't care enough to stay awake.

Later, during a break, I asked the courtroom clerk (another Margaret) about my new acquaintance. I was told that Margaret was a courtroom institution, rarely missing a day of court. All the courthouse personnel knew her well and assigned her errands, like fetching out-of-pocket attorneys if they hadn't returned to the courtroom when needed. I was also warned that she'd hit you on the arm to get your attention, something I already knew, and that sometimes she packed quite a wallop, something I hoped I wouldn't have to find out.

More composed, Sherry resumed the stand.

> Q. Ms. Wells, let me back up and ask a few questions before we get to your statement to Detective Franklin. First of all, after the anal intercourse, did the defendant do anything else at that time?

> A. He--I don't know how to say this--I can only say he pulled himself out. He took the condom off and he masturbated on my back.

Q. At the time that he had vaginal intercourse, do you know whether or not he ejaculated in you?

A. I do not believe that he did. But at the time, I was praying to God for my life. I don't really know.

Q. When you put your underwear on, was it wet?

A. Yes, ma'am.

Q. How did that happen?

A. From his semen on my back and on my legs--upper thighs.

Q. Did you see what he did with the condom?

A. He went into the bathroom--and I think he flushed it. I know he got a towel to wipe himself off, and then he threw it on the bed.

Sherry identified the towel.

Q. After he had gotten out of your car--did you say you had the strips of cloth in your purse?

A. In the pocket of my skirt. I gave them to the police officer.

Mrs. Winstead approached the witness box and held up some strips of cloth.

Sherry completely broke down.

Q. Are these the strips he said he was going to use to tie you up?

A. Yes, ma'am.

Q. When you were taken to the hospital, were you asked if you wanted to see someone from the Rape Crisis Center?

A. At the time, I was so confused, and I didn't want anybody to know. I didn't want to talk to anybody, but I needed to speak to somebody. I didn't know what to do. I said, "Yes," and they sent someone. There were so many people around--staring at me and asking me questions, and I just wanted them all to leave and go away. I never knew that--when they do that exam--I didn't know what it entailed. When you're already hurt enough, it's just like being raped again. They take your hair...they...like I said, it's just like being raped again.

The prosecutor introduced State's Exhibit Three, the statement Sherry had given to Detective Franklin the day after the rape.

Q. This statement is in his handwriting. Is that correct?

A. Yes, ma'am. I was on the couch--feeling very sick. He read it back to me and I signed it.

Mrs. Winstead faced the jury and read the statement:

"Last night about 8:00 p.m., I left Shoney's on Hillandale Road to go to our apartment, which is about ten minutes away, to change my panty hose because I thought I was starting my period, and the ones that I was wearing had a bad run in them. I left by the front door, going to my car parked in the rear. I got into my car, cranking it up, and was leaving. I saw Roland Stevens standing near some steps at the motel, waving me to come in that direction. As I drove around, he was walking in front of the car. I pulled the car up to a halt, and Roland Stevens had his hand on the door knob of the motel room door. I don't know what possessed me to see what he wanted. As I walked up to the door, I could only imagine that he was going to get something to take with him. I could only suppose [that] he was wanting me to give him a ride to the prison camp. I should have just stopped to think. I should have known not to put myself in that position. As I got to the door of Room 149, he got me by the arm, grabbing me, and then took me by the neck, choking me down. He took a steak knife from his back pocket, holding it to my face, repeatedly telling me he would kill me if I kept resisting him. Some of this time, he would be holding me by the wrist, and some of the time by the throat. I kept asking him, "Why are you doing this?" And he kept screaming, "Shut up. Shut up." He pushed me back to the bed, unbuttoning my vest. I started to cry. I struggled more, and he pushed me back, saying, "I'll fucking tie you up if that's what I have to do." That scared me even more. I told him I would stop screaming if he just wouldn't tie me up. I was crying, begging him to let me go. I knew he would kill me if I resisted. He seemed freaked on drugs or something, like he was crazy. I remember screaming when he took his pants off. He put a hand over my mouth, forcing me to stop. He kept trying to kiss me. I kept turning my head. He placed hisself [sic] inside my vagina, having intercourse for only a short period of time. He withdrew, ordering me to stand up, turn around. I was afraid to turn all the way around. He kept saying, "Turn around! Turn around! I'm serious. I will kill you." When I didn't, he threatened me with the knife again. He had evidently been putting a condom on, as he then inserted himself in my anus. He took himself out after just a second or two of this, taking the condom off, masturbating himself and ejaculating all over my back. I turned around; he put his shorts back on. I was quickly trying to get my clothes back on. He kept telling me to "Shut up, shut up. I'll kill you if you don't." I was begging him for me--to let me go or just let me take him back to the prison camp. He seemed to get madder and crazier, telling me he was raped as a child and that was the reason he had done this to me. He asked me if he could just pay me not to call the police. He told me to put the cloth strips in my pocket, as he might need them. He walked close beside me, holding my wrist with one hand, and I sensed the knife at my side with his other hand. He walked me to the driver's side of the car. I got in, [and] he climbed in over [on] top of me to the passenger's side, I guess, so I couldn't leave him. I was hoping he was going to let me take him back to camp, but I was afraid be was going to take me somewhere and kill me and take my car. He continued to show me the knife. I left by the Gulf Station, then left on Hillandale Road. He was then saying he was okay, not [to] be scared. I finally talked him into throwing the knife out the window on Hillandale Road. He kept telling me to "Slow down. Slow down." I turned right onto, I think, Carver Street, then left onto Guess Road. I was losing control of myself at this time. I was afraid I was going to have a seizure--I have seizure/panic attacks. He had me drive him around, getting crazier and crazier acting and talking. I begged and begged him to just get out of the car. He finally said, "Stop. Stop," and he opened my car door, hitting a utility pole with it. He was wanting to try and find the bus station. Before he got out, he wanted me to give him money. I told him I had none. I had one dollar. He got out. I sped away as fast as I could, finally stopping at a Shell gas where they called the police."

Basically the same story Sherry had told us from the witness stand, the written account did add some details and clarify a few points.

The prosecutor, turning to the witness, asked her to point out for the jury the person that had raped her.

During Sherry's testimony, Roland Stevens had been sitting at the defense table in the center of the room watching his accuser. Of medium height, he was slim and wiry, with roughly chiseled features and stringy, long, light brown hair. His eyes were lively and attentive, taking everything in, and his mannerisms bespoke curiosity rather than hostility. Frequently during Sherry's testimony, he whispered eagerly into his counsel's ear.

Sherry had not looked at him once, as if she could not bear his being in the same room. Now she faced him, pointed to him, jerking her arm back to her side and averting her eyes as swiftly as she could.

"He's right there."

Q. Have you seen the defendant since he got out of your car that night?

A. No, ma'am. I saw his face all over the television and newspapers, but not in person.

Q. No further questions.

It was four-thirty in the afternoon, and the defense attorney asked that court be recessed until morning. His cross-examination might be lengthy--this was the first time he had seen the statement. His request was granted.

Getting out of court early, Jack and I considered playing tennis, but we were in the midst of a heat wave. The temperature today had reached ninety-eight degrees; the heat index, one hundred and five. The entire eastern half of the country was suffering with us. The twelve o'clock news had listed heat precautions, and USA Today had quoted a policeman in Philadelphia as saying, "It's too hot for anyone to go out and commit any crimes." At least, the hot weather served one good purpose.

Tuesday morning, Margaret, wearing the same blue visor and the same blue dress, was sitting in the courtroom when we arrived. She smiled and nodded a good morning as I took the seat beside her.

Daniel Lauffer, the defense attorney, would have his turn at questioning the prosecution's star witness.

Sherry was wearing a simple, black, semi-fitted dress, which would have been striking with her pale features had she not looked so tired, her red, swollen eyes revealing her emotional strain. But she seemed more composed, thinking, perhaps, that the worst of her ordeal was over after she had told her painful story.

Not so in a rape case. More than for any other offense, the victim is also placed on trial, having to prove not only that this is the person that committed the crime, but, first, that a crime was committed. If someone takes the stand and says her house was broken into and her possessions stolen, the jury accepts that information. Their only concern is, "Is this the person that did the deed?" When someone is raped, it becomes a "she said, he said" credibility contest. If the defendant admits to sex, he will claim it was consensual, and, in most cases, the two of them were the only ones present.

The victim is scrutinized under a magnifying glass, every relevant aspect of her character and lifestyle dissected, forcing her into a defensive position, and she is victimized once more by the system.

When rape really is rape, the process is despicable, but by the very nature of the crime, there seems no other way to proceed. If the defendant is presumed innocent, she is the one that has to prove him guilty, and she is, therefore, fair game, exposed and vulnerable to attack.

Mr. Lauffer cross-examined.

> Q. In the statement that you gave to the police, you indicate that you suffer from panic attacks?
>
> A. Yes, sir.

Q. Do you want to tell me a little bit about that?

A. When I get real upset, I start to hyperventilate. I can't breathe. I lose the feeling in my hands, and sometimes I pass out--not all the time, but sometimes.

She agreed that she had been not only "real upset" on the night of the rape, but "hysterical."

Q. But you didn't have a panic attack on July eighteenth, did you?

A. I don't know what you would call it, sir.

Q. Do you take medication for that condition?

A. I take nothing now. The panic attacks are something that comes up maybe once, twice a year. It's nothing I deal with on an everyday basis. I haven't taken any medication for a long time.

Q. But you were taking medication in July of 1990?

A. Yes. I think it was Xanex.

Sherry remembered taking one on that day "about lunchtime."

Q. During the time you were working for Shoney's, how well did you know Roland Stevens?

A. Just well enough to say, "How is your day going?" But not friendly, friendly.

Q. But you did have occasion to sit down and talk from time to time?

A. To rephrase that, sir, I would be sitting down and he would sit down and talk to me.

Sherry did not remember if Roland was already working there when she began her employment in May. She had been told by Mr. Edwards, her General Manager, to take the defendant back to the prison camp one time before when he had worked past the time of his normal transportation. She described her work shift as "four to closing."

> Q. When is closing?
>
> A. Whenever you get finished.
>
> Q. Well, when did they stop serving?
>
> A. I don't remember. I've tried to forget everything. I cannot tell you.
>
> Q. But that night, you left at eight o'clock?
>
> A. As far as I can remember. That's what I've been told.
>
> Q. And you left to change your pantyhose, and you thought that you might be starting your menstrual period?
>
> A. Yes, sir.
>
> Q. And do you know whether or not you had started?
>
> A. No, sir.

The defense attorney led Sherry through the events of the night, starting with when she got in her car and saw the defendant.

> Q. When you went up to the door, you say, he grabbed you. Was that outside or inside?
>
> A. He had his hand on the door. As soon as I got right there, he opened the door--and the next thing I knew, I was up against a wall--and he had the knife.

Q. But when he grabbed you, was that outside or inside?

Sherry tried to explain again, but Mr. Lauffer was not satisfied with her answer. She gave up in frustration.

A. I can't say, sir. I'm foggy on that. He was choking me.

Sherry broke down sobbing.

Q. What time did you leave the room?

A. I have no idea.

Q. Was it dark or daylight?

A. It was still daylight.

Q. When you went into the motel room, did you notice anyone else? Weren't there other people around?

A. There were some people on the left hand side, but they were too far away. I remember a red cooler and some men drinking beer, but they weren't there when we came out.

Q. At the time you left the room and went to your car, you never made an attempt to run, did you?

A. No, sir. I was afraid for my life. No one was there to help me.

Q. Don't you think it strange that he had rented a motel room?

A. Now, yes, I do. But at the time, I didn't. I never had a reason to fear him. I've never been around a convict. I don't know how to act. I never expected anything like this to happen. If I did, I certainly wouldn't be here today.

Through the defense attorney's questions, Sherry held her head slightly to the left, away from the direction of the defendant.

Mr. Lauffer asked if she got a good look at the knife, and she described the weapon as having a wooden handle and a silver blade, "just like the knives we rolled silverware with at Shoney's."

Q. Have you ever smoked marijuana with Roland Stevens?

A. No, sir.

Q. Even at that time when you took him back to camp?

A. No, sir. The only thing I smoked were cigarettes.

Q. You never asked him where to get marijuana or cocaine?

A. No, sir.

The defense had not gained much ground with this witness; Sherry had held up well. She had steeled herself for an onslaught that had not come. But in this case, the defense attorney did not have the most usual lines of challenge open to him. He could not cast aspersion on the way she had been dressed--a white shirt, vest, tie, and skirt could hardly be called provocative. She had not been on a date with the accused; she had not "picked him up" in a bar; nor did the sexual encounter take place in the wee hours of the morning. Theoretically, none of these circumstances in any way lessens or justifies the act of rape, but, realistically, juries are less sympathetic to scantily-clad females who hang around bars or willingly accompany men to apartments at three in the morning. Given those circumstances, defense lawyers can have a field day with the accuser's morality and lack of judgment.

Nevertheless, the brevity of defense counsel's cross-examination was surprising. He did not ask why she had locked her door when she had left her car "momentarily" to see what the defendant wanted--a minor point, and explainable by "force of habit," but a question left hanging.

Mrs. Winstead wanted to clarify her witness' testimony on one point.

Q. At the time you were being held, tell us in more detail about how he choked you?

A. He was just choking me--probably not that hard. I never choked, choked--but he was--just choking me. I've never been choked before--

Crying, Sherry held both hands over her eyes. She either didn't know how to describe exactly what she meant or thought it should be obvious.

She was excused from the witness box.

Cindy Walker was called as the next witness for the State. Employed by Ed's Gulf on the corner of Roxboro Road, she had worked as a clerk until 9:00 on the night in question.

A. All of a sudden this lady just came in the store, and she was crying and screaming and hollering. She said, "Please call the police. Please, call the police." I asked her why, and she said, "I've just been raped." I took her into my boss's office, called the police, and I stayed with her until the police arrived.

Q. At any time while she was at Ed's Gulf, did you see any white strips of cloth that she had?

A. Yes, ma'am. The police kept on asking her different questions and stuff, and she pulled the strips out of her pocket. She said, "This is what he was going to tie me up with."

Q. Could you describe her emotional state?

A. She was hysterical.

Mr. Lauffer cross-examined.

Q. Do you see Ms. Wells here in the courtroom today?

A. Yes, sir.

Q. Does she look pretty much the same today as she did last
July?

The witness looked puzzled and shrugged her shoulders.

A. Well, in looks, yeah.

Q. Is her hair the same length it was then, or is it shorter?

A. It might be a little bit shorter. I don't know.

Q. How about the color of her hair?

A. Well, she might have lightened it a little bit.

Q. No further questions.

The jury looked puzzled also.

Officer Richard Clayton, a member of the Durham Police
Department, was next to testify. He had been on duty that night and had
responded to the call from Ed's Gulf, arriving three or four minutes later.
He was met by the male manager and escorted to his office.

Q. What happened when you got to his office?

A. Ms. Wells was there. She was crying and trying to catch
her breath, but she was able to articulate some of what
had happened to her. She said she was raped by a guy she
called Roland Stevens. They worked at Shoney's together,
and he was on work release. He had coaxed her into a room

at the Cricket Inn--at that time she did not know the room number. He had held her with a knife, tied her up with white pieces of cloth. Then he had forced her to drive him in her car. She didn't know where she went, but he still had a knife. She said that he threatened that if she told, he would kill her or have one of his friends on the outside kill her. She reached into her left pocket and pulled out some strips.

State's Exhibit Four, the torn strips of sheet were shown to the witness, who identified them.

Q. What, if anything, did you do with the strips of cloth?

A.. I took them to headquarters and held them in an evidence locker. They were not unsealed until yesterday in court.

Q. What happened after she showed you the strips?

A. At some point, her fiancé arrived on the scene. I asked him to ride with her to point out the room to us--the crime scene, so that we could get a handle on exactly where we needed to focus our investigation. There was some confusion as to which Shoney's, because she had said there was a motel behind the restaurant, and I thought she meant the one near the Gulf station. Once we learned the identity of the actual scene, I escorted her and her fiancé to Duke Hospital.

Q. How far was the "right" Shoney's from the Gulf station?

A. Three miles.

After Officer Clayton ascertained that Mr. Stevens had rented a room at the Cricket Inn, he turned the investigation over to Officer Franklin.

The defense attorney asked a few questions on cross- examination.

Q. Did she tell you that he had tied her up with the strips of cloth?

A. That's what I understood her to say at the time.

Q. So that's what you put down in your report?

A. That's right.

Q. And you also indicated that she couldn't give you the location of where the knife was thrown out. Isn't that correct?

A. No. She could not tell me that.

Sgt. Myron Moore was called to the stand. He had worked with the Durham Correctional Center for ten years. He verified that Roland Stevens was an inmate in July of 1990 and that he was assigned to the work release program. He explained that this particular institution was a minimum security facility and that after some inmates had been there for ninety days, depending on their crime, they were eligible for work release status if they had worked up to "level three." To reach this level, they were required to "gain a certain amount of trust."

Inmates were checked out by the front desk, and "it was common practice for the managers of inmates who were assigned to Shoney's to pick them up in the morning and return them in the afternoon." On July eighteenth, Mr. Stevens was signed out at 4:45 A.M. to return at 5:00 P. M. That night, the manager called and asked that Mr. Stevens be extended until 9:00 P. M. The extension was granted.

"At nine o'clock, when we cleared the yard and took a head count, he was missed. I called Mr. Smith, the manager, and he said he had not seen Mr. Stevens since eight-thirty. He said he had been too busy to call and let me know. I was very upset with Mr. Smith and asked him why hadn't he called and informed me. As soon as I hung up the telephone, the police called, asking if I had such an inmate and told me he was wanted for kidnapping and rape. I immediately notified the unit duty officer and put all escape proceedings into effect."

Officer David Bell took the stand and identified himself as the Prison Emergency Response Officer. He told the jury that Roland Stevens was an inmate, serving a nine-year sentence for Second Degree Kidnapping. Officer Bell's job was "to go out after escapees." His PERT Unit (Prison Emergency Response Team) was on twenty-four hour call.

"Sgt. Moore called me around nine-thirty, and I called in the unit. It took two to three days to locate him, using a minimal number of officers and a lot of overtime. We rode around and staked out different houses where the defendant might have hidden. He was picked up by the Raleigh PD near a phone booth, if I'm not mistaken, either on the twenty-fourth or twenty-sixth of July."

Mr. Lauffer cross-examined. He established that Officer Bell knew Roland Stevens well. Theirs was a small facility with a hundred and eighty to two hundred inmates, and "it wasn't hard to remember or talk to different inmates during a day's time."

> Q. Roland Stevens had not been in any trouble at the prison camp since his incarceration in 1987, had he?
>
> A. No.
>
> Q. And he was eligible for good behavior credits?
>
> A. Yes.
>
> Q. Meaning that he received one day off his sentence for every day of good behavior?

A. If I'm not mistaken, that's correct.

Allison Findley had served the Durham Police Department for nine years as an identification technician. She had arrived at Room 149 at 10:05 P. M. on that July evening of last year. After photographing the room, she was to collect evidence. She identified State's exhibits Six through Thirteen, photographs of the room, and showed them to the jury. Exhibit Number Seven showed a white towel on the bed, and Exhibit Number Five was a close-up of the bed closest to the bathroom.

"You can see a short tie underneath the pillow."

Mrs. Winstead placed a large, green, plastic bag in front of the witness, and Officer Findley put on rubber gloves before she pulled out the green and orange bedspread. Other items shown to the jury were a fitted and a flat sheet from the bed on the south wall, closest to the bathroom; two white pillow covers; a white towel taken from the bed on the north wall; a plaid short tie found under a corner of the bedspread; and a cigarette butt that had been found on the floor between the two beds. The bottom sheet of the south wall bed had been torn.

Officer Findley was excused, with the option open to recall her at a later time.

The judge gave the jury a twenty-minute break. The jurors had difficulty returning in a shorter time because the snack shop was on the sixth floor, and ten minutes had to be allowed for waiting on elevators.

Slow elevators seem to be a standard requirement in a courthouse, as if the manufacturers and installers conspire to test the frustration level of an already harried courthouse population. The Courthouse elevators in Raleigh were slow, but the Durham elevators won the tortoise award.

Margaret told me I could go to the Judge's chambers if I wanted to. I thanked her. Actually, this courtroom had no chambers that I knew of, probably because it was close to the resident judges' office. Judge Tony Brannon was in another city this week and had offered his office to Jack. Ann, the judges' secretary, who was responsible for Jack's being here this week, was friendly and entertaining.

This particular Superior Court Judges' office also was used as a pass-through to an outside-wall back corridor by other personnel who came in the front door and exited the back door, a convenient shortcut.

Unfortunately, that included defendants. With no warning, the bailiffs would come crashing in with prisoners in tow to use the rear door. On more than one occasion during that week while I was engaged in a conversation in the middle of the small inside lobby, my back to the door, whoever was facing the door took my arm and pulled me out of the way. Often the judge presiding over that prisoner's trial would also have to move from "their defendant's" path. Whoever designed this courthouse missed on the traffic flow.

Betty Hayes had been a fellow employee of Sherry Wells at Shoney's. At that time, one of her duties was to back up the dining room supervisor, Sherry.

"Sherry was one of the best we'd ever had: She would pitch in and help, rather than just telling you what to do. She came to me that day and wanted me to be in charge. She said she had to go home, but she would be gone only a short time, and she gave me the register keys. I can't remember the time, but I know it was after six."

"After she left, did you see her again that evening?"

"No. I remember I said something to another waitress like, 'I thought Sherry would be back by now.' I don't think I left until after twelve that night."

Larry Smith, the Assistant Manager at Shoney's in July of the previous year, told the jury that he had come to work at three o'clock on the day in question. He remembered that Keith Edwards, the Manager, had wanted the defendant to do some extra cleaning up that day.

Q. Did you have a conversation with the defendant that evening?

A. Mr. Edwards told me to call the camp and tell them Roland Stevens would be coming back later. At six o'clock, Roland told me, "I'm going outside to take my break," and I didn't see him anymore.

Q. Did Sherry Wells have a conversation with you about leaving work that day?

A. Yes. She said, "I have to leave for a few minutes."

Q. Did she tell you why?

A. Yes. She said, "I've got female problems." I figured from working with her that it had to be something legitimate. She said she'd be back in twenty minutes.

Mr. Lauffer cross-examined.

Q. You say that you didn't see Mr. Stevens at any time after six o'clock?

A. No. We had a real busy night. The manager had already left, and I was in charge of the whole store.

Q. And you never contacted the prison camp to tell them that he was missing?

A. By that time, they called me.

Q. Did you ever request Sherry to drive him back to the camp?

A. No.

The next witnesses for the prosecution had not arrived. But, said Mrs. Winstead, it was her understanding that they were in route to the courthouse from Raleigh. An hour went by, and everyone waited. Still no witnesses. By this time it was twelve-thirty, and the judge excused the jurors for lunch.

Brenda Brissett, a forensic serologist with the SBI for thirteen years, was the first witness to take the stand when court resumed for the afternoon. She had examined the rape-kit swabs taken from Sherry at the hospital. Ms. Brissett testified that she had found no spermatozoa on the vaginal or rectal swabs, but did find sperm on the victim's panties. The blood-grouping tests from this sperm had been matched to the victim, but the tests were inconclusive as to the defendant.

Joseph Reves, a forensic hair examiner with the SBI for four years, examined the hair given to him by Ms. Brissett, but he was "not able to establish a transfer of hair from the defendant to the victim."

Leslie Key, a Registered Nurse at Duke Hospital, was on emergency room duty on July 18, 1990, and had provided care to Sherry.

> Q. What do you recall about her appearance when you first saw her?

> A. I was actually on the ambulance pad smoking when she walked in escorted by another person. And looking at her silhouette from the back, I thought she was an old lady from the way she was walking. When I went in, I realized that she was an assault victim. My thought was that she had a saddle injury just by the way she was walking.

> Q. Once you were able to meet with her, what observations did you make?

Ms. Key read from her nursing assessment and a *Sexual Assault Data* form.

A. She was teary. Her teeth were chattering. She was emotionally upset, but appropriate--handling the situation.

Q. Did she tell you what had happened to her?

A. Oh, yes. She was able to tell me the man's name. Apparently, they were both working at Shoney's. She also told me that he was white and the nature of what happened.

Q. Did she say anything about a knife and being choked?

A. Yes. And that he had made threats.

Ms. Key had also asked Sherry when she had last had intercourse. Her answer had been "one month ago."

Dr. James Thomas Roth, an OB/GYN resident at Duke Medical Center, took the stand and explained to the jury that he had been on call in the emergency room on the night in question.

Q. Was it one of your duties to examine women who had been sexually assaulted?

A. Yes.

Q. How often does that occur, doctor?

A. In the past year, one to two times a month.

He told the jury that he had seen Sherry that night close to 11:00 P. M. He read from his notes.

"She appeared upset and agitated. She told me she had been sexually assaulted close to her place of work. She said she had been penetrated vaginally and anally, but not orally. There were no biting or wounds, but a knife was used, and the assailant grabbed the patient by the throat and choked her."

On examination, the doctor found a "small perineal tear" and a rectal tear accompanied by blood. He also noted that his patient was "appropriately tender" in the areas involved.

> Q. The vaginal and anal tears--would you expect to find them in consensual sexual intercourse?
>
> A. No.
>
> Q. Did she tell you who had assaulted her, doctor?
>
> A. She said he was on work release and working at Shoney's, I think, as a dishwasher or in some similar capacity.
>
> Q. What was her demeanor when she told you about what happened?
>
> A. I have noted that she was "appropriately upset, clear as to details, and consistent."

On cross-examination, Doctor Roth said he had been told that June twenty-fourth was the date of the victim's last menstrual period.

> Q. Was she having a menstrual period at that time?
>
> A. There is no indication of that. I didn't list it.

The defense attorney asked that one question too many.

> Q. Is it your testimony that there is no way that the tears could have occurred other than through forced intercourse?
>
> A. I would say it would be very unusual.

Officer Allison Findley was recalled to the stand. This time she had the victim's clothes that she had collected from the hospital and sent to the lab. Another package contained the bed clothes from the motel room, and she unfolded the remnant of the sheet from which the strips had been torn to show it to the jury.

Sherry, seated on the front row of the audience, buried her head in the shoulder of the woman next to her.

Piece by piece, Officer Findley held up Sherry's white blouse, bra, pantyhose, green skirt, and green vest, still bearing her Shoney's identification tag.

Sherry and her companion left the courtroom.

Her clothing was passed to the jury.

Although these items bore no tell-tale signs of what had happened, the jurors inspected each with interest. A hands-on examination of articles that you have heretofore only heard described, somehow confirms the reality.

The State rested.

Robert Franklin, the detective with the Durham city police who had been sitting at the prosecution table throughout the trial, had never taken the stand. In a departure from "normal" procedure, instead of calling him to read the statement he had taken from Sherry to the jury, Mary Winstead had read it herself while Sherry was still on the stand.

Had this course of action just been easier, or did she not want him subjected to cross- examination?

In a surprise move, Mr. Lauffer began his defense evidence by calling Detective Franklin as his first witness.

Detective Franklin had been on call on July eighteenth of last year and had responded from his residence to the police communications call, driving first to Duke hospital, where he had talked with Sherry for about twenty-five minutes. He had taken no notes that night, wanting "to wait until she calmed down."

Answering Mr. Lauffer's questions, Detective Franklin said he had gone to the motel after leaving the hospital and had spoken with the managers at Shoney's. He had also spoken with "two gentlemen that were evidently staying at the motel at the time this incident occurred," but he had not spoken with them that night. An employee of the motel had told him that out-of-state construction workers had stayed in the room next door to Room 149 that night and had been out in the parking lot after the police cars arrived. Calling the construction company, Detective Franklin had learned the men's names and tracked them down, but it had not been easy:

"They were hard to find. I think they work something like three twelve or fifteen hour days a week, or something or other. Anyway, they are not in the Durham area but like about three or three-and-a-half days a week when they are working here." Finally, he had made contact, locating them at their new job site.

Q. Did you take any statements from them at that time?

A. I did.

Q. I show you what has been marked as Defendant's Exhibit Number Three. Would you take a look at that, please?

A. This is a photocopy of a statement I took from them on August twentieth, 1990.

The statement was in this detective's handwriting, written in the two men's presence, and bore the signatures of both. That was the problem--but just one problem. The defense attorney asked the officer to read the statement, the prosecutor objected, and the jury was sent out.

The judge addressed the defense attorney:

"First of all, Mr. Lauffer, on what basis do you feel that you are entitled to introduce the statement of non-testifying witnesses?"

Unless he presented evidence to show that the witnesses were not available, the defense attorney should have known that the detective could not read the statement which was not his testimony but someone else's. Before this could occur, the defense first had to show certain criteria to meet this exception to the hearsay rule.

Mr. Lauffer belatedly explained to the court that one of the men, Mr. Dunbar, could not be reached--all attempts on his part to find him had failed. Subpoenas to his home address and work address had come back unserved--"He has not been employed with that company since October," and even his mother "hasn't seen him since October [and] has no idea where he is."

Verbally, he had covered some of the necessary factors; however, no affidavit from the mother or returned subpoenas were offered as verification.

Mary Winstead, arguing for the State, maintained that the first factor under this *hearsay* exception, written notice to her that the defense intended to use this statement in the absence of a witness, had not been received. Most importantly from the prosecutor's view, if the statement of an absent witness was allowed, she could not cross-examine a piece of paper.

But, the defense countered, the State had been in possession of the statement for nearly a year, while he had received it only two months ago, not knowing until then that he had two witnesses to look for and not knowing that he would have trouble locating them.

The rules of evidence, even when clearly spelled out, sometimes are not followed--due to misunderstanding, inexperience, failure on both sides to communicate effectively or adhere with discovery motions, or what have you. The list of possible scenarios is endless. Sometimes, the results can be harsh and seem to thwart the process rather than help it. But in this instance, the trial judge had some leeway to sort it all out, decide how crucial the evidence was, and, most importantly, determine if "the interests of justice" outweighed the technicalities that governed. There are twenty-four statutory exceptions to the hearsay rule, and all of them have multiple components that must be met.

Somewhere in the arguments from the two attorneys, it was the prosecutor that revealed that one of the men would be present tomorrow as a defense witness.

For the moment, the judge decided to sustain the State's objection and disallow the statement because written notice had not been given to the prosecutor. But he would reconsider his ruling after the witness testified tomorrow. At this point, the statement could be read only into the record (for appellate purposes), but not to the jury.

The jury was summoned, and the prosecutor had a few questions of her own before releasing Detective Franklin.

> Q. You indicated you spoke with Sherry at the hospital. Is that right?
>
> A. Yes, ma'am.
>
> Q. Would you describe her emotional state at that time?
>
> A. Very unstable, crying, confused, surprised, probably verging on going into shock.

Mr. Lauffer had run out of witnesses at four-fifteen.

The judge was not happy. He had adjourned early Monday for the defense and had waited half of this Tuesday morning for the prosecutor's witnesses; now the defense wanted an early dismissal again. At the bench, he notified both lawyers that at nine-thirty in the morning, he would expect this case to go forward with no more delays. Yes, he understood the inconvenience to a witness having to wait in the courtroom, but that inconvenience was compounded twelve times more when the jurors were kept waiting. This was a court of law. Some things took precedence.

Court was adjourned.

Even this late in the afternoon, the temperature outside was a hundred degrees, and as we made the short walk from the parking lot into the hotel, hazy spirals of moist, sticky air rose to wilt every cell in our bodies. Too early for dinner and too hot for much else, we chose to shed our shoes, prop our feet on the coffee table, and talk in the comfort of our air-conditioned room and discuss the case.

A most intriguing puzzle was forming--a question alluded to only once so far by Mr. Lauffer: why had Roland Stevens rented a motel room? Renting a motel room for a few hours is a pretty hefty expense on a dishwasher's salary.

He knew he had to return to the prison camp for the night, so he could not stay overnight in the room without becoming an escapee...and escape didn't add up...why stay next door to his place of employment, the first place searchers would look? And, according to Sherry, he had told her to drive him back to the prison camp. It was possible he planned to escape and changed his mind, but not too likely.

According to Sherry, her decision to leave work was spontaneous. If she had no idea she was going to leave at eight o'clock, how could he have been waiting for her? If he had rented a room with any plans for Sherry in mind, their meeting would have had to be prearranged, and that would mean Sherry had not told all. On the other hand, Sherry could have had nothing at all to do with his registering at the motel. Could he have rented the room planning to rape whomever--any woman who happened along in the parking lot that night? Possible, but not probable, and a rather expensive and erratic gamble.

The defense had brought up marijuana and cocaine. Had he rented the room to conduct a drug deal? Was it such a big deal that it required the privacy of a room instead of a dark corner in the parking lot? If so, had Sherry gone there to buy? Or had she haplessly appeared, a pawn of fate, just as he was leaving the room after concluding his business, and, on impulse, had he seized the opportunity and taken advantage of her being alone?

There seemed no plausible explanation for Roland's renting a room, not from the testimony so far. Jack didn't make me any happier when he pointed out that the truth, if incriminatory and known only to the defendant, might never surface during the trial. The only conclusion I reached was that my reasoning, in and of itself, could be the problem in trying to find an acceptable answer--who said it had to be logical to me to have made sense to the defendant?

What I didn't know at this time was that on my list of "possible reasons," one may have hit the mark.

And I had learned something else that the jury was not entitled to know at this point. Brandishing a knife was not new to the defendant. This had also been his choice of weapon when he had committed the second degree kidnapping he was currently in prison for.

Jack asked if I'd I like to go to Pyewacket's for dinner.

Pyewacket's was in Chapel Hill, not Durham, but close by, and we'd not likely run into any jurors.

"However, they won't have 'the most wonderful sandwich in the whole world' on the dinner menu," he added, and we both laughed.

In the past, we have planned our arrival to the Triangle area, business or pleasure, to coincide with lunchtime at this restaurant on Franklin Street, home of what I had dubbed the "most wonderful sandwich in the whole world." My excessive praise for the sandwich had something to do with its combination of ingredients (fresh mushrooms, avocados, sprouts, cucumbers, homemade creamy cucumber dressing on freshly baked whole wheat bread), and, perhaps, something more to do with the glass of wine that accompanied it the first time I ordered this culinary delight several years ago. I would later blame it on my lack of sleep during an especially exhausting week, so that by

the time we had arrived that Friday at lunchtime for Jack's weekend seminar,
an ordinary glass of chardonnay had effected me like a liter bottle, my copi-
ous praise for the sandwich vastly compromised. I fell into a deep sleep at the
pool while he attended his meeting.

We had been to Pyewacket's only once before for dinner, a real treat,
and I readily agreed to eat there tonight, sandwich or no sandwich.

Wednesday morning, Carl Wood took the stand for the defense.
A resident of West Virginia, he worked as an electrician on various job
sites in North Carolina and other neighboring States. He was working in
Durham in July of 1990 and staying at the Cricket Inn.

"They moved us around--didn't keep the same room for us." On July
eighteenth, he was staying with his co-worker and friend Allen in Room
147, and they had come straight to the motel after work, arriving between
five-thirty and six o'clock. Carl was getting ready to take a shower, while
Allen was standing by the front window near the open door.

"There was a young lady in a parked car brushing her hair. I don't
remember the car now except that it was silver or light blue and it was a
new model."

> Q. Can you describe the lady?
>
> A. She was young, sort of blonde-headed, with hair down to
> her shoulders.
>
> Q. Did you see how she was dressed?
>
> A. She was wearing green, I think.
>
> Q. What, if anything, did you see her do?
>
> A. I saw her start to get out of the car, and I took my
> shower. That's basically all I seen."

He told the jury that he had been in the shower for three or four minutes, and then he sat on the bed with his head against the wall. He had heard two bumps on the wall, and a few minutes later, the same thing again.

> A. We laughed it off. We thought somebody was having a good time.
>
> Q. Did you hear any screaming or loud noises?
>
> A. No.
>
> Q. Do you think you would recognize the young woman again if you saw her?
>
> A. I doubt it.

Sherry was still seated on the front row of the spectator section and directly in his line of vision. The defense attorney started to ask if the witness saw her in the courtroom, but stopped himself, not wanting to take the chance that Mr. Wood could not identify her.

> Q. Did anything else unusual happen that night?
>
> Ms. Winstead: Objection.
>
> Court: Sustained.

Mr. Lauffer was looking at his notes, and the witness was looking out into the courtroom while he waited for the next question. His eyes stopped on Sherry and flashed recognition. He had picked her out, but the defense attorney had missed this eye to eye contact and never again asked this witness the identity question he now knew he could answer.

Instead, Mr. Lauffer questioned Mr. Wood about the detective who had found him a month later on another job.

Q. Did you make a statement?

A. Yes.

Q. And you signed it?

A. Yes.

Q. And this officer talked to both you and Mr. Dunbar at the same time?

A. Yes.

Q. He didn't prepare separate statements?

A. I don't remember. It was too long ago.

Q. But that is your signature?

A. Yes, sir. Sure is.

Q. Would you please read the statement?

Mrs. Winstead: Objection.

Mr. Lauffer asked to be heard, and the jury was sent out. Mrs. Winstead objected on the basis of hearsay because it was joint statement, and Mr. Dunbar had seen things Mr. Wood had not testified to.

Hearsay can be admitted as evidence under numerous exceptions to the hearsay rule. The specific criteria governing this instance are spelled out in State v. Smith, the first of which is notice to the other attorney (in this case, the prosecutor from the defense) in writing that this evidence will be presented.

There had been no written notification. The defense argued that this statement was pertinent to their case, "the best evidence we have as to Mr. Dunbar, and there are no grounds to say he was partial."

The Judge decided that because the prosecutor had had this information "for some time and could reasonably expect the defense to proffer it, proper notice has occurred." In addition, he found that the statement was essential to the defense in this case and its admission would "best serve the interests of justice." The statement would be allowed.

Carl Wood now read the account he and his friend Allen had given Detective Franklin and which both of them had signed:

> "Several weeks ago, we were staying at [the] Cricket Inn,
> Hillandale Road, [in a] room next to where we understand a
> rape took place. That evening, I [and] Allen Dunbar was coming
> from the shopping center and saw a silver Grand Am pull up
> and park in front of our room. There was a white female with
> blonde hair in it. We saw her sit there for approximately five to
> ten minutes, some of the while brushing her hair. She then got
> out of the car and went into the room next to ours. About fifteen
> to twenty minutes later, we heard two thumps from next door.
> At no time did we hear any yelling, screaming, fighting, nor any
> noise that would make us think anything whatsoever was going
> on. We didn't see the people leave. I recognized that the girl had
> on a Shoney's uniform. We normally stay at this same motel every
> week, as we work for Overcash Electric out of Mooresville and
> are now working at the new shopping center under construction
> at Roxboro Road and Old Oxford Highway. We think that if there
> was any screaming or yelling, we would have certainly heard it, as
> you can easily hear noises at this motel from room to room. We
> heard no such noises."

The jurors appeared puzzled. Some of them were looking at the prosecutor. They wanted her to explain this turn of events.

Mary Winstead cross-examined. She wanted to make sure the jury understood that Mr. Wood himself had seen the woman in the car for only a minute, did not see the car pull up or the girl get out of the car--in other words, the statement had been mostly his friend's observations because Mr. Wood had been in the shower. She also established that the air conditioner was running in his room, suggesting that the "lack of noises" could be explained by the unit's muffling effect.

After Mr. Wood was excused, Mr. Lauffer recalled Detective Franklin to the stand and verified that he was the one that had taken this statement.

Mary Winstead briefly cross-examined.

> Q. Detective Franklin, do you recall what Mr. Dunbar told you about when he first saw the person [in the car]?
>
> A. He told me that he had walked to Winn Dixie from the motel room which is about--I would estimate it about two hundred yards north of the motel room at the shopping center there--to get a two-liter drink to mix mixed drinks with, and that upon returning, he saw this vehicle parked there adjacent to their room.
>
> Q. Did he tell you that he was drinking during the time they were in the room?
>
> A. I don't know that he told me that he had already begun or was intending to begin once he got back to the room.
>
> Q. I don't have any further questions.

Mr. Wood's testimony was certainly damaging to the State's case, and in the light of all the evidence so far, it could possibly be true. The victim had said she saw a red cooler and some men drinking beer, so one could deduce that these were those men.

She could have willingly gone into the room with Roland, and he could have turned on her once there--still rape. Vaginal and anal tears do not spell consent. But this hypothesis may be difficult to believe--Sherry's testimony was too convincing. After Detective Franklin's added testimony, a more likely explanation might be that if these two men had been consuming beer and mixed drinks for two hours, they could have reached the point that they weren't paying strict attention to what was happening around them. Sherry had walked up to Roland, obviously knowing him, and there was no reason for their suspicions to be aroused. And if the defendant had pulled her into the room and choked her against the wall, they couldn't have seen that--or could they? This is an instance when drawn layouts of specific locations become significant to what we can accept as reasonable. The jury had been shown such a diagram during Sherry's testimony, but at that time they had not been looking for answers relating to this statement.

This last testimony had cast the first ray of doubt about Sherry's story, maybe only a twinge.

The State's main witness had been Sherry. Now the defense would call theirs, the defendant.

Roland Stevens took the stand.

He was eager to testify. His attitude posed throughout the trial by his non-stop whispering in counsel's ear indicated that neither a battery of attorneys nor wild horses, nor a battery of attorneys riding wild horses, could have dissuaded him from his turn to talk. It was as if someone had shouted "It's show time" and raised the curtain to a full house of anxious fans awaiting the star. From the moment he took his seat in the witness box, he began cutting his eyes to look at Sherry in the audience, instead of keeping them trained on his lawyer right in front of him.

Sherry buried her head in her companion's shoulder, not wanting to meet his gaze.

Mr. Stevens told the jury that he was originally from Richmond, Virginia, but his present residence was Central prison.

Q. Directing your attention to July of last year, where were you at that time?

A. I was in Guess Road--Guess Road in Durham, minimum custody camp.

Q. Guess Road Prison Camp?

A. Yes, sir.

Q. How long had you been there?

A. Since September first of '89.

Q. And what were you serving time for?

A. Second degree kidnapping.

Q. When were you sentenced?

A. I believe it was November 5th of 1987.

The witness testified that he had been on work release and working at Shoney's since June of last year as a dishwasher and a busboy. Turning his head to the left to talk directly to the jurors, he explained that only the store manager was allowed to pick him up from the camp and bring him to work, but anyone was allowed to take him back--"your wife or your mother or your father and your grandmother"--as long as he was back by nine-thirty if he had obtained permission to stay after six.

He spoke easily and casually, as if he had just encountered these people on a picnic in a public park and was anxious to make friends and share their fried chicken.

The jury eyed him coldly, however, believing at this point that he had no right to be friendly.

"Yes," he knew Sherry from work.

Q. Would you tell the jury what kind of relationship you had with her?

A. Friends. Just friends.

Q. Would you sit down and talk with her on occasion?

A. Yes, sir.

Q. What kind of things would you talk about?

A. When it started out, you know, we just talked about just bullshit things, you know, just to pass the time away...you know. Sometimes she would be sitting in there going over her--her paperwork, you know...getting ready for work and everything...Then some days I would be in there and she would come over and sit with me, and vice-versa. Like that. We just talked about, you know, whatever went on, you know...

Q. How many times would you say you sat down and had conversations with Sherry Wells?

A. Probably a total of ten times.

Sherry was shaking her head.

He told the jury that Sherry had taken him back to the prison camp "a total of three times," the first time "about a week and a half before July eighteenth." Describing their first trip, he claimed that she asked him about all the people that visited him at work, and he told her they were bringing him "reefer" to sell so he could "try to make some money that way."

Q. By reefer, you mean marijuana?

A. Yes, sir.

Q. Go on.

A. Next thing I know, I opened the ashtray of her car...and I looked down and there was a big fat joint... We'd get high. You know, we'd smoke and drive around Durham because I didn't have to be back to the camp 'til nine-thirty.

Sherry was crying and shaking her head, holding on to the woman beside her.

The witness testified that two or three days later, Sherry asked him if she could take him back to camp. She was even more interested in the people that came to see him, telling him she was "no fool and knew what was going on."

"'By the way,' I said, 'I got a little something for us tonight.' So I pulled out some of mine, and we got high and we go through the same things. She drops me off."

Q. What did you pull out?

A. Just a joint. And that was it. Nothing else. I'd say about three days later, Sherry was sitting in the little small room where she was doing her paperwork when I came up to her and started talking to her, and she put her paperwork aside and she tells me--she asks me--she says, "What do you think? Do you think that you can get me anything, anything good? She says she didn't have any connections in Durham. She didn't know anybody. I say, "Well, what do you want?" She said she wanted an eight-ball and she wanted an ounce of reefer.

Q. What is an eight-ball?

A. Cocaine. And an ounce of reefer. I said, "Yeah," I gave her a price. She said, "That's a little too steep."

Q. What price did you give her?

A. Four-fifty.

Q. Four hundred and fifty dollars?

A. Yeah. She said, "That's a little steep...This is...I had this conversation after the third time that we went back to camp...

He realized he had mixed up the sequence of events. He backtracked now, telling about the third trip back to camp with Sherry. On this occasion, he said, they sat in the car at the camp for half an hour smoking marijuana, and the officer had come over to the car to see what the delay was. He, of course, didn't want the prison guard to know what they were doing, and she had asked Officer Jones if she could pick him up early the next day, but was told "no" because Thursday was his regular day off.

Roland rambled on and on, mixing times and places and leaving boulder-size holes in his story. Was he having trouble with the sequence of events or was he making it up as he went along?

This last account was to have happened on Wednesday. It was Friday or Saturday that he saw her again.

Q. Did you have a conversation with her?

A. Yes. We went--we went over--we went over everything. We went over--we--this--this now--this is where we started talking about was I--was I to get anything for her. So I told her, "Yeah. I could get--the price was four-fifty." She said that was a little steep. I said, "Well, Sherry, you and I known each other a while." I said--I said, "You know, maybe we'll work something out." And she's--she says, "No. I know what you're thinking and no." So I say, "Okay. Suit yourself." So approximately the sixteenth--I believe it was July sixteenth, she came to me this time. I was sitting in the room. She came to me and told me that we'll work something--we can work something out. She told me she was

going to give me forty-five dollars. We'd get a room at the
Cricket Inn.

*Two men on the jury turned to their left, searching for Sherry in the
audience, and glared at her. They had to be wondering why he had rented a
room, and now one explanation had been offered.*

*The witness continued, saying Sherry had brought him the money the
next day, but he had asked her to keep the forty-five dollars because he wasn't
allowed to have that much money at the camp. The manager had walked in
just as he was handing the money back to her, and she told him not to worry,
that he wouldn't know what the money was for. The next day he had arrived
at work early and Sherry had come in at her usual time, shortly before four
in the afternoon. He kept talking:*

"She goes to her car, and it was raining a little bit--because I had
asked her...I said, 'Sherry, go get the money for me.' And she said, 'Wait 'til
the rain lets up a little bit.' The next thing I know, I turn a corner and she
hands me the forty-five dollars. This was, I don't know, maybe between
four and five o'clock. I go, 'I don't want to take your money.' [I] walk all
the way to the Cricket Inn hotel, see this woman named Peggy standing
behind the desk. I asked her. I said, 'I'd like to have a single room.' She
says, 'We have no single rooms.' I said, 'Well, give me a double room.' I
said, 'How much would that be?' She said--I believe she said it was thirty-six dollars— between thirty-six and thirty-eight dollars. I gave her the
money and she gave me the room key." He registered for the room in his
own name, but gave a false residence because he was afraid the clerk would
recognize his "Guess Road" address, and, besides, "you ain't allowed to do
that on work release."

The jurors were fascinated, hanging onto every word.

And he kept talking.

"I gave the key to Sherry Wells. We had already done planned everything. I told her--I said, 'I'll leave at eight o'clock, so you come shortly after

that.' She said, 'Okay.' I said, 'Now you're sure you're going to get away?' She said, 'Yes.' I go--you see--I go back to her at approximately twenty minutes to eight, ask for the key. She says--she starts looking. She can't find the key. She done lost it. I'm hunting all around Shoney's ... now it's about a quarter to eight--and I remember looking at that clock. I remember this well... I was on my hands and knees by the--around the dish area where I usually work at. Larry Smith, the manager, came around the corner. Larry Smith seen me on my hands and knees. This was a quarter to eight, and he seen me on my hands and knees looking for this key. Yeah. He said, 'What are you doing' I said, 'I'm looking for a key.' He didn't say nothing. I knew exactly--I remember this well. I remember looking at the clock exactly five minutes to eight--Larry Smith asked me would I install a light, a fluores-cent light, above the line. I'm thinking now, Ain't no way in the world I'm going to do this and get over to the motel. I say, 'No.' So I told Sherry--I said, 'I'm going on over. And she looks at me. The place was packed. I mean it was--it was jam-packed. That's what I was worried [about], that she could get away.

Roland, still facing the jury, recounted his second conversation with Peggy at the motel, telling her that he had lost his key. She asked for his driver's license, and he told her that he had left it in the car. So she asked him to sign for another key and handed him a duplicate. He then described, with help from a diagram from his attorney, his exact path to the office and then to Room 149.

I went inside the room--opened the door and went inside the room. Wasn't more than three or four minutes, I hear a...*Roland made a knocking sound on the witness box with his fist.* I go to the door, open it up, Sherry comes into the room, closes the door. That was it. We get inside the room. She asks me have I—have I--have I got the stuff? I said, 'Yeah.' I said, 'I got it.' She didn't ask me to see it or look at it or anything. We take our clothes off."

The same two men on the jury sought Sherry out with their eyes. Their facial expressions conveyed a clear message: "You didn't tell us this part."

"She says, 'We got forty-five minutes.' She said 'I told them that I'd be gone forty-five minutes.' I said, 'What kind of excuse did you use?' She said, 'I used the excuse I had a run in my hose and I was on my--and I'm on my--and I was on my menstrual period and I had to go home and change.' That left us forty-five minutes. It was perfect. Her...for us to take care of our little business, she could take me back to the camp, for her to take--in her mind to take that stuff home with her, drop it off, and she could come right back. That would allow the forty-five minutes--that's perfect. Okay. We go ahead--we take our clothes off."

Sherry was sitting on the edge of her seat, hugging herself, rocking back and forth, tears running down her face.

He continued:

We get on the bed, on the back bed--didn't even undo the bedspreads or nothing, just right on top of the daggone bedspread. We were both naked. We were laying--I started kissing her--and I am kissing her. She says I didn't, but we daggone did. Okay. I enter her vagina. I go exactly three--how do you say--three strokes. She says she don't want--she does not want me to come inside of her. That's what she said. She said, 'I don't want you to come inside of me.' I said, 'All right.' I said, 'Okay.' I said, 'It's all right with me.' This was three times, three little strokes. Okay. I'm half-way mad, and she--I said--I said, 'All right, you.' I said, 'Get up.' And she says--damn--she says--damn--she says--she says, 'Oh, no.' She says, 'Oh, no. Not that.' I said, 'Sherry'--I said--I said, 'You're getting your money's worth.'

The Defendant's demeanor had changed, suddenly and substantially, from obliging and gregarious, to hostile and combative. He had transformed from a friendly, bouncy puppy who wants to crawl in your lap to a seasoned German shepherd confronting a stranger, and he wasn't aware of the effect.

The courtroom had remained totally silent, but somehow it seemed even more hushed now. He had sensed that some of the jurors were giving his story some credence, and his confidence had built. It was his show, and he was playing it to the hilt.

Sherry, arms wrapped around herself, was still rocking.

Margaret turned to me. "He's talking trash," she whispered.

Still facing the jury, Roland continued:

"And she says, 'All right.' I reached down in my pants. I got a little package of--a little Preamer [sic] pack. I had a little bit of Vaseline in that preamer pack. I did not have a condom at all. I didn't have no condom. I put a little Vaseline on my penis and entered her in her--in her--in her--in her anus three times. She says, 'I don't want you to come inside of me like that.' I pulled off, you know, just ejaculating right on her back. She's mad, and I'm mad-- disgusted. And I don't understand this here at all. I get a towel. I just go--I go--I say--She's standing right here inside the room just like you've seen those pictures--right at the back bed where the--You' all remember where the cover was turned up? She's standing right there. I go back, get my--get the towel. I start wiping myself. She says, 'Well, have you got the stuff?' I says--she says, 'Give me the stuff.' I told her--I said, 'Sherry, I haven't got it.' She scratched my face on the side of my face, goes off and tells me she's going to go to the police and say I raped her.

Roland was talking excitedly, gesturing with his hands and waving his arms, acting this scene out for the jury.

Sherry was hugging herself tightly, crying, rocking back and forth.

I pushed her up against the wall, the side--here's the door coming in, the side wall right here. I push her up against the wall. I grabbed her by the throat, and I say, 'Sherry, don't say that stupid shit.' I said, 'Don't say that stupid shit.' I said--I said, "I'm going home in a month and a half.' I said, 'Please don't say that.'

Roland paused, caught his breath, and continued in a lower and dejected tone.

"She's all mad. I'm disgusted. She still said she's going to go to the police. I go to the corner of the bed, the side of the bed, sit there. And she's standing up right here. She's at the front bed. I'm at the side. I'm at that back bed. I pull up. I sit down, grab the end of the sheet, take out my fingernail clippers and poke a hole in the sheet and rip it. I've made my--I think I even made two or three strips and held them up to her like that (*demonstrating*), and she told me--she says, 'Aw, I'm not going to say nothing.' I look at her--I look at her. I said, 'Well, we'll see.' She said, Let's get dressed. I will take you back to the camp.' I said, 'Fine.' We get dressed.

Roland had slowed down now, talking more calmly.

Sherry was still rocking.

"She walks out of the door first. I close the door behind me. As soon as we got outside, she says she's going to go to the police and say I raped her. In my mind now--I'm going over this in my mind. I'm sitting there thinking in my mind, 'I got twenty-four hours to go back to that camp, twenty-four hours. All they'll get me for is unauthorized leave--unauthorized leave, and I--they'll remove me off work release, but I'll still go home in September.' I go to the driver's side, but I say nothing to her. I open the driver's side. I get into the seat myself. I get into the seat. She says, 'Oh, no. You're not driving.' I said, 'I know I'm not driving.' I move over. She gets in beside me and closes the door. I'm quiet. She's quiet. Neither [of us] saying nothing. She pulls out and starts heading on back. She goes down--it's Hillandale, and, I guess, on Carver, and starts going down Guess Road. All right. I'm sitting there and thinking, 'Daggone man, she's--she's mad. She said she's going to go to the police.' She's getting ready to start to turn--to turn up to the little side road that leads to the camp. I take the steering wheel--just like she said--I take the steering wheel--hit the steering wheel and said, 'No, Sherry, just take me on downtown.' She rode up the road a little bit. She ain't saying nothing now. She goes up the road a little bit, turns and starts heading downtown. All right. We get down there. All this stuff about she's speeding and all that stuff--that's bullshit. We're going on downtown. I tell her, 'Just drop me off at Brightleaf Square or near there.' This is a one- way street. She drops me off. The last--let's see--as we close the--see, I--as I'm getting ready and go out the door, the last thing she tells me is--is, 'You better get yourself checked. Have yourself--have yourself checked.' and I said, 'Why?' She said, "Because I've got some woman problems.' And in a voice just like that! I said, 'Yeah,' and I close the door and then went up to Brightleaf Square."

Mr. Lauffer interrupted.

> Q. Okay. Let me stop you there just for a minute. At any time while you were in the room with Sherry or while you were in the car with her, did you have a knife of any kind?
>
> A. No, sir. I did not have no knife. No. No. Do you want me to go ahead?
>
> Q. Yes. Go on.

Continuing with as much animation as before, Roland launched into the history of his thought processes and bizarre flight from the police. First, he had gone to a Mexican restaurant and ordered a Budweiser, and considered his present situation:

"Four hours ago, I'm doing just fine. Everything's good. Damn. I'm going home in a month and a half. What's going on?"

He decided to call a "certain person" to pick him up, explained "everything that happened" to her, and she took him to her home while making futile attempts to talk him into returning to the prison camp. Later, she dropped him off at a ball field.

"I slept--I slept in the--in this portable bathroom--in the john all night long. The next morning, I woke up, started walking down the road, and I was figuring, 'I got to find something out here ' I went down to this--these people I know at a bar, and I walked in there."

Telling the owner/bartender, whom he knew, his problems, she reassured him and left to see "what she can find out." Then he received a phone call.

"I don't know how the person knew how to find I'd be there, but he did. 'Man,' he said, 'You've got to get out of Dodge. They got your picture in every police car in Durham. The PERT team is down here. They said the Highway Patrol is down here at the camp.' He said, 'They said that you took that girl in the parking lot and took her over into a motel and raped her.' I said, 'All right. I appreciate it.'"

He paused, thought a few seconds, and backtracked again.

"Excuse me. That was before I went to the bar. This guy I knew, he-- well, he picked me up and told me some things, and anyway, I--I left the bar. I figured it wasn't safe to stay there because it's a drug area. The cops would be there eventually probably looking for me. I went in the woods and stayed in the woods and this person come and picked me up and took me down to an Interstate and then just dropped me off. Then--then I was caught--you know, later on in July, I was caught."

But Roland had left out a few days. His lawyer was offering little guidance through the story. He let his defendant tell it his own way--he might not have had much choice. Roland Stevens was probably not an easily controlled client.

Q. What happened after you got to the Interstate? I mean, where did you go?

A. I went--he dropped me off at a sign saying New Hill on the Interstate on Highway 70. I went down into the--like into the embankment, like trying to figure things out in my head, going over things.... Anyway, I was down there in the embankment, and I figured, "Ain't like no way in the world." Because the guy that dropped me off, he said he's going to go back and see what he could find out...he said he wanted to see if they could find her and talk to her-- talk to Sherry. I couldn't depend on him coming back...he said he'd try to be back at eleven o'clock with some money and figure out what to do. Well, I couldn't sit there and wait. It was about six-thirty. The mosquitoes were eating me up. I couldn't stay down in that damn old gully, so I got up out of the ditch and walked to the sign--right there--at that sign saying New Hill and figured my best thing was just hitch-hiking and hope for the best."

He told the jury that "a person" that he didn't know picked him up. He told "her" he was "on the run," and she asked if he wanted to "hang" with her--she was on her way to New Bern to buy some cocaine. He stayed the night with her at someone else's house in New Hill until five-thirty the next morning, when they left together.

"We went back to Cary, where she lived at. She took me back to her apartment, washed all my clothes--my blue jeans, my red shirt . She said she'd get me a job in Cary working for construction. The guy would pay me out of his pocket. I said, "Okay, that's fine.""

But until something happened, Roland needed a place to hide out during the day, and his new-found friend took him to Jordan Lake, telling him she would pick him up at six o'clock that afternoon. He waited until mid-night, but she didn't return. He decided that either she was high on cocaine or that she had seen his face on the news and "just got plain scared." Starting out at midnight, he hitch-hiked again, this time with a man in a pick-up who took him to a point three miles outside of Cary. He walked into the city, look-ing for the woman who had promised to return, but he couldn't recognize her apartment. Then he walked to the shopping center where she had stopped to buy a pack of cigarettes before taking him to Jordan Lake.

"So this was on a Saturday morning that I got there. I stayed there looking for her, hoping to God she would come up there so I could straighten all this bullshit out. She--she never came."

Roland's next move was to call "the person" that had initially picked him up, and she tried to talk him into going back to the camp.

"I said, 'Please, go try to find the girl and talk to her.' She said she doesn't want to get involved. Something strange about her voice. I said, 'Damn. Something ain't right here. This don't sound like her.' I told her I'd call back later on." He did call her back, but a man answered the phone. "He says, 'Operator, what area code is this?' And the operator says, 'Will you accept a call from Roland?'" The man repeated his request for the area code, and Roland grew suspicious and hung up.

He looked at the jury almost pleadingly.

"I want to turn myself--hey, I want to turn myself in. I had to. I knew that...My twenty-four hours had done gone out, you know. I mean, they had printed this stuff in the paper, and they had done everything they could, and it was too late. The procedure would sort of be that if you were work release and you didn't come back-- you've got twenty-four hours to come back. If nothing would have been said, I could have gotten back to the camp. But since I didn't have the daggone shit, she wanted to get even with me...I can't help why I didn't have it. I told her while I was in the car, 'I can get it. ' But she didn't say nothing. She didn't say nothing. She was mad. She didn't say a damn word."

Most of the jurors looked skeptical now, but a few of the men looked like they were still trying to give him the benefit of the doubt.

His lawyer interrupted.

> Q. Let me direct you back to the time when you were in Cary, after you made the phone call. What did you do next?
>
> A. Want to know everything about it? Everything?
>
> Q. Everything.
>
> A. Okay.

But Judge Thompson decided that "everything" would have to wait. The jurors were due a mid-morning break. He instructed them to return at eleven-thirty.

Margaret informed me that she didn't need to hear any more. She had made up her mind a long time ago.

Although the jury was intrigued with Roland's story, fiction or non-fiction, nothing he had recounted after he had left Sherry had anything to do with proving his innocence to the charge of rape. Perhaps, there was a point to all this--they just had not heard it so far.

When damaging evidence is inevitable, further travesties are better admitted than hidden, seeming worse if revealed on cross- examination. But the pitfalls can be fatal without guidance when you tell "everything."

After the break, however, the defendant was allowed to race on, all valves open, full steam ahead.

"Why don't you just pick up where you were and continue?" defense counsel suggested.

Roland led the jury on a merry chase. Saturday, he had stayed around the shopping center all day, hoping his mysterious good Samaritan would show up.

"I had seven or eight dollars in my pocket. I spent it at the record center. I should have held on to it, but I didn't."

But he had enough to sit at Appleby's and "get drunk, trying to figure out what I'm going to do... Nobody wanted to get involved, so I just walked around. I found a little park over in Cary. I stayed there and slept on the park bench all night Saturday...I woke up the next morning...aching a little bit."

Sunday, he tried the shopping center again, "hoping the person would show up. Never came." He went to Rose's and shoplifted a "pair of trunks and a muscle shirt....You know, it was hot, and I tried to fit in....I was all over TV and everything, so I figured if I looked like a jogger or something, nobody would notice me." He changed clothes in the woods.

"It's late Sunday evening, and I'm walking around hungry and trying to figure out what I'm going to do....I go in the park and go to sleep again. This stuff's starting to get old. [She] never returned. I can't talk to nobody in Durham.... Can't call nobody. I just felt like going off."

He was really laying it on, and some of the jurors looked sympathetic.

Monday was a playback of Sunday, except this time he pilfered orange juice and food.

"By then I'm looking real scraggly."

Again, he spent the night on the park bench.

"Tuesday morning I wake up about seven o'clock...It's cold. You know, the summer nighttime gets a little chilly out there, and all I had was shorts covering me.... I see this car pull off at a school in Cary. I see this old woman get out [of] the car. She walks to the school. I'm sitting in the park about two football lengths from the park bench to the school. I see her walk up in there and I think to myself, 'It's perfect.' Snap my fingers like that [*demonstrates*]. A ride and some money. So I walk over to the school--tripped over to the school. She comes around the corner. I grabbed her by the throat, and I said to her, 'Do you have any money?' She said, 'No. I left my pocketbook at home on the kitchen table with my husband who's waiting for me.' I said, 'Well, give me your car. Give me the keys to your car.' She handed them to me, and I said, 'You got to come with me.' She said, 'Oh, no. Please don't take me with you.' I said, 'Lord, I can't leave you here. You'll call the police.' So she gets in the car."

Margaret and I looked at each other. Neither of us could believe what we were hearing. Any ground that he had gained with the jurors--if he had gained any--was turning into a mud slide. They were wide-eyed. Later they would find out that this victim was the Assistant Principal of the school from which he had abducted her.

But he didn't seem to know the damage he was doing, and he kept going.

"We get in the car. I said, 'I'll drop you off and everything will be fine. I ain't going to hurt you.' We drive a little ways down through Cary or out on the outskirts of Cary, pull up an old dirt path road. There's a house up there. I said, 'Hell, I can't drop you off here.' She bit my finger and jumped on out of the car and went up to the house."

Margaret bowed her head and softly giggled, probably hoping the woman had drawn blood.

"Now I take the car, go back down the same driveway."

Roland rambled on, saying nothing of value, wondering how he's made such a mess of things, and concluding again that it's all Sherry's fault:

"The bitch has ruined my life."

Driving back to Cary, he parked the car just three blocks from "the same park bench."

Q. Why did you go back to the park?

A. I don't know. Beats the hell out of me.

While sitting on the park bench contemplating his dilemma, Roland spotted police cars arriving at the school, and decided he'd better leave.

He's still talking.

"So I walk over to Kentucky Fried Chicken. There's a girl in a Shoney's--I mean, a Kentucky Fried Chicken uniform ....She's got like a little pouch on the side. It's the middle of the afternoon--sun beaming down. She walks around the side of Kentucky Fried Chicken like a fool [to] where I am. People all around. I grab her by her throat and I say, 'Give me your money.' She says, 'I ain't got no money.' I turned and say, Hey, I'm just kidding. I'm just kidding.' She goes one way. I go the other way."

The jury had had enough. The only question in anyone's mind was why he was still talking, tightening the rope around his own neck.

But Roland seemed to be enjoying his big day, somehow perversely expecting sympathy for his plight from this captive audience.

Getting back into the car, he drove to Shelby Lake and spent the rest of day "walking around, playing volleyball, and trying to figure out what to do." That night he slept in the car.

"Next morning, I woke and said, 'Well, what in the world am I going to do?' I'm standing outside of the car. See--I'm standing---facing this way, just looking out and trying to figure out what's going on. A Raleigh police officer pulls up. Didn't even--I didn't hear him. I mean, daggone--surprised me I didn't hear him--he was so quiet, I didn't hear a car."

The police officer asked his name. He gave it.

"Now, aren't you the person that left out of Durham?"

"Yes, sir."

"You've been all over T. V. Didn't you know that?"

"Yeah."

"You didn't hide yourself very well, did you?"

"No."

"Well, somebody called in and said that they had seen you on T. V. and had seen you over here at the lake."

"Yeah."

Roland continued excitedly with this play-by-play narration of his arrest.

"All of a sudden there's some daggone cameras and reporters and everything. Damn. There's reporters and everything all around every- where. I said, 'Daggone, how did this all happen?' Anyway, I'm in the car. The police officer tells me, 'You're my biggest catch in a year and a half.'"

Margaret was only half successful when she tried not to laugh out loud.

The witness now read the statement he gave to police, which was basically the same story he had told the jury without the extraneous lengthy details: that he had agreed to buy drugs for Sherry; he had rented a room with money she had provided; she had agreed to exchange sex for the drugs; when he told her he didn't have the drugs, she became mad and threatened to go to the police; and he had threatened to kill her, had choked her, and had torn the sheets to frighten her because he was afraid she would go to the police.

Q. Were you telling the truth to Detective Franklin?

A. Yes, sir.

Q. Are you telling the truth today?

A. Yes, sir.

Roland stated that he had already pled guilty to two counts of second degree kidnapping, theft of a motor vehicle, and attempted common law robbery, the offenses committed during his flight period. He added, erroneously, that he had also pled guilty to Habitual Felon (that would be decided by the jury after this trial if he was convicted). In return for his pleas, the State had dismissed one count of second degree kidnapping and assault on a female, and he had received a forty-year consolidated sentence.

Q. Did you rape Sherry Wells?

A. No. I did not.

Q. Did you kidnap Sherry Wells?

A. No. I did not kidnap Sherry Wells.

Q. No further questions.

Mary Winstead had probably filled more than one legal pad with notes from the defendant's testimony that she could attack with and had gathered a stockpile of ammunition. She began calmly, asking him about the employment checks he had earned. He admitted that he had not turned the money into the prison as he was supposed to, but he had given it to a "certain person" for drugs. She led him through his activities for the day of July eighteenth a year ago.

Q. Now, you told Larry Smith that Keith Edwards asked you to work late?

A. I certainly did.

Q. But that he had forgotten to call the prison unit and--

A. Oh, he called.

Q. You didn't tell Larry Smith that Keith didn't call?

A. Oh. No. No. No. No. I--I--to tell you--to be perfectly honest with you, I lied--I lied to Larry Smith. I lied to him.

Q. What did you lie to him about?

A. About saying that Keith said I could stay over.

Q. Keith didn't say that?

A. Oh. No. No. He did not say that at all.

Q. That was just part of your little plan?

A. That was part of me and Sherry Well's plan.

He had told Peggy, the desk clerk at the motel, that he had to drive to Hillsborough later that night.

Q. So you lied to her too?

A. Yes, ma'am.

Q. Now, you say that you did not ejaculate in Sherry because--

A. No. No. I did not, because she said, "No." She didn't want me to.

Q. Have you talked with anyone in the Department of Corrections about these charges against you, Mr. Stevens?

A. Everybody knows about the daggone charges. [It' s] been all over TV. That's why they're dragging me down over there--because of all this bullshit.

Q. Well, my question to you, sir, was have you talked to any- one in the Department of Corrections?

A. More than likely, I probably have--probably talked to them. Yeah.

Q. And about the facts of the case?

A. It's a good possibility, probably.

Q. Have you told anyone in the Department of Corrections, sir, that you didn't shoot off in her because they could take sperm from her and it would match up to you?

A. No. I sure did not.

He admitted that the anal intercourse was not part of their agree- ment, but when he told Sherry that she was "getting her money's worth," she had said, "All right." He insisted that he did not use a condom, only Vaseline from his "preamer" pack. Mrs. Winstead asked him what type of pack he was referring to, and he told her it was a pack containing Vaseline that he had brought with him to treat an injured finger.

Q. Didn't you call it a primer pack earlier?

A. No. It's a creamer pack--like, you know--a creamer pack where you can tear it and put a creamer in the coffee.

Roland denied again having a knife or throwing a knife out of the car.

Q. Well, have you ever carried a steak knife on your person?

A. Have I ever?

Q. Yes, sir.

A. Yes, ma'am.

Q. And specifically in 1987, the offense that you're serving time for--

A. Second degree kidnapping. I went into the store ... I was drunk on cocaine...that can be verified...went into the store, asked for a carton of cigarettes, put my wallet on the table--on the counter—asked for a carton of cigarettes. Now, I first went in there, asked for a pack of cigarettes, went back out to the car, got my wallet and got the knife off the dashboard, came back into the place, asked for a carton of cigarettes, and then--I don't know--I just--I don't know. I guess, I just blanked, took the woman out to--put her in the pickup truck. Then I said, "What in the hell am I doing?" I told her to get out of the truck, and then that was it.

Q. And you took her out into the woods too, didn't you, Mr. Stevens?

A. Oh, no.

Q. You dragged her to the truck and you didn't take her into any wooded area?

A. I did not take her to no wooded area.

Q. And then you fled, did you not, in your truck?

A. Yeah. I fled and had a wreck.

Q. And a Raleigh police officer came up to you, searched you and found--

A. I don't know. I was knocked out. I don't know.

Q. --in your back pocket, a steak knife, didn't he sir?

A. Oh, yeah. There was one there. Yeah. Yeah.

Q. What were you going to do with that woman?

A. I wasn't going to do nothing .... Why do you think I let her go? I told you I was drunk and everything else.

Q. None of these offenses that you've told the jury all about--none of those involve men, do they?

A. No. No.

Q. You always kidnap women?

A. That's what the record shows.

Q. That's the truth, isn't it, sir?

A. That's what happened ... that's why I'm guilty-- I mean, I am guilty.

Q. Now, when you went to Cary and you kidnapped the Assistant Principal there, do you remember what you said to her?

A. Yes, ma'am. I do.

Q. You said, "Shut up."

A. I might have. I probably did.

Q. Did you say "Shut up" a few times maybe when you were in the motel room with Sherry?

A. Oh, no. Oh, no. Oh, no.

Q. You never said "Shut up" to her?

A. No. No. I did not say "Shut up" to her.

Q. But you did threaten to kill her?

A. Oh, yes. I did. yeah.

Q. How many times?

A. Just that one time.

Q. Now, Mr. Stevens, you were also convicted of rape in--

Mr. Lauffer objected and asked to be heard. The jury was sent out.

The attorneys argued back and forth as to whether a conviction for rape in Pennsylvania in 1975 was admissible. The defendant had served ten years in prison for that charge. The defense contended that it was over ten years ago and should not be admissible. Although his release date was not more than ten years ago, the only documentation Mrs. Winstead could provide to the court showed a parole date but did not mention the offense he was paroled for.

The judge told her she could question the defendant, still sitting on the stand, about when he had been released. Roland "couldn't remember."

The prosecutor also wished to show a conviction for attempted rape in Richmond, Virginia, in 1971. She contended that the defendant himself had opened the door on convictions more than ten years ago when he had testified that he had pled guilty to "habitual felon." (*In fact, Roland had not pled guilty to this charge, but he thought he had. If convicted in this rape case, the jury would consider whether or not to label him such, but he had apparently misunderstood and thought this charge was part of the plea bargain for the other charges related to the rape.*)

The defense, of course, objected.

After much discussion, the court allowed the Pennsylvania conviction, but ruled that the Virginia conviction was not admissible. The jury returned, and the prosecutor resumed her cross-examination.

Q. Mr. Stevens, were you convicted, sir, in 1975 in Crawford County, Pennsylvania of the offense of rape?

A. Yes, ma'am.

Q. And you alleged that that was consensual also, did you not?

A. No. I pled guilty.

Q. Didn't you claim that it was consensual?

A. At first. Then I changed my mind.

The prosecutor asked him about the alleged marijuana that he was supposed to get for Sherry. He contended that she had asked about it upon entering the room but had not asked to see it.

Q. And she didn't want to smoke it either, did she?

A. No. We were on borrowed time, anyway--only had forty-five minutes.

Q. All right. Even though you had smoked marijuana with her on other occasions and she was obviously very anxious to get some marijuana from you on this occasion--since she changed her mind about the sex from the time you originally talked with her and approached you about it--she didn't want to smoke any marijuana when you got to the motel room?

A. No. Like I said, we was on limited time.

In response to Mrs. Winstead's questions about who else had taken him back to camp and the number of times for each person, Roland named Barbara (three times), Eddie (three--no, maybe four times), and Sherry (three times). He wasn't positive about the number of times for Barbara or Eddie.

> Q. But you're positive Sherry took you back exactly three times, is that right?
>
> A. Yep. Sure am.
>
> Q. Now--

That's as far as the prosecutor got with her question because Roland was talking again, but not to the prosecutor. He was looking at Sherry.

"Why are you shaking your head for? You know daggone well you did."

Sherry spoke up from the audience:

"Don't start---"

"Don't start? What the hell is she bugging--"

Judge Thompson interrupted and told the jury to go to their room.

"Mr. Stevens, I don't want you to make--"

"I'm sorry, your Honor, but they're back there shaking their heads, smiling and everything--"

"Just listen to me, Mr. Stevens. I will not have any comment from you to anyone else in this courtroom other than to answer the questions that you are asked. Do we understand each other?"

"Yes, sir. Yes, sir. Yes, sir."

"Do you think you can do that?"

"I can do that."

"Bring the jury in."

Mrs. Winstead reviewed the prison camp procedure for work release inmates and asked how many times he had requested to stay late at work and not return to the prison camp until nine-thirty.

"I don't know. I'd say three."

"Three times for that also?"

"Um-hum."

"Three" seemed to be the magic number. He had just testified that people had driven him back nine to ten times. Mathematics was not his forte`.

Roland insisted, even though the information was not in his statement, that he had told Detective Franklin about Sherry taking him back to the camp on three occasions, that he had ridden around Durham with her "getting high" on marijuana, but he had not told the detective that Sherry wanted cocaine from him.

> Q. And how much was it that you were originally going to charge her?
>
> A. Four hundred and fifty dollars.
>
> Q. But she came to you with the idea that she would give you Forty-five dollars?
>
> A. For a hotel room. Yeah. But I don't have no money.
>
> Q. She had the idea about the motel room too, is that right?
>
> A. Yeah.
>
> Q. She would give you Forty-five dollars?
>
> A. Yes, ma'am.
>
> Q. And you agreed that you would then get her an eight ball of cocaine and an ounce of marijuana and have sex?
>
> A. Yeah.

The prosecutor led him through his testimony about his confused flight from captivity, and Roland tangled and tripped over his own feet more than once. He could not keep names, times, places, or sequences straight. Any sense of chronology was out of the question, but he didn't seem to notice.

In response to questions about the events of that night, he reacted heatedly twice: once about the steering wheel and once about the knife.

Although the word "grabbed" was used in his written statement, he insisted, almost yelling at the Assistant District Attorney, that he had only "hit" the steering wheel to deflect Sherry from the prison camp. He picked up the Bible and used it as a pretend steering wheel, demonstrating the difference between "hit" and "grab" for the jury. Irately, he accused Mary Winstead of "trying to make me a little mixed up."

When asked about the torn sheets, he said Sherry must have taken the strips as part of her plan to go to the police and accuse him of rape. He backed up this assertion by bringing up the knife himself as a parallel effort to defame him--after all, she must have been out to get him if she claimed he had a knife.

To "prove" his point, he related a conversation that had taken place after his arrest and during Detective Franklin's questioning. He had denied having a knife. Fibbing, Detective Franklin told him that they had found the knife the next day by the mailboxes that Sherry had described. But he stuck to his story--he didn't have a knife. Playing devil's advocate, the detective asked him if he thought Sherry was mad enough at him to have put the knife there herself. He had agreed, latching on to this idea and accepting it as a perfectly logical explanation:

"That's exactly what happened--me and him said--we was talking about it," he angrily told Mary Winstead.

> Q. But at any rate, you didn't tell her to take the strips of sheet with her?
>
> A. No. I did not tell her to take no strips of nothing with her.
>
> Q. But you did tear the bed sheet?
>
> A. I tore the strips myself to scare her.

Q. Why were you trying to scare her?

A. From saying the daggone thing that I raped her.

Q. How were you going to scare her with those?

A. I don't know. I just tore the daggone things. I never told her I'd tie her up. I never done nothing. All I did was tear the daggone things. That was it.

These small torn strips of cloth from an ordinary sheet had become extremely important. Even Roland couldn't attempt to explain them. Although there was ample evidence without them, the strips were a bonus-- the cherry on top, the cream on the coffee, the proverbial icing on the cake--no way around them. The prosecutor knew there was no point in letting him go on with his self-destruction. She had taken the mild approach, giving him room, allowing him to talk, and he had done an admirable job of convicting himself--the game was over.

Mr. Lauffer did not ask any more questions.

The defense rested.

The jury was excused early for lunch and told to return at two-thirty, but the lawyers remained where they were for the charge conference.

The issues were fairly clear-cut, however, and decisions were made quickly, so we were pleasantly surprised to find that we still had time for a leisurely lunch before the jury returned.

We decided to go to the hotel restaurant which overlooked the lake that we had had so little time to enjoy. The heat wave had continued, but the wall of glass gave us the illusion of being outside. After listening to Roland all morning, I felt as if I had fallen down Alice's rabbit hole and the Queen of Hearts was gaining on me. The change of scenery--that and the rational conversation--reassured me, and I chose to believe that, like Alice, I had awakened from an impossible dream.

But my delusion had not long to live. After lunch, the Mad Hatter was still there--not a figment of my imagination.

The judge charged the jury, giving them the following choices and explanations of each:

> First Degree Rape or
> Second Degree Rape or
> Not Guilty;
> First Degree Sexual Offense (anal rape) or
> Second Degree Sexual Offense or
> Not Guilty.

The difference between First and Second Degree hinged on the alleged knife--whether or not the jury believed that the defendant had a knife which the victim saw and believed to be a dangerous and deadly weapon.

The jury would also decide:

> Second Degree Kidnapping and
> Felonious Escape or
> Not Guilty of either.

As soon as the jury was isolated in that special room where monumental decisions are made, court continued, a new charge conference was underway, in anticipation of a possible guilty verdict. If the defendant were convicted, the jury would be asked to continue their service. They would consider Roland Stevens's past record and decide whether or not he should be labeled an *Habitual Felon,* a title that could make a substantial difference in his possible sentences.

After the proper charges were agreed upon, the court stood "at ease," no formal recess being declared. The judge requested that counsel remain close by in case the jury had any questions.

An hour later, the jury passed a note to the bailiff who passed the note to the judge.

The clerk asked Margaret if she would round up the missing lawyers, and she bounded from her seat on the second row to accomplish her mission like a bench warmer in the ninth inning.

Five minutes later, all parties assembled, the judge addressed the attorneys:

"I have received two questions from the jury that read:

'Do we stay in here until we reach a decision?' and
'We need clarification on first and second degree rape.'

Because of the late hour--ten minutes to five--Judge Thompson suggested that he recharge on the elements for these two offenses and dismiss them for the evening. Both attorneys agreed.

Everyone seemed grateful to leave the courtroom after a tedious and emotional day. Especially Sherry, who looked exhausted.

Jack and I had no previously conceived ideas on how to spend the evening. We were tired as well, but felt that we needed to salvage some undefined loss. We had heard of a restaurant called Marco Polo, and we confirmed its existence by that hierarchy of reference material all obedient Americans turn to for ideas, the Yellow Pages. The promised cuisine was intriguing: Chinese/Italian. Under the same roof. And authentic: The Italian chef was Caligahir from Venice, and the Chinese chef was Chan from Hong Kong. My whole day had been spent somewhere in <u>Wonderland</u>, and it somehow seemed appropriate to give an Italian waiter my order for wonton soup, ivory shrimp and scallops, and hot tea.

Thursday morning the jury met once again at nine-thirty.

At ten-fifteen they had a verdict:
Guilty of Felonious Escape.

Guilty of Second Degree Rape.

Guilty of Second Degree Sexual Offense.

Not guilty of Kidnapping.

The judge now informed the jury that they would have to make an additional decision: whether or not the defendant was a *Habitual Felon*.

The State submitted records of his three prior convictions of attempted rape, rape, and kidnapping as evidence. The defense stipulated to those documents.

The jury returned to their room. Five to ten minutes later, the verdict was guilty, and the jurors were thanked for their service and excused.

The Habitual Felon conviction elevated the possible sentences the defendant could receive for the convictions from this trial. For example, felonious escape, usually three years, could now be extended to life. It was up to the judge.

Mary Winstead asked the court for consecutive life sentences "to protect the public by restraining the defendant....He has absolutely no regard for the law and no regard for other human beings....He has been convicted of three other violent crimes against persons, all against women....And I think this Court can be absolutely assured that if Roland Stevens ever walks out on the streets of any State in the United States again, that he is going to commit more violent crimes. I would ask your Honor to treat each of the offenses separately because they are separate distinct offenses."

The defense had nothing to say.

The judge addressed the defendant:

"Mr. Stevens, prior to my entering the sentence in this case, do you wish to say anything to the Court? You have that privilege."

His lawyer answered.

"No, sir."

The judge asked the Clerk to record the following sentences:

Second Degree Rape--Life to run at the expiration of the forty
years previously sentenced as a result of his guilty pleas.

Second Degree Sexual Offense--Life to run at the expiration of
the rape sentence.

Felony Escape--Life to run at the expiration of the sexual
offense sentence.

"Any further matters?"

The defense gave notice of appeal.

"The defendant is in custody."

*After the defendant had been led from the courtroom, Sherry stood
from her seat behind the rail that separated her from the prosecutor's table,
her eyes on Judge Thompson. Relief was visible on her tear-streaked face. She
smiled tentatively.*

"Thank you," she said softly.

*With three life sentences on top of forty years, Roland Stevens would
not bother her again--or anyone else.*

*Mary Winstead had brought her case to a successful conclusion.
Dropping into the Judge's office to bring Ann some paperwork, she looked
considerably more relaxed. She lingered to talk with Ann. Mary was happy
and relieved that Roland Stevens had been convicted. She had worked with
Sherry for a year, not knowing if she would ever be emotionally capable of
taking the stand and facing her attacker. Roland Stevens had a long criminal
history and needed to be stopped.*

*Presuming that Mary did not believe Sherry had arranged to meet
Roland as he had claimed, Ann asked if she knew or had an opinion as to
why the defendant had rented a room that night at the Cricket Inn. This
loose end was still raveled, and maybe she could neatly cauterize the frayed
strands. She replied that she did not know that answer, but wished she did.
The only clues she had lay in his previous charges. Two of his victims had been
gas station attendants, which implied that they were random-- vulnerable*

accessibility playing a key factor in his choice. And he had procured a third victim by hanging around in a parking lot waiting for a female--any female--to appear.

Bingo.

What had seemed like an implausible explanation was distinctly parallel. From the list of multiple choices, this choice had seemed the least plausible. Now elevated to a precedented probability, this scenario was the most terrifying: Roland Stevens was a professional rapist. That's what he did.

Mary also told us that Sherry was considering bringing a lawsuit against the State of North Carolina because this defendant had been granted work release despite his record of violence. In addition, Shoney's may find themselves in court for hiring him and subjecting her to what should have been seen as a calculable risk. Although North Carolina State law is clear on when the State can and cannot be sued, a try wouldn't hurt. If the State was held accountable for a prison system policy that endangered their citizens, maybe they would tighten the leash and someone else would not have to suffer the way Sherry had.

No amount of money could compensate this young woman who would have to deal with the devastating side-effects that had altered her personality forever and would torture her if she lived to be a hundred.

Society would also punish her. A male reporter for the New York Post has labeled this effect "the Bloomingdale scenario: five years from now she would hand a credit card to a clerk who would say, "Oh, you're the one who was raped."

Another judge had entered the office and stood listening to this conversation. He waited until there was silence and then offered his appraisal:

"This case is a clear indictment of the prison system in general and the work release program in particular. What employers don't realize is that, given the short amount of time prisoners have to actually serve on their sentences because of overcrowded conditions, most inmates are paroled before they are even eligible for work release. So those who are hired have committed

enough offenses or at least one of the more serious offenses to have been in prison long enough to obtain work release status."

He had a point, an obvious point, if people were aware of the current parole practices. Clearly disgruntled with the realities he dealt with every day, he added, "The only good thing right now about the court system is that my pay check comes regularly the first of each month--and this year the Legislature tried to mess that up."

Somehow, even though Roland Stevens would not be able to prey upon the general female populace until he was old and out of practice, any woman listening to this case would not feel that much safer the next time she found herself alone at eight o'clock at night in a parking lot.

There were other professional rapists out there waiting; if this case was in any way typical, one or two convictions wouldn't stop them.

How many women would be violated before the accrued magic number of ruined lives earned their attacker a sentence long enough to mean anything?

And this case was not necessarily "typical."

Many rapists are more cunning, able to avoid capture for many years, raping again and again and again.

Many victims of rape do not report it.

All rapists are brutal.

Some are also killers.

Their victims don't live to testify.

CHAPTER FIVE

August–October: State v. Bonnie Lou Locklear

The Stevens case behind us, we made our annual trip to Charleston under the auspices of attending a weekend-long party on Sullivan's Island. "Beach music" enthusiasts gather from several States to listen, mingle, and dance. The party starts on Friday night and continues on Saturday from noon until midnight, the hardiest souls returning for more on Sunday afternoon. The revelry takes place in a large, World War II-era rectangular, white, wooden building with wide porches fronting on the ocean, at once reminiscent of what we think of as a simpler time when "God and country, mother, baseball, and apple pie" were at the center of existence. I can easily visualize the handsome young officers in their starched uniforms taking their sweethearts for a good-bye stroll on the sand, their privacy guarded by the tall, sea-oated dunes blocking the view from the picture windows and the rocking chairs on the clubhouse porch.

We were enamored with Charleston on our first trip, even though Hurricane Diane (1984) made a pass and tried to chase us away; we would return each year even if there were no party.

Charleston was devastated by a direct hit from Hurricane Hugo in 1989, and this year, reconstruction was almost complete. The brave, never-say-die residents have survived hurricanes, earthquakes, and the Civil War, and their gracious city continues to thrive even more splendidly after each disaster. Many visitors bestow upon this beautiful Southern-to-the-core and historical city the ultimate compliment: "I wish I were from here."

This year we arrived a few days earlier than the two couples that would join us on Friday. Regardless of how many times we came, there was never enough time to explore. I had just read a mystery novel about a couple making the transition from the concrete of Washington D. C. to a tiny community just outside of Charleston where the husband had spent his childhood summers. The author had described the fictional town in such detail that I felt sure it had existed under another name. After studying the map, however, I was unable to determine which town she may have used for a model, and I chose the "next best adventure" on my list. Much of the book centered around a swamp. So it seemed a perfectly natural thing for me to say, "Walk through a swamp," when Jack asked me what I wanted to do. After he recovered, he smiled in resignation. "You're on," he said, "Let's find one."

As it turned out, one of the plantations open to the public has a wooden-slat walkway through an adjoining swamp. We were the only ones there except the full-time residents: alligators, snakes, herons, other exotic birds, and a myriad of "things" we didn't want to know about. Unseen insects filled the sun-filtered air with their singing, while others darted around the brightly colored lilies and wild flowers. The planked walk sat only inches above the slick, green fungi-covered water, and a long black snake directly in our path reared its head in imitation of a cobra to protest our interruption of his afternoon nap. We left more quickly than we came. Not one of my better ideas.

The food in Charleston is considered an art, especially anything from the sea. Shrimp is almost always served with sausage, and those who love "hot and spicy" have multiple choices. Culinary creativity abounds--where else can you order quail stuffed with collards or creamed grits (that taste like anything but) for an appetizer? I can't speak for the crawfish-- this delicacy is plentiful, but it is served to someone else.

Undeniably, we consumed our share of rich food, enjoyed the party and our friends and departed too soon--always too soon--on Sunday. "Next year" was already creeping into our conversations.

Jack's current assignment to Robeson County was postponed for another week when he was commissioned instead to the small town of Albemarle in a rural county that holds Superior Court only one week a month. His mother had grown up in Stanly County, and many of her relatives still lived there. I elected to stay home this week and catch up on commitments put off far too long.

Jack's Monday was spent with routine administrative duties and picking a jury for the first case. Tuesday was different.

"How was your day?" I asked when he called.

"Strange," he said.

"Strange how?"

"Well, as I told you last night, we picked a jury yesterday for an indecent liberties case. Today I had to question the little four-year-old boy to make sure he was qualified to testify, and I decided he was. When I finished, the defense attorney asked him some questions, and he got real upset. We took a fifteen minute recess, and the District Attorney said we'd try again, but he wasn't sure how it would go. So I came down from the bench to talk to this little fellow--we had put a chair in front of the witness box to make it easier for him--and the minute I got to him, he broke down again."

"Do you think it was the black robe?" I asked.

"That may have had something to do with it. The District Attorney had to dismiss the case."

"I'm sorry." I could tell he felt partly responsible.

"Well, I doubt if he would ever have been able to go through with it. Anyway, that was just the first thing. We started picking a jury for another case, and when someone asked if any of them knew any of the parties in the

case, one man said, 'Yeah. I know the defendant. I think I took out a warrant on him for a worthless check.'"

"Oh, no," I sympathized. "There went the whole jury."

"Oh, not just the twelve. They don't have a jury pool room, so he contaminated the entire panel of forty people. He didn't mean to do anything wrong, but I still had to declare a mistrial. So we spent what was left of the day doing pleas. To top it off, the third thing was that I found out this was a dry county."

Sounded like he was in for a long week.

Wednesday was better.

"I had a great time today," he started, "I had lunch with a bunch of women."

"Sounds like I needed to go with you after all," I laughed.

"My clerk invited me to lunch along with several other of the courthouse personnel. On the way to the restaurant, I mentioned that my mother's maiden name was Burleson. Would you believe my clerk is related to me? I haven't been able to contact my mother's brother, though. I've decided that he must be out of town. So I called Aunt Lena on a morning break. I knew she would have my hide if she found out I was here and didn't call. It's been years, but she remembered me immediately and seemed happy to hear from me."

"Good. I'm glad you got in touch."

"Oh, that's not all. This afternoon, we were in the middle of a plea, and in walked Aunt Lena through the courtroom doors, walking-stick and all. She's over eighty years old, still drives herself, and felt that she had to see me in person. She's arranged lunch with all the aunts, uncles, and cousins she can round up for tomorrow."

Having a strong sense of history, tradition, and family, Jack loves small towns, where he can sit around talking about old times and listening to colorful relatives recount their lives. His stay was refreshing, but the memories of his week in Albemarle would soon contrast sharply with those of another small town of an entirely different nature.

He would spend the remainder of these six months in Lumberton, the Robeson County seat.

It's difficult to describe Robeson County, just forty miles to the south of us, fairly. Some have even referred to this portion of our State as "a third world country surrounded by the rest of North Carolina." Some exceptional people do live and work there with no ill will toward anyone, but they live among others who exhibit little regard for human life and mold the prevailing environment.

Regrettably, the dark side is the only side you see in a courtroom.

The mix of population per se should not cause the problem: one-third black, one-third white, and one-third Indian. After all these years, you'd think the three races have had ample opportunity to learn to understand each other and live peacefully. Unfortunately, resentment festers like an open wound.

These three distinct groups have chosen to remain detached for the most part--a mix of unyielding cultures with different values--and old habits are tenaciously preserved as "rights." The most visible results are an extremely high illiteracy rate, and a propensity for weapons--knives, the most popular choice; guns, a close second. Among some residents, violence is an "accepted" way of life, the traditional means of settling arguments or "saving face," especially with family members or "loved ones."

The Indians call themselves Lumbees, but their tribal heritage remains a matter of dispute, both locally and on the Federal level. At this writing, the Federal government has recently once again refused to recognize them as a tribe, thereby continuing to classify them ineligible for the Federally-funded programs granted to "official" tribes. Some historians believe they are Croatans, descendants of Roanoke Island, from where Virginia Dare, the first English child born in America, vanished along with the rest of the first English settlement. The colonists' fate remains a mystery to this day, and their story is told in a symphonic drama by Paul Green, <u>The Lost Colony</u>, staged outdoors each summer in Manteo on the site of their settlement and disappearance. Around 1950, however, our State legislature declared the Robeson County Indians to be a branch of the Cherokee tribe. Still others suggest they are related to the Tuscarora.

What is known for certain is that they were here first.

John Oates, a local historian, wrote:

"These Indians were found in this same section when the Scotch first came up the Cape Fear [River] and settled in Bladen and Cumberland counties. They have been loyal to this Country and all of its wars and have furnished many fine soldiers in the armies of America" (327).

And we also know that "out west" was not the only place the Indians retaliated against "the white invaders."

Lew Barton, a Lumbee historian, wrote about their local hero, whom he called the "Robin Hood" of this region, the leader of "a bloody Indian 'uprising'" during the Civil War and the following reconstruction years:

"For ten years Henry Berry Lowry and his 'outlaw' gang ran free in Robeson and surrounding counties, living, as Chairman Mao put it later, 'like a fish among the people.' Before his 'reign of terror,' as the white historians called it, was over, he and his band of sixteen men--poor white, Black, and Indian-had taken the lives of twenty-nine of the rich whites in the county. Shortly after Lowry disappeared, never to be seen again, the state legislature restored the right to vote, to bear arms, and to own property to the Lumbee Indians, rights which had been taken away in 1835. As a result of his battles, the first school for Lumbee Indians was founded in 1886, and it later became the first Indian college in the nation."

But for many generations to come, the one-third white population ruled, and the Indians and Blacks in this county were suppressed. Although they work together, the three cultures remain separate in their churches, social activities, and neighborhoods.

Even our Legislature took particular note of the situation and attempted to even the score by creating a "special minority district." This brought about an Indian lawyer filing to run for Superior Court Judge. The District Attorney, who was white, however, also lived in this district and filed to run against the minority candidate. But the chance for an Indian to attain this office became moot--he was fatally shot at the door to his home before the votes could be cast. The immediate feared assumption was that his death was political, but the killing, like so many in this region, was the final settlement of a "domestic dispute" of sorts. The victim had attempted to help his girlfriend keep her daughter from the clutches of a young Lumbee man they disapproved of. The young man "took care of it."

Undaunted, the legislature created a second minority slot and carried it two steps further. They provided the means to appoint a judge of Indian heritage, and they amended a statute, adding a special provision (for Robeson County alone) to allow this newly appointed judge to appoint the Public Defender, an appointment usually made by the Senior Resident Superior Court Judge who was now the white former District Attorney.

But even with these unusual and extreme measures, coupled with larger numbers of "minorities" who have achieved higher educations and returned to their community, the violence goes relatively unchecked.

On February 1, 1988, Indian activists Eddie Hatcher and Timothy Jacobs protested the treatment of their people by taking over the local newspaper office and holding the employees hostage to draw attention to what they claimed were corrupt county officials. Their siege captured international news attention, and they were tried and convicted a year later, their cause unheeded and forgotten.

Only people not familiar with the area were shocked at their behavior. Lumberton had been a powder keg for a long time.

As a court reporter, often traveling the forty miles with local lawyers to take depositions, I had grown familiar with the disquiet in this quaint, innocent-looking town where most of the downtown streets were named for hardwood trees.

I had also taken court proceedings on several occasions, and tension virtually saturated the air of the courthouse corridors. One could feel the animosity radiating from the surrounding faces. Even many of the courthouse personnel acted cold, angry, or distrustful to people they did not know.

And the courthouse is where it all comes together--the blasting cap to an eternally lit fuse.

I warned Jack.

"You don't understand. You will think you've been transported to a walled city out of the past where people cut each other to leave their 'mark' like a boy scout earning a badge."

He had heard all the bad press, but I could tell that he didn't really understand. It did not take him long, however, to learn. The first week's court calendar consisted of three typed pages of ADWITKs (Assault with a Deadly Weapon with Intent to Kill).

His first trial that week was a cutting case, which amounted to a free-for-all fight between Rabbit, Bear, and Wahoo. The victim had over five-hundred stitches on his face and back.

Three different versions--the victim's and those of the two defendants--left the evidence so confused that Jack had no idea how the jury could sort out the facts--he couldn't. But the jury quickly found the victim's girlfriend's brother guilty of Assault With a Deadly weapon Inflicting Serious Injury, a lesser charge, but still a ten year felony. The co-defendant was found guilty of simple assault, a misdemeanor. The jurors' deliberations had taken twenty minutes.

The jurors had no trouble understanding what happened. They lived with it. In fact, they understood the law "as to intent" better than did the District Attorney who applied the charges. They knew the defendant had no "Intent to Kill." If he had, he would have, and the charge would have been murder.

Also in his first week there, Judge Thompson accidentally learned that he was to preside over a capital case the following week. That he wasn't notified, he assumed, was just an oversight. But it soon became apparent that the District Attorney's office didn't know from one day to the next what they were going to try. The Assistants were fortunate to get the file for their next case two days before trial, so notice to anyone else was not an option.

The District Attorney had won election on a "no plea bargaining" campaign platform in a county whose middle name was criminal violence. With no pleas, no cases were closed, and the court docket was hopelessly backlogged.

The Thursday before the capital case was to begin on Monday, two assistant public defenders from Fayetteville drove over to Lumberton and requested a meeting with Judge Thompson in chambers during a break in the "cutting case." They were accompanied by the public defender in Lumberton. They were concerned about the appointed defense lawyers in the upcoming case, charging that they had fallen short of what was expected from them. The two public defenders from Fayetteville had represented this same defendant, Gardener, in Cumberland County, where he had been convicted of murder, and they had subsequently written the Lumberton defense team offering their help in the Robeson case by sending copies of their motions. They had never received an acknowledgement of their offer from the two attorneys. Then the defendant's family in Michigan had notified them that something was amiss and wanted to know what kind of justice we were meting out in North Carolina. Gardener's family told his former lawyers that when they had contacted their son's new lawyers (for the new case) after receiving a subpoena to appear, they were told that their travel expenses would not be paid. The reason for this, they were told by one of the new lawyers, was that he had not bothered to apply for expenses because their son "was going to be executed at some point" anyway. Their attitude amounted to "Why bother with properly defending him?"

So this "Thursday emissary" had come to warn the judge that, at the request of the defendant, they would file a motion the next day to have the two Lumberton defense attorneys removed from the case. The motion would come before his court on Monday morning, and the two public defenders from Fayetteville would be called as witnesses. The Public Defender from Lumberton agreed to represent the defendant temporarily at the hearing.

This was an explosive situation. For lawyers to stand up in court and ask that other lawyers be removed for reasons of incompetence is not an ordinary occurrence. It is unheard of. Somehow the press had learned of the motion even before it was filed, and the newspapers had a field day with what was supposedly known only to the parties involved.

Monday morning, when time came for the hearing, the two Lumberton defense lawyers whose talents had been questioned had had the weekend to think about it. They "quit" before they were "fired," asking to withdraw from the case. They cited their reason: interference from other attorneys had caused a rift in their relationship with their client. When the Lumberton Public Defender, now representing Mr. Gardener, joined in their motion to withdraw, the hearing was no longer needed, and the judge had little choice. The "new lawyers" were excused from the case and the case was continued.

The defense attorneys may have thought they saved some face in their home town papers, but the legal community wasn't as gullible.

The only light moment during this first week was a telling one. Judge Wiley Bowen was also in Lumberton this week, and he told Jack what had happened in his courtroom. Evidence and charge concluded, he had sent the jury to their jury room even though it was well after five o'clock. He told them to stay just long enough to pick a foreperson, and then they would be excused for the day, to start their deliberations the next morning. After ten minutes, the jurors returned. Judge Bowen inquired if they had been successful in electing a foreperson. No one stood to say, "Yes." Instead, they collectively nodded. Puzzled, the judge requested, "Would the foreperson please stand, so I'll know who you are?" There was a moment's hesitation, as the jurors looked back and forth to each other. Four persons stood.

After a month of listening to one "cutting" story after another, Jack came to the same conclusion as the jury had in the "Rabbit, Bear, and Wahoo" case.

"They have no 'intent to kill.' Obviously, they want to leave their victim alive, but scarred and/or maimed," he expounded one night, shaking his head. "A scar or mark serves as an everyday reminder of who put it there and why."

Now he understood why other judges and lawyers across the state, upon learning that his next assignment was Robeson cynically quipped, "Oh, the heart of 'misdemeanor murder" or "shooting into occupied clothing territory." Boyfriend-shoots- girlfriend and Saturday-night-brawl murders were so commonplace that macabre humor was one way of dealing with the madness of a violent climate.

The illiteracy rate became apparent, as each new case brought fresh surprises. One witness after another would take the stand to say he had completed the eighth grade but could neither read nor write.

On October first, when Jack had a murder trial scheduled, I decided to go along. We pulled into the courthouse parking lot at the same time the jail bus arrived, so we hurried into the back elevator before the prisoners had time to unload.

I recognized some people from my working days, including the court reporter who lived in Fayetteville and commuted to Lumberton each day.

For the first ten minutes, Judge Thompson "called" the calendar. The names were Martin, Blackhorse, Oxendine, Locklear, Locklear and Chavis. Still another Locklear was the defendant in the trial that was to begin today: Bonnie Lou.

But court would now be recessed for at least twenty minutes before jury selection. Someone had erred, and prospective jurors had been told to report at ten o'clock instead of nine-thirty.

The bailiff, Jimmy, had a ready smile amidst the confusion.

"How do they have enough first names to go with all the Locklears?" I asked during the break. How do people keep them apart?"

"No idea. Maybe that's why so many have nicknames."

At ten o'clock, the judge spoke to the jury pool, filling up the side of the courtroom wooden benches.

"Jury duty is one of the highest responsibilities of a citizen. This is your courthouse. Jury duty is democracy in action, democracy in its purest form... The fact that the defendant has been accused is no evidence whatsoever of guilt... As a juror it is your duty to render a verdict that speaks the truth."

After running through the requirements that made them eligible for service, Judge Thompson asked:

"Is there anyone who is not qualified?"

One man stood. "I'm hard of hearing."

That was not on the list of requirements, but probably should have been.

"We'll get to that in a moment, sir. But I must tell all of you that only in a case of extreme hardship will I excuse you."

As a general rule, most people shy away from openly asking to be excused, even if they want to be. But two more men immediately stood, and their boldness encouraged another man and a woman to join them and approach the middle aisle. They lined up in front of the judge's bench to be heard individually.

The man with the hearing problem was first. He said he could hear the judge fine, but the judge spoke clearly--some people didn't, and he would have to read their lips. He was excused.

The line grew longer.

A student who had just started classes this week was allowed to postpone her jury duty to another session.

The next man was also allowed to postpone his scheduled week when he told the court that he was a production manager with one hundred and fifty people under his supervision, and this was the peak of their busy season.

The line grew to within a few feet of the door.

The next man said he was a logger. Six men would be out of work if he wasn't there, and no one could take his place--but, no, this was not his first jury date--he had postponed it until today--and, no, his situation would be no different two weeks from now. The judge gave him a choice: today or two weeks from today. He chose to stay today.

Half of the people standing abandoned their places in line and returned to their seats.

Two more prospects in what remained of the line were excused. One woman had been a resident of another county for ten years, but still received her mail at this county's post office; therefore, she wasn't a resident and did not meet a basic requirement.

Twelve names were randomly picked by the Clerk and called to the box, beginning with Mr. Smith.

"Please take seat number one."

I had not paid any attention to the jury box until now, but as my eyes naturally followed Mr. Smith, I saw that the jurors seats were literally numbered with six-inch-high, white decals on the front of each black leather chair. I had never seen this before, but Jack later said he had seen numbered juror seats in one other county, except the numbers were closer to the chair color and more subtly applied. I supposed the reason it struck me was that we had joked for a month about placing large posters on the doors of the two courtrooms, designating Courtroom One and Courtroom Two. The lack of specificity was causing a problem. Every day the judges were having to rescind numerous "orders for arrest" for defendants who had not shown up for their cases; unnecessary paperwork for the clerks and waste of deputy time, because the reason given every day was the same: the defendant had waited in the wrong courtroom. Jack contemplated donating plaques for each courtroom outer door bearing an oversized number, or maybe one of those old-fashioned drawings of a hand with one index finger extended for Courtroom One, two fingers for the second one. Maybe they should flash...In the end, he decided that if they could not figure it out for themselves, it wasn't his problem.

The first twelve prospective jurors in the box were told that Bonnie Lou Locklear was charged with first degree murder, stabbing another woman to death. However, this case did not fit the capital category, so the death sentence would not be a factor. Now they would be questioned by the lawyers.

The first question by counsel was improperly open-ended.

"Is there any reason, based on moral or religious convictions, that anyone of you cannot sit on a murder case?"

Two women raised their hands. The first said that she had lost three people in the last year, including her mother. She didn't say how. Her mental state would not be conducive to hearing this case.

The second said that her cousin also had died after being stabbed. In addition, she had "no right to decide" because of her religious convictions.

A man now raised his hand and stated, "I've been born again. It's in the hands of the Lord."

The judge asked his questions, and all three were excused for cause.

The next question was if any one of them had been the victim of a crime, and from the remaining nine, three hands shot up. A woman on the back row said she had been "cut" by her husband. The case was still pending.

Two businessmen had been victims of multiple break-ins.

Not all of the above were dismissed for "cause" and both attorneys used peremptory challenges to excuse them. (*A peremptory challenge requires no reason to be given.*) But two had been black, so the black Public Defender raised "Batson." The white prosecutor was not about to be left out. He raised "Batson" also; his opponent had removed "the only white male juror left."

"Batson" is the name of a U. S. Supreme Court case that has opened the proverbial Pandora's box, rendering peremptory challenges obsolete--in theory, a lawyer can still excuse a juror because he doesn't like the way his hair is parted or the color of his tie, but in reality, "juror instinct" is a luxury of the past, a relic belonging to a legal museum. There were good reasons for the Batson decision that stated that attorneys could not excuse jurors based solely on their race. But the original ruling was the result of a "pattern" of racial bias by a prosecutor in Kentucky which had taken place over an extended period of time and involving numerous cases. Subsequent decisions had expanded this original rule to jury selection procedures in every individual case, but a "pattern" of some sort was still necessary. Two blacks by one side and one white by the other side did not establish a pattern, especially when legitimate concerns had been apparent.

"Batson" was the newest and most popular hue and cry, but it appeared quite often that the attorneys crying it had never actually read the governing cases. It was obvious that some raised it because they were afraid not to. When asked by the judge to back up their position, they "recited their vowels," not having the vaguest idea of what they should say.

It's true that the case law is unclear: you-can't-do-this, but-we're-not-going-to-tell-you-what-you-can-do rulings, so confusion abounds. In the meantime, unwarranted "Batson" motions were attempted so often they were beginning to have the same effect as crying "wolf."

I could see the judge bristle. Frivolous motion or not, he would have to make "findings of fact" and "conclusions of law" for the record.

"My assessment of the initial composition of the twelve prospective jurors is four Black, three Indian, four White, and one person from India. Would you agree with that assessment?" he asked both counsel.

They agreed. They also agreed that the racial make-up fell in direct line with the racial make-up of Robeson County.

After further exploration and several knowing glares from the bench, the Public Defender withdrew his Batson motion, and the prosecutor followed suit.

By lunchtime, twelve jurors and one alternate had been chosen.

We ate quickly and took a long walk on the downtown streets. We stepped into an antique store which was packed to the gills-- we had to do some careful maneuvering around and between the owner's newly acquired purchases from two estates, beautiful additions to his already outstanding collection of unusual and expensive period furniture pieces and silver. Jack decided it was best for me not linger, so we finished our walk.

Immediately following the lunch break, the prosecutor, Stan Todd, brought to the judge's attention the fact that a juror had been approached by a witness during the lunch recess, but with good reason. The juror had not recognized Mr. Chavis when she had replied during questioning that she didn't know any of the parties in the case. Now she remembered that his deceased wife had computed her taxes for many years, and she had been to his house several times for social occasions.

She was excused.

Judge Thompson sent for six prospective jurors from the other courtroom and said it was his intention to replace the newly excused woman with the alternate juror and pick another alternate. But only one prospect answered his summons--the rest of the jury pool had been dismissed four or five minutes ago, and no one had consulted the court.

The lack of organization was getting embarrassing.

While the court was waiting for new jurors, another defense attorney (not connected with this case) asked the judge to strike an order for arrest for his client who had been in the wrong courtroom yesterday. I smiled at Jack. He didn't smile back.

Then the one available juror was questioned. He had been a police officer for two years, knew all the other police officers, and, yes, he had previously worked with the officers involved in this case. Excused.

Judge Thompson looked miffed. He was wondering why he had come to work today.

"Empanel the jury," he told the clerk. "We will proceed without an alternate."

Stan Todd, a squarely built, brown-haired man of medium height, was the Assistant District Attorney representing the state. He began his opening argument. He told the jury that on June 6, 1991, Bonnie Lou

Locklear and Rosemary Chavis had been drinking together. At some point, Rosemary had slapped Bonnie Lou. Later in the evening in the living room of the Chavis house, Bonnie Lou stabbed Rosemary in the neck with a butcher knife.

Angus Thompson, the head Public Defender of Robeson County, was a large framed, tall, black man with a voice that matched his stature. He spoke to the jury next, filling in background and more details:

The defendant, Bonnie Lou Locklear was thirty-three years old, and although she had completed the ninth grade, she could "read very little." At the time of the murder, she was living with her sixty-eight-year-old boyfriend, Willie Chavis, and his thirty-five-year-old daughter Rosemary Chavis. On the evening of June the sixth, after a few drinks together the two women had visited their mutual friend, Pamela. Rosemary began calling Bonnie Lou names and Pamela tried to mediate, but the verbal assaults continued during the walk home and finally escalated to physical assaults.

The defendant was extremely petite. Her long, jet-black, wavy hair contrasted with her pale lilac shirt and framed her attractive, angular face which was unadorned by make-up. Sitting to the left of her attorney, Angus Thompson, she was just a few feet away from Detective Oxendine at the prosecutor's table.

Officer John Ammons of the Red Springs Police Department was the first witness. On June sixth of this year, as commander of the Red Springs Rescue Squad, he had received a call to respond to the Chavis residence at eleven-thirty at night. He arrived ten minutes later. As he approached the screen door of the trailer, he was met by Willie Chavis, who told him that he thought his daughter Rosemary was dead. When the detective went into the trailer, he saw the victim "lying in a massive amount of blood." She had no pulse, no vital signs. There were "no weapons on or near the body." He went back outside to radio the sheriff's office and did not return inside until a deputy arrived.

Q. Was the defendant there?

A. Yes.

Q. Did you talk to her?

A. No. She was sitting on the porch crying. She never reentered the residence.

Willie Chavis was also on the front porch.

The pathologist was Dr. Marvin Thompson of Southeastern General Hospital. He testified that death was caused by the severing of the right subclavian vein and penetration of the right lung. (Translation: she had been stabbed in the lower right neck and had bled to death.) Showing a picture to the jury, he pointed to the knife wound, which was gaping, less than an inch wide and two inches deep. There were no other cuts or bruises, "just that stab wound." An inch either way would have missed this vital vein, about the size of a pencil, and although her lung would have collapsed, she could have survived with medical attention.

Q. How long would an individual continue to live with that type wound?

A. Long enough to bleed to death--four, five, or six minutes-- with the vein completely severed.

The wound showed clearly in the police photograph.

Q Would you expect, doctor, an absence of blood on the neck?

A.No. It appears to have been cleaned as I see it here on this exhibit.

No photographs were taken at the autopsy.

From the Medical Examiner's Report the jury learned that Rosemary's blood alcohol level was equivalent to .15 on the breathalyzer. (.10 is considered legally under the influence).

No blood alcohol test was performed on Bonnie Lou.

> Q. Would the wound be consistent with a long, slender butcher knife?
>
> A. It would be consistent with it.

Detective Oxendine had arrived that night at the Chavis trailer along with Detective Strickland and several other officers. He told the jury that he was in charge of the crime scene.

Bonnie Lou was already in a patrol car, and he entered the trailer to find a "female subject on the floor in the living room." He had a brief conversation with Willie Chavis and later accompanied him to the police station for a longer conversation, taking his statement. He had not talked to the defendant at all when she was in his car, but he did interview her later at the Sheriff's Department. After being informed of her rights, "she talked briefly."

> Q. Did she tell you what happened?
>
> A. She said Rosemary slapped her, and she got a knife and stabbed Rosemary in the neck. Then she said, "That's all I'm saying at this time."
>
> Q. Did she mention anything about Rosemary beating her?
>
> A. No.
>
> Q. Did she mention Rosemary having any weapons?
>
> A. No.

Q. Did she say she had been slapped and cursed at and beaten all evening?

A. No, sir. But she was talking right much. She was right rowdy.

Q. What do you mean?

A. She was loud and cursing, calling everybody a M. F. and S.O.B. When I was getting ready to finger-print her, she started talking about killing her again. No one said anything to her.

Her first statement was taken at two in the morning. Less than a half hour later, "She started talking again. She said she went and got a knife. She meant to kill Rosemary. Killing did not bother her. Something told her to kill the bitch for slapping her."

Q. What was Ms. Locklear doing when you first arrived?

A. I parked about seventy-five yards from the trailer. As I got nearer, I could hear a female voice hollering, cussing, and carrying on coming from the patrol car.

There would be much confusion about the murder weapon, starting with its present location.

Q. Do you have that knife with you?

A. Yes, sir. It's in your office.

"Just a moment, your Honor," Assistant District Attorney Todd said as he headed out the side door of the courtroom. Detective Oxendine unwrapped both plastic wrap and a cardboard container to get to the huge knife.

It was established that at one point the knife had been unsealed since the murder and that the cardboard sheath had been added before it was resealed, but the defense attorney and a police officer had been present. "Why" was not explained.

Also, how it was obtained was somewhat of a mystery.

Detective Oxendine said Willie had showed it to him in the kitchen sink.

Was there blood on it? If there was blood on it, was it sent for analysis? No one asked, and no one said.

Angus Thompson cross-examined for the defendant.

During Detective Oxendine's twenty-two years in law enforcement, he said he had investigated between twenty and thirty homicides.

Q. Did they all result in arrests?

A. That's the ones I based it on.

The detective did not know Willie Chavis before going to his residence on the night in question. When he arrived, several other officers were there ahead of him, along with emergency personnel. He had talked to Mr. Chavis briefly at the scene but did not write anything down at that time. His field notes observations were written down later *(much later, but the jury did not know that yet)*. He did not talk to the defendant at the scene.

Q. When you walked in the house, did you see Rosemary Chavis?

A. Yes, sir. She was laying on the floor.

Q. Did you go into any other room?

A. I went to the right from the living room and down the hallway to Rosemary's bedroom.

Q. What did you observe there?

A. The bed looked like somebody had been on it. There was blood coming out of the bedroom--heading out toward the living room in the hall.

Q. Do you remember if there was a television in that room?

A. I don't recall. I was looking for blood stains.

Q. And you didn't go into any other rooms off the hallway?

A. No. Other officers had checked.

Q. Did you observe anything turned over?

A. No. Not that I remember.

Q. Did you go into the kitchen?

A. Yes, sir. I went to the sink and recovered the knife.

Q. You picked up the knife at that time?

A. Yes, sir. Well, after it was photographed.

Q. Did you make any notes with respect to the home?

A. Yes.

Q. Did you make any notes on the scene?

A. No, sir.

The jury had to wonder how the knife got into the sink and why they were learning through the defense that there was blood in the bedroom.

Detective Oxendine had taken two statements from Mr. Chavis (eighteen days apart) and two statements from Bonnie Lou. He had also interviewed Pamela. Some were signed. Some were not.

Q. Why did Bonnie Lou say that she stabbed Rosemary?

A. Because she slapped her.

Q. What was the argument about?

A. She wouldn't comment on that.

Q. Did you ask her where she had been that day? Had she been drinking that day? Had Rosemary been drinking that day?

A. She wouldn't comment on that.

Q. And you didn't think that Mr. Chavis' second statement and Pamela's statement were important enough for them to sign?

MR. THOMPSON: Objection.

JUDGE THOMPSON: Sustained.

Q. What else did you collect besides the knife?

A. A twenty-two bolt-action rifle on June 25, 1991.

Q. So this was two and a half weeks later. Is that when Mr. Chavis told you...

MR. THOMPSON: Objection.

JUDGE THOMPSON: Sustained.

Q. Where were you when you got that rifle?

A. At Mr. Chavis' residence.

It appeared that Willie Chavis could be testifying for both sides. And it also appeared that the police had taken a rifle that had something to do with this case and they had not presented this evidence themselves.

The prosecutor, Mr. Todd, asked the detective a few more questions.

Q. When you took the statement from the defendant, why did you not write down all the questions you asked her?

A. Because she had no comment...no answers.

Q. Did she ask you to add anything or mark out anything?

A. No, sir.

Q. Did she say anything at that time about another weapon?

A. No, sir.

Q. But she did tell you that she meant to kill Rosemary?

A. Yes, sir.

Q. And that she would kill her again?

A. Yes, sir.

Q. And that it didn't bother her that she had killed her?

A. Yes, sir.

Q. Did she tell you why she killed Rosemary Chavis?

A. Only in the first statement.

Q. Why?

A.. Rosemary slapped her.

The defense wanted another turn.

Q. Did you ask her how many times she was slapped?

A. She said one time.

Q. Did you see any bruises or scratches on her?

A. No, sir.

Q. You didn't see any bruises, Detective Oxendine?

A. No, sir.

Mr. Todd's turn.

Q. Did she complain of any wounds?

A. No, sir.

Q. What was she wearing?

A. A pair of pants and a top with three-quarter sleeves.

Q. Did you see any obvious wounds on her?

A. No, sir.

The hour was late, and before recessing court for today, Judge Thompson warned the defendant's family and friends in the audience that if any overnight attempt was made to contact a juror, he would conduct a contempt hearing, and if contempt was found, the offender would be sent to jail. After the jury was excused, he addressed the lawyers.

"I realize you have asked for full recordation of these proceedings and that, of course, includes bench conferences. But due to the physical make-up of the bench (very high) and the physical make-up of the court reporter (five feet, one), bench conferences will not be physically possible. We will have to send the jury out instead."

They laughingly agreed that he had a valid point. Sherryl, the court reporter, laughed with them.

Wednesday morning I talked to Sherryl before court started. She had taken the proceedings in Robeson County for a number of years, and I hoped she could give me some answers as to why I was hearing only half a case.

"What about the blood in the bedroom? Doesn't that open up all sorts of possibilities, including self-defense? Or is that why the State left out that part?"

"Probably. Here, self-defense is the usual claim because so many people are armed. So when one guy says something to make the other guy mad and the other one pulls out a gun and shoots the guy who insulted him, he can still say self-defense, because the person he shot was armed," she replied.

"And blood analysis on the knife? Is it just assumed that blood was on that knife and that it was the victim's?"

Oh, that's a given," she told me. "There is no comprehensive investigation any more. A few years ago, the SBI investigated the Sheriff here, and even though no charges were brought, there is no love lost between the two agencies. Since then, the SBI is no longer called in to assist; therefore, no physical evidence, no tests. They've got a body and a confession."

"Do you know anything about the rifle?"

"More than likely, Willie is going to say that his daughter had a rifle and Bonnie stabbed her in self-defense. Of course, nobody said anything about a rifle until two weeks later--so, you can draw your own conclusions."

"So Willie could have been thinking this over, knows he can't bring his daughter back, but doesn't want to lose Bonnie too?"

"Could be."

"And is anybody going to tell us how the knife got from the living room into the kitchen sink?"

"*Probably not. When one of the first officers got there and wanted to know where the murder weapon was, Willie took it out of the drawer. It had been cleaned.*"

"*Well, isn't the jury going to wonder why the State is letting some of the police evidence come out through the defense? I mean, wouldn't the average person suspect all the State's evidence if it appears that some of it is 'withheld'?*"

"*They might. More juries have been coming in with 'not guilty' verdicts. They're letting them off all the time.*"

Having more understanding of the situation was more depressing than helpful.

The defendant was led down the hall in shackles. Her ankles and feet were so tiny that it looked like the iron rings would slip right off if she wasn't wearing shoes. This morning, she wore the same black pants and a crisp, cotton, red-and-white striped shirt.

The seven women and five men on the jury were seated.

Deputy Strickland was the first officer on the scene that night, arriving after the rescue squad. He testified that Willie Chavis and Bonnie Lou Locklear were both sitting on the front porch. He asked Mr. Chavis to accompany him inside, which he did. Then Deputy Strickland searched the trailer "to make sure no one else was there." He and Mr. Chavis went back outside, at which point, he had asked, "Who done this?" and Willie Chavis pointed to Bonnie Lou.

"No," he had no conversation at that time with the defendant. The deputy had used his car radio and was told that more officers were on their way.

Q. What was the defendant doing at this time?

A. She had been sitting quietly on the porch, but when I got back from using my car radio, Ms. Locklear was walking around in the yard, cursing loudly, and making statements. She had walked a couple of hundred yards down the road. I drove to her location and arrested her. She was very verbal and abusive. She started kicking the inside of my car. She made the statement that she'd "killed the bitch" and said she'd do it again.

Q. Did she appear to be intoxicated to you?

A. Very much so.

Angus Thompson cross-examined.

Q. Did you keep any notes from that night?

A. No, sir.

Q. You never reduced to writing the statements Ms. Locklear made to you?

A. I wrote a statement up later, a week or a week and a half ago.

Although Strickland had turned in a one-page written report that night, he had recorded this three-page statement only ten days ago; it was from his recollection.

Q. Where is that statement now?

A. The D. A.'s got it.

Angus Thompson was most upset. The jury was sent out. He told the court that he had not received a copy, and as defense counsel, he was entitled to any statement made by the defendant to a law enforcement officer. The prosecutor, Mr. Todd, was asked if he had any other statements by the defendant that had not been disclosed. As a matter of fact, he did. Officer Wilkins had heard what she said. He hadn't given copies of either documents to her lawyer because "they contained nothing new in content."

"My feeling was that this was the same thing over and over again," the prosecutor said, defending himself.

After the jury was brought back, Angus Thompson continued to cross-examine.

Officer Strickland testified that he himself had never had possession of the knife.

> Q. But you did see the knife?
>
> A. Yes. I saw Mr. Chavis take it out of a drawer and lay it on the kitchen counter. I took it and laid it on the table.
>
> Q. So you did have possession of the knife?
>
> A. Momentarily.

Officer Strickland told the jury that he had kept the scene secured that night "to keep it from being tampered with."

> Q. But it certainly could have been tampered with before you arrived?
>
> A. Yes, sir.
>
> Q. Officer Strickland, what would you have known in the report written ten days ago that you would not have known on June 6, 1991?
>
> A. Not much. Other than what Detective Oxendine told me.

The defense attorney was shaking his head in frustration.

He asked the court not to excuse this witness; he might wish to recall him.

The prosecutor protested, saying the officer had been up all night.

The defense attorney said he had been up all night too.

The court instructed the officer that he would have to remain available.

Willie Chavis took the stand for the prosecution. He was a nice look-ing, neatly dressed man, and his bearing and facial features denied his six-ty-eight years.

I wondered how he was going to handle this. I felt safe in assuming that he had loved his daughter. But he had also loved the defendant. Was he going to help convict his lover for killing his daughter? If he still cared for Bonnie Lou, he was caught in a most unenviable position. He spoke calmly, and his tone was matter-of-fact.

Q. Do you know the defendant?

A. Yes.

Q. How well?

A. We was living together.

Q. How long had you been living together?

A. Nine months.

Q. Was Rosemary Chavis your daughter?

A. Yes.

Q. Did she also live there?

A. Yes. She did.

Q. Were you home around nine o'clock that night?

A. Yes. I was.

Q. Tell us what happened.

A. Rosemary and Bonnie Lou had a half case of beer. They walked down to the trailer park and came back about nine-fifteen. They were both well intoxicated. Bonnie was hollering that Rosemary had slapped her. Bonnie had a knife. I took it away from her. Rosemary told Bonnie to settle down. I went back to my bedroom. Later on, I heard them scrambling, and Bonnie said, "Let me up." I got up and went in the hall. Rosemary had the rifle and told me, "That girl cut me." I think she wanted me to shoot her.

Q. Was the rifle loaded?

A. No. It was not.

Q. What condition was it in?

A. The bolt was pulled back.

Q. Please continue.

A. Rosemary was bleeding. I pushed her behind me. Bonnie was standing in the hall with a knife. I took it away again. I turned around to help my daughter and saw there was nothing I could do, so I got in the car and drove to Shannon and called 911.

Shannon was approximately two miles away.

Q. How long was it between making the call and someone arriving?

A. Oh, ten minutes.

Q. Did you have the opportunity to observe the defendant before you called?

A. Yes.

Q. And was she injured in any way?

A. Not that I could see.

Q. She didn't have any scratches?

A. Well, I wasn't--I couldn't say yes or no.

Q . When you got back, did you see the defendant?

A. Yes. She was standing over Rosemary, wiping the blood off and telling her to get up.

Willie Chavis was shown a picture of his daughter lying on his living room floor. He said her position was not the same as it had been when he left to summon help.

"She was laying with her head up near the air conditioner--where the blood is," he said, voice breaking for the first time.

Q. Mr. Chavis, how long was it between the time you took the knife away from Ms. Locklear the first time until you saw her again with the knife in her hand?

A. Approximately two hours.

He had hurt the defendant, but he had also helped her.

Cross-examination by Angus Thompson would reveal how far he was willing to go to come to her aid.

Q: Mr. Chavis, you testified that your daughter and Ms. Locklear had a half a case of beer. How did you know that?

A. I seen them.

Q. Then you had been drinking with them?

A. No, sir. I don't drink.

Q. You said that they left the house after they had been drinking and returned around nine o'clock. How long were they away?

A. Two or three hours.

Q. When the two women got home, were you home?

A. Yes, sir. Sitting in the living room when they came back.

Q. Were they arguing?

A. Yes. They were.

Q. Could you ascertain what they were arguing about?

A. Me.

Q. Was Rosemary angry because Bonnie said something about you?

A. That's right. Bonnie said Rosemary slapped her.

Q. Did you tell them to stop arguing?

A. You don't stop Bonnie when she's drinking. Rosemary listened to me.

He said he had taken a knife away from Bonnie in the living room and put it in its proper place, the kitchen drawer. The women had gone to the back bedroom and talked. They "settled down." Twenty minutes later, he went to his bedroom and fell asleep, waking up around eleven. That's when he had heard Bonnie tell Rosemary to "let her up." He told the same story again, saying he had gone into the hallway to go to the back bedroom when he encountered Rosemary with the rifle and Bonnie with the knife.

Q. What did you do?

A. Rosemary handed me the rifle, and I moved her behind me. I took the knife from Bonnie and put it on the coffee table.

Q. Where was Rosemary?

A. She was laying down on the floor. I told Bonnie to help me get her up and put her in the car. She come over and tried to help. But we couldn't. She wouldn't stop bleeding. So I left. Bonnie had a towel. She was telling Rosemary to get up. She wasn't mad with her.

Mr. Chavis went to Shannon to call for help.

Q. Did you ever go back to the back bedroom?

A. Yes. After I came back.

Q. Were things knocked over?

A. Yes. I straightened them up.

Q. Wasn't there a fan turned over as well as other items?

A. I don't remember. Just stuff knocked around.

Q. Had Officer Strickland already been back there?

A. Yes.

Q. Do you remember being interviewed by Mack Woods from my office?

A. Yes.

Q. Do you remember telling him that you saw "Rosemary whipping Bonnie"?

A. Yes, sir. They was whooping at each other, like with dukes (*demonstrating by putting his fists in front of him*) --hitting at each other.

Q. Do you remember telling Mr. Woods that you didn't know what the argument was about?

A. I could have.

Q. Do you remember telling Mr. Woods that you had never seen either of them that drunk before?

A. I did.

Q. Do you remember telling him that they might have been on something besides beer?

A. Yeah. I still say it.

Mr. Chavis was not volunteering much. It was apparent that he was not going to give anything to the defense lawyer. He would have to dig for it.

Mr. Thompson showed him several pictures of his daughter lying in a pool of blood. He had already seen them one time. He told the defense lawyer, "I wish you'd stop pushing them on me" before acknowledging that Rosemary's head had been moved while he was gone to phone for help, and a towel had been placed underneath it like a pillow.

He did say that Bonnie was "as nice a person as you'd want to meet," when she had not been drinking and that Rosemary underwent the same personality change.

Q. Wasn't Rosemary almost drunk when she got back?

A. No, sir. They wasn't almost drunk. They was drunk.

Q. Both Rosemary and Bonnie?

A. Yes, sir.

Q. But you can't say who got that knife after you put it in the drawer because you were in your room asleep?

A. No. I can't.

Q. Anybody could have got that knife?

A. Yes, sir.

Q. And you did hear Bonnie say, "Let me up"?

A. Yes, sir. I did.

The State rested.

Their case was a body, a confession, and maybe a murder weapon--a knife that a third party had told them was the murder weapon.

The defense called Pamela as their first witness. She lived next door to Bonnie's sister. She testified that Bonnie, her friend of ten months, and Rosemary, whom she didn't know well, walked down to her trailer around six-thirty or seven that night. Also present were her fiancé and her sister, who was babysitting for several small children.

"Bonnie walked in with a Natural Light beer in her hand, and Rosemary pulled her shirt up and showed me two more hot beers she had stuck in her pants." Rosemary was calling Bonnie names.

"Bonnie was high, not drunk, but getting upset because Rosemary was cursing her in front of other people. Rosemary pushed Bonnie, and I got in the middle--sat down between them. Rosemary was still cursing and I asked her to leave because of the kids. Rosemary said something like, 'I'm going to have to bust her face tonight.'"

Rosemary left, and Bonnie followed five minutes later.

"Yes," she remembered talking to Detective Oxendine several days later.

Q. Did you read the statement he wrote down?

A. No. He did not let me read it. The first time I read it was this morning when I talked to you.

Q. Did he ever ask you to sign any statement you gave him?

A. No, sir. I didn't sign nothing.

Q. But did he ever ask you to?

A. No, sir.

The defense called Detective Oxendine, who was sitting at the prosecution table, back to the stand to read the statement he had taken from Pamela. His written account was essentially the same thing Pamela had just said, but with less detail and with one addition:

"Bonnie did not want to go home because she was afraid Willie would beat her because she'd been to her [Pamela's] house."

He had interviewed Pamela ten to twelve days after Rosemary died, had given the narrative to the D. A.'s office, but did not talk to the D. A. about the statement "because she was not going to testify for the State."

Q. The twenty-two rifle--is that still in the D. A.'s office?

A. Yes, sir.

Q. Would you go get it?

The detective came down from the stand and left the courtroom, returning with the rifle, which he described as bolt action, clip fed. He told the defense attorney he had obtained it from Mr. Chavis.

The District Attorney had some questions of a different nature.

Q. Detective Oxendine, you have been sitting here beside me in this chair since the beginning of court this morning, have you not?

A. Yes, sir.

Q. Have you heard the defendant make any comments about Rosemary Chavis?

Objection. The jury was sent out.

The judge would have to hear the rest of this testimony to decide whether or not the jury would then hear it.

Q. What did you hear her say?

A. When you and Mr. Thompson were at the jury box showing photographs to them, I heard the defendant say, "She had no business beating me. I'd do it again."

Q. How far were you from the defendant?

A. Four feet.

Q. At the time, was the statement made to anyone in particular?

A. No.

The defense attorney addressed the judge.

"May I inquire of the court reporter if she heard and recorded that statement?"

"You may inquire."

"Madame Court Reporter, did you hear the defendant make that statement?"

"Not that one," Sherryl replied.

The prosecutor argued that the comment was a "spontaneous utterance" and should be admitted.

The defense attorney claimed that this testimony would "substantially prejudice" his client.

The judge ruled:

"In the discretion of the court, the objection is sustained. And I will ask you, Mr. Thompson, to instruct your client not to make any further statements. If she does, from this point, my ruling may not be the same. Do I make myself clear?"

The jury returned, and the prosecutor had a few more questions.

> Q. On the occasions when you talked with the defendant, has she ever mentioned a rifle?
>
> A. No, sir.
>
> Q. Has she ever mentioned another weapon to you besides the one she used?
>
> A. No, sir. Just the knife.

The detective came down from the stand and leaned the rifle beside the witness box.

The jury was left to wonder if Rosemary had the rifle in her hands while she was profusely bleeding. If so, there most probably would have been blood on the rifle. No one had asked. Would tests have shown traces of blood if it had been wiped? Would Willie have wiped the rifle clean? Why had no one asked him? If Willie had made up the "rifle" story, why hadn't he "loaded" it too?

Brenda, Bonnie Lou's sister, was the next witness for the defense, but she added little information. She said she had three more sisters and five brothers, and she had met Willie Chavis only twice. The only questions that may have given the jury some insight were not allowed:

Q. Was Bonnie Lou an adult when her parents died?

Objection.
Sustained.

Q. Do you know whether or not Bonnie Lou has been gainfully employed?

Objection.
Sustained.

Q. Who was Bonnie Lou living with before Willie Chavis?

Objection.
Sustained.

Q. Do you know if your sister has physical or mental problems?

Objection.
Sustained.

Q. Did you serve in the capacity of Guardian for Bonnie Lou?

Objection.
Sustained.

These were questions that could have been appropriate to show "mitigating" circumstances in the sentencing phase of a trial. But this was not sentencing, and her background was not relevant to guilt or innocence. Whether her sister was her guardian or not and whom she had previously lived with had nothing to do with whether she had murdered Rosemary Chavis.

Brenda was excused.

The defense asked to break for lunch. He said he would present one more witness, a doctor.

Heading out of the courthouse for lunch, the two men who got on the elevator with us were having a conversation. The elevator was very small, we were facing each other, and one was telling the other about the fair. He said that he had gone last night, mainly to see the mules jump. The other man laughed.

"Mules jump?" I couldn't help but ask.

"Well, not really 'jump,'" he answered. "They walk a plank, then fall thirty feet into a huge water tank."

Jack was chuckling.

"Why?" sounded like a reasonable question to me.

"So people will watch, I guess," the man laughed. "It's the funniest thing I've ever seen."

"Okay," was all I could manage, nodding.

We got in the car.

"Is it me?" I asked Jack. "Those poor dumb creatures," I was trying not to sound too indignant. "I bet the animal rights people are standing on their heads."

Jack's chuckles were turning into full blown laughter. "Probably," he got out. "But you've got to admit, that would be pretty funny." His laughter was past control.

"Jack--" I admonished.

"I know. I know. You're right," he admitted through hysterical tears.

After lunch, it was decided that the doctor would not testify after all. He had performed the psychological evaluation on the defendant to determine if she was competent to stand trial.

The State had tried earlier to call him as *their* witness, but after some discussion, it was apparent that the State had inadvertently received the full report on the defendant's psychological evaluation, a report they shouldn't have had access to, since she was found competent to stand trial.

The defense wanted to use the doctor as if he were their hired expert psychologist, but insanity was not an issue in Bonnie Lou's defense--besides, by saying she was capable of standing trial, the doctor had in effect said she was legally sane. And if the defense questioned the doctor, the State had a right to cross-examine, and evidence damaging to the defense could come in as well. Their conclusion was not to ask this witness, who had driven from Raleigh and sat in the courtroom all morning, any questions.

The defense rested.

The case was over. All that remained were closing arguments and the judge's charge before the jury deliberated.

They did have a body and a confession, and testimony that indicated that Bonnie Lou had killed Rosemary, and a possible murder weapon, even though the circumstances were hazy at best.

The lawyers made their arguments.

The defense lawyer asked the jury to consider all the details the State didn't tell them. "The State says it boils down to a few simple sentences, but use your common sense."

The prosecutor countered: It's not necessary for you to know every detail of what happened that night. What you do know is who came out of the bedroom with a knife in her hand."

The jury charge from the judge started shortly after five o'clock, and at its conclusion, the jurors were dismissed until the next morning.

At nine-thirty the next day, the jury filed in.

One of them carried a cooler.

At four o'clock that afternoon they had agreed.

Not Guilty.

Bonnie Lou's sisters and friends hugged her, and they walked together from the courtroom.

One could only suppose from the verdict that reasonable doubt hinged on the rifle, the implied scuffle in the bedroom, and the undis-closed-by-the-State-until-they-had-to-and-had-never-investigated-the-bedroom = self-defense.

The prosecutor talked to some of the jurors later, and this analysis was correct.

Jimmy, the bailiff, handed the judge a partial sheet of paper torn from a legal pad that had been left on the jurors' table. It read:

FACTS

Dead Body--R. C.

Knife--Stab wound--Death--B.L.

Rifle in R.C.'s possession

Statements---> 1 signed, 1 unsigned

The defense attorney had implied self-defense often enough-- arguing that the defendant was not the aggressor, there was only one wound, no indication of murderous intent because she placed a towel under the victim's head, telling her to get up--just never actually saying "self-defense."

But she had confessed.

And she had said she'd do it again.

And the rifle was unloaded.

And if they were listening closely, they heard, more than one time, the defendant say out loud from the defense table, "I'd kill that bitch again."

I had.

Perhaps the jury was sending a message to the State regarding their haphazard investigation.

Or perhaps this case could be chalked up to "*the peculiarities and inequities of the law.*"

Judge Johnson once said he had "borrowed" this story from his former contracts professor and had used it several times in private practice when he was not left with much else to say in a defense final argument.

A new lawyer, having just passed the bar, rented an office in a small building housing several other lawyers and hung out his shingle. Confronted with his first case and not knowing what to do, he sought the advice from a more experienced lawyer down the hall. The older and wiser lawyer listened to the facts and then told the young lawyer that "due to *the peculiarities and inequities of the law*, you'll probably lose this case." The young lawyer did, in fact, lose the case.

Hired for his second case, he again did not know how to proceed, so he walked down the hall again to ask the more experienced lawyer his advice. The older and wiser lawyer listened to the facts and again told the young lawyer that "due to *the peculiarities and the inequities of the law*, you'll probably lose this case." He did.

After this same advice was given for the young lawyer's third case, he could stand it no longer.

"How are you so sure that I'm going to lose this case?" he asked the older and wiser lawyer in frustration.

"Well," the older and wiser lawyer explained, "I used to have a successful practice, a nice home, several nice cars, a wife, and three kids. But last year everything changed. My wife filed for divorce on the grounds of impotence. At the same time my secretary filed a paternity suit against me. And due to *the peculiarities and inequities of the law,* I lost both."

In State v. Bonnie Lou Locklear, however, instead of "the law," perhaps this case could be attributed to the "peculiarities and inequities" of Robeson County.

The prosecutor had said first degree murder.

The defense had *kind-of-said* self-defense.

The jury had said not guilty.

The truth may have resided somewhere in between.

Or maybe this was a "typical" cutting case, and Bonnie Lou had missed, inflicting a fatal wound instead of a mark.

CHAPTER SIX

———————

November: State v. McCollum

For the remainder of Jack's term in Robeson County, the cases were routine--depressing but nevertheless, routine--and it was just as well. I stayed at home, and the forty-five minute commute for him was no problem, and once again, we had a regular dinner hour and schedule akin to that of our neighbors. Some normalcy, whatever that is, was welcome.

After several delays, the most chilling trial of Jack's year started in early November. Although a Robeson County case, the venue had been changed to Cumberland County and, therefore, to our hometown of Fayetteville, which has earned the privileged status of "All American City." It is also a city that is automatically pigeonholed as a "military" town because Fort Bragg and Pope Air Force Base are adjacent.

Native Fayettevillians take exception to this lone label, boasting a proud history in the fashioning of America.

Christened early on as Campbellton by the large Scottish settlement in the mid-seventeen-hundreds, we narrowly missed becoming the permanent capitol of North Carolina, losing to Raleigh by one vote. Though the Scots remained loyal to the King when the break with England came, thirty-nine "patriots" signed the Liberty Point Declaration of Independence as early as June, 1775, just two months after the battle of Lexington, Massachusetts. The town was later renamed in 1783 in honor of General La Fayette, the French nobleman who, despite great risk to his career and reputation in his own country, helped us win the Revolutionary War. The general paid us a visit forty-three years later, an occasion for much pomp and circumstance, which is recorded in detail in John Oates' *Story of Fayetteville.*

"Sherman's Hell-hounds" came through our city in 1865, destroying the strategic U. S. arsenal that had been captured by the Confederates and used to supply Southern soldiers with Yankee ammunition.

And it was here that Babe Ruth hit his first professional home run.

Our downtown area literally circles around the Market House, which was just what its name implied in the olden days--a central hub--selling meats, fish, produce, and various goods shipped up the Cape Fear River. Our town fathers insist that slaves were sold there on only two occasions when an estate was being settled or personal property auctioned, and not in the normal course of business as is commonly expounded .

The first Market House (destroyed by fire in 1831) was the temporary State Capitol building and the site of the North Carolina ratification of the United States Constitution. A brick replica stands in its place, retaining the open arches on four sides, allowing one to see through at street level. The copper cupola with its four-sided clock is visible from each of the four streets that spoke out from the circle. The best view can be seen coming down Hay Street from Hamont Hill--our only hill of any significance, which is why locals call it "the Hill."

My grandmother claimed that the bottom of Hamont (also spelled Haymount) Hill marks the beginning of the Blue Ridge Mountains, some four to five hours away, and she was right. The bottom of the Hill is the dividing line between the Piedmont and Coastal plains. Traveling east from that point to the coast, the land is as flat as a Salvador Dali clock.

Although Jack was born and bred here, I'm half and half. Originally from Boston, my father met my mother while he was stationed at Fort Bragg. After fighting two wars, the big one in Germany and the conflict in Korea, he opted for civilian life and chose to live here, my mother's birthplace. Developing a taste for grits (but still passing up the collards), he is a converted Southerner, in spite of retaining his Yankee trait of announcing exactly what he thinks whether his listeners want to know or not. Missing only the winter sports he grew up with, he passionately pursues the game of golf and plays every day, now that he's semi- retired. My mother is the epitome of the gracious Southern lady-- friendly but reserved, open but private, and magnanimously hospitable. She acknowledges no four-letter words. Untiringly dedicated to her family with an open heart and an abundance of forgiveness, she rules with her head. Only the flashing of her cornflower-blue eyes signals disapproval.

So I have lived in various environments, as a child having the advantage of traveling to other states and foreign countries, and since the age of eleven, establishing permanent roots.

Our city and populace owe the two military bases a large debt. Perhaps because of the great number of personnel who retire here, people who have travelled the world and expect more from us, we are not the sleepy southern town we might have been. We have our own technical college, a private university, and a state University. Culturally, we make a valiant effort to keep up with our growth, our Arts Council, Fayetteville Symphony, Cape Fear Regional Theater, Fort Bragg Playhouse, and Methodist College staging an array of quality performances that belies our size of a hundred thousand. The people who live here are indeed varied, many of them staunch, Scottish, self-reliant individualists. While mainly a blue-collar town, we have our share of professionals and entrepreneurs, large and small. Still, our county auditorium draws its greatest crowds for wrestling matches and rock stars. Our old courthouse is a marvelous building, boasting a wide flight of marble steps, huge pillars, a marble facade with a quotation from Shakespeare's *Merchant of Venice* carved on the front facade of the building: *Though justice be thy plea, consider this, That, in the course of justice, none of us should see salvation; we do pray for mercy.* The interior boasts marble floors and staircases, and the high-ceilinged courtrooms look stately, as courtrooms should look. The building is presently occupied by various city offices.

Our "new" courthouse, new since 1978, stands in the center of town, appropriately just a block east of the Market House and diagonally across the street from Liberty Point. The building is modern and the courtrooms are far more sterile, having no trappings of a by-gone era.

The razing of the two-hundred-plus-years trees and historic homes on Green Street awakened us to preserving what was left of our downtown heritage, and it is now fashionable to restore and convert rather than tear down. Many of the charming old homes within walking distance of the courthouse have become law offices.

This "new courthouse" is Judge Thompsons's home base, regardless of his schedule.

The McCollum trial had been originally calendared for late October and moved to Cumberland County for trial because of the publicity the case had received in Robeson County.

A last minute deposition of an expert had prompted the defense counsel to ask for a current psychological evaluation of their client, and the trial was delayed a week to allow them to accomplish this.

When the new trial date arrived, however, the Assistant District Attorney from Robeson County had forgotten to request formally that the defendant be transported to the Fayetteville jail from the Raleigh prison where he was held. Jury selection once again was delayed until that afternoon when the defendant could be present, and no jurors were seated.

The shaky start was a portent of things to come.

The prosecutor was Mr. Carter, the Assistant District Attorney from the Robeson County District Attorney's Office. Tuesday, the first black juror the prosecutor excused had an attitude problem-- answering on his questionnaire that his hobby was "sex," putting his feet on the jury box rail, and asking, "Where do you get a drink of water around here, anyway?" All of this had added up to sufficient grounds for the prosecutor to excuse him, but the Defense team raised "Batson" anyway.

The Batson motion is raised by attorneys if the opposing counsel shows a pattern of excusing persons from the jury on the basis of race.

After some discussion, the defense withdrew their motion due to the juror's demeanor. But the prosecutor, falsely encouraged, pushed his luck. He excused two more black jurors, although he did accept a Hispanic male. The two black jurors he excused had given all the "correct" answers, and because he had now excused the first three black persons that had been called into the box, the defense counsel raised the Batson issue again, this time, perhaps more justifiably; a "pattern" of systematically excusing black jurors could have been established.

However, Mr. Carter's "articulate, believable, race-neutral explanation" or reason required to combat Batson, was that the jurors had "hesitated" when asked about the death penalty. His Honor instructed him that his reason was insufficient; capital punishment is not an easy question for anyone, and it is only natural for people to hesitate. The result was that the entire jury pool of forty people had been "tainted," and were now excused, and jury selection started anew from square one.

The prosecutor asked for a mistrial--on what grounds, no one could fathom--there was no trial with an empaneled jury underway. Well, if he couldn't have a mistrial, he would appeal. Appeal what? The day finally ended with only one juror in the box and a very irritated Judge.

Wednesday seemed like a rerun when the prosecutor did exactly the same thing. His reason on this day for excusing the first three black jurors called into the box was the same as it had been yesterday: they "hesitated."

When the defense team raised Batson this time, a bailiff was sent to chase down the black woman who had just been excused to come back and wait in the jury room. The Judge ruled that the prosecutor was not entitled to excuse her peremptorily; he could further question her if he wished and try to find another reason to excuse her, but, the Judge explained once again, "hesitation" was not a sufficient reason to justify raising Batson. He pointed out that one of the reasons that the jurors were hesitating was the convoluted and confusing manner in which the prosecutor was asking the questions--it took the juror a while to understand what was being asked.

Mr. Carter dug his hole deeper.

To the astonishment of all, he asked the Judge to recuse himself from the case because his rulings were prejudiced to the State.

The Court of Appeals would have a merry chuckle from this one. Mr. Carter was the State.

His Honor gave Mr. Carter half an hour to submit a written motion stating his grounds. Returning in a half hour without a written motion, the prosecutor asked for a transcript of the past three days of attempted jury selection, and the Judge refused his request.

The lines were drawn.

By this time it was late afternoon, and the Judge told the prosecutor that he had until tomorrow morning at 9:00 A. M. to prepare for a hearing on the matter.

Again, Mr. Carter asked for a transcript.

Denied.

An hour later, the Court Reporter, not knowing what to do, found Judge Thompson in another judge's chambers. The prosecutor had asked her to type up the transcript anyway, without cost to the State, and she had told him she would. But now that she'd thought it over, she did not want to taint her position of neutrality. Judge Thompson told her to do what she wanted; he would not decide for her. However, she was advised by another Superior Court Judge listening to this conversation that since she was paid by the State, her actions could also be the subject of appeal by the defense. She decided not to type the transcript.

The fact that the prosecutor had asked the Court Reporter for the transcript after it had been twice denied by the Court angered the judge greatly. Even-tempered, thinking before he speaks, he is civil even to those who oppose him in a not-so-civil manner and does not exhibit anger often. But when the occasion arises, he confronts head-on, face to face, not behind anyone's back.

For the second day in a row, Jack came home with his blood pressure at a non-measurable level.

Twice he had explained the law to the Assistant D. A., and twice it was obvious that the prosecutor either didn't understand or didn't care. To allow the Assistant D. A. to disregard Batson blatantly was just begging for a reversal of the case--something the prosecutor, too, should want to avoid.

That had already happened once in this case. This trial was a retrial, seven years after the first go-round, an all too familiar story. The crime had occurred in 1983 and was tried in 1984. The N. C. Supreme Court had waited four years, until 1988, to reverse, not just the sentencing phase, but the guilt/innocence phase as well. The Robeson County District Attorney's office had waited three more years to try it again.

Henry Lee McCollum had been on death row for seven years, and a crucial witness for the prosecution was dead. Two of the perpetrators of the crime were still free, never having been arrested; the reason, according to the Assistant D. A., was that they had not confessed; ergo, "no evidence." Henry's brother would also receive a new trial.

The scenario would have been keystone-laughable except for the abhorrent nature of the crime.

At the hearing the next morning, the prosecutor presented an affidavit stating that the Judge was not being "fair and impartial" and should excuse himself from the case. The affidavit stated new reasons other than hesitation for excusing the jurors, reasons that he had not expressed in court the day before. His motion was denied; an Order to that effect stating the reasons would be forthcoming.

The appellate courts lean to "citizen" rights, and in the criminal court that "innocent citizen," unless or until proven guilty, happens to be the defendant. Therefore, you could take this premise one step further and say appellate courts lean to the defense, although many defense attorneys would disagree and would like the presently conservative courts to lean more.

There are many reasons for this seemingly one-sided bent. One of the primary reasons, and the most illustrative, is that in the past the police departments have been notorious for coercing confessions and abusing their power. Before the 1991, now famous, Los Angeles tape, showing gross police brutality, the general public did not believe that such abuse happened. If it was alleged, they thought the defendant was exaggerating; "He probably deserved it" was the prevailing attitude. There were few wins from juries against police officers, who have historically represented citizen protection.

Judge Thompson had seen police abuse on a regular basis twenty years ago when he was the District Attorney. Some officers didn't even try to hide it. Then the prosecutor, he took aside one officer, who kept bringing in banged up prisoners to court, and told him that he wasn't fooling anyone and if he brought anyone else to court who had "resisted arrest," he'd be prosecuted himself. The officer took the warning wisely and cleaned up his act. Ten years later, the same officer would testify against the police department for Judge Thompson's law firm in a civil case brought against the city of Fayetteville.

The trial showed a pattern of police brutality over a long period of time--an unpopular lawsuit, to say the least. However, the plaintiff's lawyers turned around a doubting Federal judge and a doubting jury who found for the plaintiff, but awarded him only a thousand dollars. When asked by reporters why the monetary value was so low, some of the jurors replied that they were afraid of retaliation by the police department!

The plaintiff's attorneys won an appeal for damages only, and an out-of-town jury in Wilmington didn't have any qualms about rewarding the plaintiff nine hundred thousand dollars. The up-hill-battle case was significant, and the firm was a hero--but only to a few.

The city manager, mayor, and city council were undone. Fayetteville was in the running for the prestigious "All American City" award that same year, which status they did attain, but this was not the image they wished to present. Many of our local citizens also disagreed with the verdict and thought the police had every right to beat up on a "criminal that was holding quaaludes." Besides, said criminal had smart-mouthed the officer, so there was nothing wrong when the officer put his hands on the arrestee's shoulders for leverage and kneed him in the groin with such force that the man's testicle had burst, requiring surgery and rendering him sterile. The fact that the prisoner's hands were handcuffed behind his back did not seem to matter.

In truth, there are a great many law enforcers who are dedicated professionals, who do their frustrating and sometimes sordid jobs well, and who receive inadequate compensation and little thanks. We owe them a lot. But, as with all organizations, there can be a few bad oysters in the steam pot that ruin the roast. The minority who do not follow the rules generate more rules for the rest to deal with.

Unfortunately, as will happen, additional unforeseeable circumstances arise, allowing some defendants to manipulate the system, thus using their new protections to a height not intended. It also took time for law enforcement to become educated to these rights and not to botch the cases before they came to trial. The "Burger" Supreme Court, trying to stop these gaps, had swung the other way and was labeled conservative.

Batson came about for another reason, but a related one. The primary reason was to give each citizen his chance at jury duty, but the defendants were effected as well. Just as police brutality most often happened to minorities, minorities were quite often the defendants in trials. In many instances, the prosecutor, concerned that a minority would not convict "a brother," would summarily dismiss all minorities from the jury on the basis of their skin color alone. Someone finally challenged one District Attorney for this practice, and in 1986, the Supreme Court handed down new rules for picking a jury.

Although the pendulum is still swinging, the Appellate courts lean toward the defense to quell minority abuses and to ensure a fair trial to each and every citizen. Trial judges take this "leaning" into account when making their rulings. They certainly cannot outguess the appellate court, especially on close questions, but they give the probable reaction of the higher courts heavy consideration.

In this light, an appeal to a necessarily defense-oriented appeals court claiming that the trial judge is prejudiced against the State falls just short of incredible. The State still deserves a fair trial, but Batson is a citizen protection, and however ludicrous a prosecutor thinks this decision is, it is law, and he has no choice but to obey it.

Once again, jury selection began and absorbed the last two days of this week and most of the next week.

I accompanied Jack to court Friday morning for the beginning of State's evidence.

Ten years before, I had worked in this courthouse, and many of the same personnel were still here. While getting my necessary coffee, I talked to two of the bailiffs, and one of them handed me some photographs because I was one of the subjects. The bailiff and I had been "extras" in the movie BILLIE BATHGATE, and the courtroom scene had been filmed in our old courthouse across the street. Of Nineteen-twenty vintage, the formidable building housed stately courtrooms with high ceilings and mahogany paneling decorated with oil portraits of former judges.

The movie crew had spent a week reconstructing a Superior Court courtroom, restoring its original luster, and placing the seal of New York State above the judge's bench. I had watched a few cases tried in this room when Jack was District Attorney, and I was still in awe of its imposing atmosphere; it looked the way a courtroom should. Apparently, Hollywood agreed with me.

Amanda, the resident judges' secretary, had helped the film crew locate the judges' portraits from their family homes, and she had been rewarded by being selected as an extra for the filming. Several of us, myself included, had been selected initially as court reporters, because the director had wanted people who could actually type on the steno machine and would therefore lend authenticity by having their fingers on the right keys for what was being said.

But by the time we had been fitted in Nineteen-thirty garb, the director had learned that only men were court reporters during that era. Well, they said, we would be selected to sit in the jury box. Wrong again. Same story. It was not until 1940 that women were allowed to serve on a jury, and this movie pre-dated that. So we became "courtroom spectators," and after reporting to "wardrobe" and "hair" at 5:30 A. M., we sat and waited, constantly rolling our hose back into our garters, for the rest of the day. I spent only twenty minutes actually on the set at 4:30 that afternoon, and we were released at 7:30 P.M.

For all of our patient labors, we knew even then that we probably would wind up on the cutting room floor. I was extremely thankful that I had never considered acting for a career.

Now, a year later, a bailiff was handing me a picture of the three of us, Amanda and another court reporter and myself, minus makeup and modern hairstyles. We were not a pretty sight.

The first order of business on this morning that the trial finally began was administrative. Judge Thompson wanted the racial composition of the jury pool from which the seated jurors had been selected to be placed on the record. According to his notes and aided by the questionnaires filled out by the prospective jurors themselves, the composite was determined to be as follows: Fifteen black males, eighteen black females, twenty white males, twenty-three white females, one male Hispanic, one Japanese-American, one Indian, and one "other," who the judge thought appeared Eurasian, although no one else, including the attorneys and the clerk, would venture a guess as to ethnological origin.

This breakdown by race was being placed on the court record out of an abundance of caution for the appellate court, especially if the defendant was given the death penalty. In the courts attempt to "equalize," however, they also had forced the trial courts to highlight the differences by prejudicially expecting *prejudice in the very process of taking precautions against prejudice.*

The courts were in effect saying that those involved picking a jury expect a black man to vote differently against a black defendant, that they do not trust a white male to judge a black defendant, or that they assume all Blacks think alike and will acquit a black man and convict a white man, or vice-versa for each scenario--no benefit of the doubt, no room for the unbiased juror, no acknowledgement of the pre-existence of the equality they are propounding. And they may be right. One can assume there are as many biased prospective jurors as there are unbiased jurors; some would argue, more.

If the jurors had known that the appellate courts automatically assumed the lawyers' decisions to seat them was based on the color of their skin, they would have been insulted. But the jury was safely tucked away in their jury room while their ethnicity was under discussion.

The record completed, Mr. Carter, prosecutor for the State, began his opening argument. He was of medium height and extremely thin, a forty-year-old black male with a short haircut and thick glasses that seemed large on his narrow face.

He told the now racially equal and acceptable jury that this trial would not cover the entire life of eleven-year-old Sabrina Buie, the victim in this case, but only her encounter with the defendant, Henry Lee McCollum. She had not planned or initiated this encounter with Henry Lee McCollum or the three other young males who had taken her life.

"They took her to the woods, stating, 'We are going to take some of that pussy,' and violated that young girl's body. They agreed that if they let her go, she was going to tell, so they had to kill her, and the method they chose was probably the most brutal and vicious that you've ever heard... The most important part of the State's evidence is the defendant's own statement, although there is physical evidence to corroborate.... You decide whether this defendant is mentally competent to know what he was doing. He may have a low IQ, but he knew right from wrong... This case is not a 'who-done-it'... the question is not whether he was involved. You will hear in his own words that he was. The question is what he did and what he didn't do."

There were three defense lawyers: James Fuller, a well known attorney from Raleigh; Bill Davis, a Robeson County attorney; and Marshall Dayan of the North Carolina Resource Center, a Division of the Office of the Appellate Defender, located in Raleigh, and authorized by statute to assist attorneys in the trial and appeal of capital cases.

The big gun, however, was Fuller, a large man, around forty- five, with full, longish gray hair, sideburns, and glasses. He had tried a number of capital cases during his long and distinguished legal career. In recent years he had focused on civil litigation. Just a few weeks ago, one of his clients had been executed, all appeals exhausted. Mr. Fuller had chosen to be with his client on the day of execution and had witnessed his death.

How difficult it must be for him to turn right around and try another capital case. Whether a defense attorney believes in the innocence of his client or not, he has come to know him well during the long appeals process, and execution becomes a personal blow as well as the ultimate, irreversible, final defeat.

The defense team elected to defer their opening statement until the end of the State's evidence and the beginning of theirs.

Ronnie Lee Buie, Sabrina's father, a small, neat, graying, black man who had worked for J.P. Stevens in Wagram for twenty years was the first witness for the State. He was wearing a tuxedo-like suit. His daughter had been killed in September, 1983. At that time his household consisted of his wife, one of her nieces, five-year-old Ronnie, Jr., three-year-old Juanita, and eleven-year-old Sabrina. He had been working the twelve noon to twelve midnight shift. On the morning in question he had left home about 11:20 for work.

> Q. Did you see your daughter--see Sabrina that morning?
>
> A. Yes.
>
> Q. Did you notice what she was wearing?
>
> A. Yes. She had on blue pants, sneakers, a flowered shirt and a vest-like jacket.
>
> Q. Did you notice her hair?
>
> A. It was the way my wife kept it. She would plait it up--braid it and put these beads like...
>
> Q. Do you recall what color beads might have been worn by your daughter?
>
> A. Red. I know--red.

State's Exhibit Five was identified by the witness as Sabrina's hair clasp.

> Q. What is different about it today than when you saw it in September, 1983?
>
> A. It's all torn up. One of the ends is missing.

The next exhibit was her flowered shirt. Mr. Buie had last seen it "when Officer Floyd called me to the police department and said he found it in a ditch covered with stain."

> Q. Do you know what kind of stain?
>
> A. Blood stain.

Mr. Buie similarly identified Sabrina's blue pants, tennis shoes, and jacket, all of which he had seen her wearing on the Saturday she disappeared.

Leaving his workplace that Saturday at midnight, it had taken thirty minutes for Mr. Buie to drive home. His wife was not there and Sabrina was also not there.

> Q. Did you talk to anyone about where Sabrina was?
>
> A. Yes. My wife's grandmother. I went out in the car and started asking. I went to James Shaw's house to tell my wife that Sabrina wasn't home and we had to find her. I was worried. We rode around town--it might have been fifteen to twenty different houses--and asked.
>
> Q. How long did you search for her that night?
>
> A. Two or three hours.

Mr. Buie had given up the search that Saturday night and "went back home and went to bed."

> Q. How long did you sleep?
>
> A. I got back up at 8:00.
>
> Q. What did you do then?
>
> A. Sometime that day I went to the police station and filed a missing person's report. Then I rode around to different houses to see if anybody had seen her.
>
> Q. Did you search anymore?
>
> A. Yes. We searched in the woods.
>
> Q. How long did you search for her on that Sunday?

A. Until 5:00 A. M. Monday.

James Shaw, his brother-in-law, had assisted Mr. Buie in the search.

"Me and James Shaw went all through the woods. I looked one way, he went another. We went through by Alice Roger's house. He found her."

Q. Where was she found?

A. In a ditch right next to a soy bean field.

State's Exhibit Six was a photograph of the soy bean field.

Q. Did you go over there?

A. No. I didn't want to see her dead. I like to passed out.

Q. Did you know what her condition was?

A. No. I didn't.

The State had no more questions. Defense attorney James Fuller stood, "Your Honor, I have no questions."

Alice Rogers was the next witness. She had known the Buies and Sabrina "all of her life." She had heard that Sabrina was missing and "that Monday afternoon about one o'clock, I was washing dishes and saw a shirt in a ditch." She went to the ditch and noticed that the shirt was blood-stained, so she didn't touch it and asked her neighbor to call Officer Floyd. He came, and she showed him the shirt.

Again, James Fuller stood, "Your Honor, we have no questions of this witness."

Sergeant Larry Floyd of the Red Springs Police Department took the stand. He testified that at nine o'clock on that Sunday morning, September 24, 1983, he had received a radio message from the dispatcher "to go around on Brewer Street to take a missing person's report from Mr. Buie." After taking the report, he "put it out" in the surrounding counties and towns-- her description and a small picture attached to the missing person's report. "Mr. Buie told me they were to continue to check with other people."

On Monday, he had checked with Mr. Buie early to see if his daughter had been found. Later that afternoon, he received a call from Ms. Rogers that she had found a blouse in the ditch next to the bean field. "I picked it up, initialed and dated it, and put it in a bag. I took it to Mr. Buie, but he wasn't home, so I left word for him to get in touch and took it to the police department. Mr. Buie came thirty-five minutes later and identified it as Sabrina's. I knew the red stains on the blouse meant there had been some trouble. We wanted a thorough search of the area, so we called the rescue squad."

Sgt. Floyd then heard a radio message for an ambulance. The body had been located, and he proceeded to this area where James Shaw led him to the spot.

"I saw the body of an eleven-year-old girl lying on her back in the bean field with only a bra around her shoulders and no other clothes."

This officer had also known Sabrina "approximately six or seven years."

A large aerial photograph of the soybean field area that included a residential neighborhood was shown to the jury. Henry Lee McCollum's street and house were pointed out. Officer Floyd testified that he had called the station and requested deputies to secure the area. No one else would be allowed into the area until it was thoroughly searched for evidence. The chief of police called the SBI to assist.

Mr. Carter asked the witness to identify State's Exhibit Eight, a photograph of the remains of Sabrina Buie.

Sabrina's father, wiped his eyes with his handkerchief.

This picture of the dead child was passed to the jurors; it would prove to be the least graphic photograph they would be asked to examine.

Officer Floyd testified that he had stayed on the scene until after dark. The SBI had arrived and started processing the scene.

Mr. Davis handled the cross-examination.

> Q. Did you have an occasion to transport the defendant somewhere?"
>
> A. Yes. The morning of the arrest.
>
> Q. Who was in the car?
>
> A. Just the two of us.
>
> Q. Did he tell you he didn't kill her?
>
> A. Yes. He said he didn't kill anyone, and the only thing he did was hold her hands.

Mr. Davis then asked Officer Floyd about Chris Brown, Darrell Suber, Lewis Moore, and L. P. Sinclair. The witness confirmed that Mr. Suber still lived next door to the ditch where the blouse was found, Mr. Sinclair lived four or five blocks away, and Lewis Moore currently lived "out on Mt. Tabor Road, five to six miles out of town."

What about Chris Brown? The jury was having to think hard. They had been told in opening argument that the defendant had not acted alone; four men had been involved. They had to assume that these were the others' names--and they would be wrong. But names were all that were offered at this time and addresses, all near where the body was found, and the fact that these people were free.

The jury looked confused. The defense team was more or less admitting that their client had participated by "holding her hands." But the defense

knew what the evidence would reveal. Fuller, who headed the team, was playing it low-key; let the evidence come on through and try to save his client's
life. Some would be hearsay, but Mr. Fuller knew that it didn't hurt him, so
he didn't object. The strategy was to try to lessen this defendant's culpability,
to portray Henry as a minor player led by the others, not as a leader or principal participant. When the jury realized that two of these men had never
been arrested, would they be more hesitant to hold Henry McCollum alone
responsible and impose the death sentence?

There was a chance, and right now, they needed every chance they
could get. The evidence had just started, and it would get far worse.

Agent Leroy Allen, a crime-scene specialist and ten-year employee
of the SBI, came to the stand. In 1983, he had been assigned as a local crime
technician. On September 26th of that year, he had been called at 4:45 P.
M. to go to Red Springs. Going through the town, he had turned right on
Maxton Road and arrived at 5:30 in the housing development when it was
still daylight. There, he saw a crowd of people behind the houses, and he
was met by Sgt. Floyd. The houses were separated from the bean field by
a ditch, and there was a small tree line. He did a visual examination of the
body and the surrounding area before taking photographs.

"The body was covered with a brown jacket--one of the men had
covered her. She was on her back. One arm was up behind her head and
one to the side. Her legs were in a "V" position--in other words, they were
open. Her bra was pulled up behind her neck, up over her head. That was
the only clothing she had on." Agent Allen described State's Exhibit Nine,
a close-up photograph of the victim's head, pointing out to the jury the
blood from her nostrils and mouth, insect activity, and vegetation--twigs
and sticks that were caught in her hair. The debris corresponded with the
vegetation in another area on the edge of the bean field where there were
briars and small cedar trees.

State's Exhibit Ten was a photograph taken the next day by the Medical Examiner in Chapel Hill. The numerous scratch marks down her back were parallel. Also visible were leaves, twigs, and part of her bra.

"I helped cover the body with a white sheet to preserve the evidence on the body and assisted in putting her into a body bag."

Exhibit Eleven showed scrapes and scratch marks to the left side of her body and part of her face. Twelve showed the "drag marks" on her opposite arm.

Agent Allen left the witness box with the photographs to stand in front of the jury to show them what he had described.

The courtroom full of people was totally quiet.

Agent Allen resumed the stand.

Q. After these photographs were taken, what did you do with reference to processing the crime scene?

A. I went to another area--back toward Harry's Store-- where there were high weeds and overgrowth. Located within this area was an old trail that had now been grown over. I found several sticks, wooden matches, a cigarette butt, beer cans, and a piece of plywood.

The judge announced a morning break, and I walked down the hall to Jack's office.

Three stories up, the three large rectangular windows overlooked a large area of downtown and a profusion of trees not so noticeable on the ground.

Two streets over, the tall white steeple shining in the morning sun announced the historic First Presbyterian Church, a town landmark, set amidst towering trees still displaying their autumn orange and gold leaves.

Two sparkling red fire engines, ready to roll, sat in the fire station drive-way directly across the street.

To the right, a gingerbread Victorian house, sporting a bright red-tiled roof, dominated the corner. A black wrought iron fence around the back yard, overshadowed by a huge, ancient oak tree, clashed with the sterile courthouse parking lot it backed up to. A few years ago, this magnificent specimen of an era gone by had been scheduled for demolition when a local law firm had bought the abandoned structure and resuscitated it. The project had required massive reconstruction and a great deal of money and patience. It now stood as a proud monument to the older generations that came before us. I had taken many a deposition in that splendid house, but each time I saw it, I studied its round towers, upstairs balconies, and needle-pointed spires, and always found something new. Although this two-story structure was dwarfed by the six-story courthouse, I realized that every time I drove down that street, it was not the courthouse that caught my eye.

Jack had removed his robe and was walking around the office, tired of sitting all morning.

I had a question.

"I heard that Henry McCollum's brother, Leon, would also receive a new trial and that he could no longer be tried for the death penalty because of his age. Is that correct?"

"Yes. He was tried as an adult the first time, but now the statute has been changed. I've been told that the change was due largely to his case."

"Okay. That was my first question. Now, somewhere I picked up that Leon's last name is Brown?"

"Right."

"But he is Henry McCollum's brother?"

"Yes."

"Well, is Chris Brown also Henry McCollum's brother?

"No."

"Chris Brown is Leon's brother?"

"No."

"So Leon Brown is Henry 'Buddy' McCollum's brother, but Chris Brown is not Henry's brother, and he is also not Leon Brown's brother?"

"Right."

"Okay. Who's on first?"

Recess over, the defendant was brought into the courtroom.

Henry Lee McCollum was of medium height with a lean muscular build, a handsome young black man with almost sculptured features, looking more like a model for Ralph Lauren than an inhabitant of death row. Security was tight in our courthouse, the judge's bench "swept" with a metal detector each time before he entered. A special procedure was followed for bringing in a prisoner:

The defendant would face just inches from the inside wall beside the back door of the courtroom while his handcuffs were being removed by a bailiff standing immediately behind him. Another bailiff to the side watched and blocked the rail in front of the spectators and the path to the front door of the courtroom, while a third bailiff stood behind the chair the prisoner would occupy.

The defendant, robot-like during this procedure, did not move so much as a muscle before he was told to do so, and the same bailiff who removed his handcuffs accompanied him to his seat amidst his three lawyers.

Agent Allen resumed the stand before the jury was brought in.

A trial was like staging a show--the jurors were the VIPs, with backstage duties performed before they entered.

Before the recess, Agent Allen had mentioned finding a piece of plywood in the woods, but he had not indicated its size. The six-feet-long by one-foot-wide board was now brought to him wrapped in brown paper and marked as State's Exhibit Thirteen. Allen testified that he had not found it in the same location as the body, but at the opposite end of the soybean field in "an area with overgrowth on top of honeysuckle vines."

> Q. After you found the board, did you notice anything about it?

> A. Yes, sir. A brownish red stain.

Q. What did this stain appear to be?

A. Blood.

After the stains tested positive for blood, Allen then delivered the board to David Hedgecock, a specialist in blood and body fluids at the SBI lab in Raleigh.

Allen had continued his search "as one would travel through vegetation," on an old path. The wood was to the left of the path; to the right, he found a small stick, wooden matches, a cigarette butt, beer cans, a small area that had been "flattened," and a larger stick of wood like a broken limb that appeared to have blood on it.

"I did not test it because it was not a large amount and I did not want to destroy it."

The two sticks were now shown to the witness, along with the matches, what was left of a Newport cigarette, and three Schlitz Malt Liquor beer cans. Allen had processed all of these items for fingerprints later that same night at the Red Springs Police Department. He had found several latent prints, which he turned over to the lab.

At yet a third location, "back toward the housing development where little vegetation droppings from cedar trees were on the ground, I found a red hair braid in a drag-marked area where the vegetation had been disturbed...At the end of the drag area, the ground is pulled up some." Showing a photograph of the area he was describing, he called it a "dug mark in the ground."

The following day was Tuesday, and Agent Allen travelled to Chapel Hill to the Medical Examiner's Office for the autopsy of Sabrina Buie's body.

Q. Who performed the autopsy?

A. Dr. Deborah Radisch. Dr. Page Hudson was there for part of the time along with another pathologist... Sabrina's body bag was placed on the table, and the body was removed from the white sheet and photographed. Then it was cleaned of debris and maggots. Post- mortem finger-prints were taken, using printer's ink on all her fingers.

Allen showed another photograph to the jury, this one of Sabrina's head, taken during the autopsy. The body "had been cleaned, somewhat," and showed abrasions and bruising around her neck and face. Twigs and leaves were in her hair, and "cedar tree droppings" were visible where the remainder of her hair-braid was still located.

After completing the examination of the outside of her body, the doctor opened her remains.

> Q. Before her body was cut open, did you know what the cause of death was?
>
> A. No.
>
> Q. After the internal examination was started, what did you observe?
>
> A. As I observed her, the doctor first opened her chest cavity and then the neck area and removed the inner part of the throat area.
>
> Q. Were photographs taken at this time?
>
> A. Yes.
>
> Q. Using State's Exhibit Twenty-Six to illustrate your testimony, after Doctor Radisch removed the inner throat area, what, if anything, did you observe?
>
> A. A pair of panties and a small stick.

The witness's voice had cracked as he answered the last question. All the years in between had not erased his emotions of that moment.

Q. Were these items visible at all before Doctor Radisch
opened the inner throat area?

A. No, sir, *was the whispered reply.*

The picture was passed to the jury.

Some of the autopsy photographs had been the subject of pretrial
motions. The defense had presented a Motion in Limine to prohibit the
State from introducing these photographs, labeling the pictures as "gruesome, ghastly, and grizzly," whose only purpose would be "to inflame and
disgust the jury." The U. S. Supreme Court had reversed death penalty
cases because they felt selected photographs had prejudiced the jury to the
defendant, and there was a chance that the verdict was based on emotion
rather than reason. The decision of what photographs to allow was a judgment call and left to the trial judge. Judge Thompson had allowed some,
and not others. Whether or not he had decided correctly would be up to a
higher court.

Q. After Doctor Radisch removed the panties and stick
from Sabrina's throat, what did she do with them?

A. I took possession of them.

The panties and two-inch stick were now identified by Agent Allen,
and then presented to the jury in an open bag.

The jurors quickly passed from one to another what the Doctor had
removed from this child's throat.

The Doctor had also given Agent Allen the bra that had been left on
Sabrina's body and a rape kit "which contained a blood sample and slide
smears taken from the victim's vagina, rectal area, and oral cavity."

Returning to Red Springs on Wednesday, the day after the autopsy,
Agent Allen went back over the crime scene area.

"In the same area where I found the hair-braid and beer cans, I now also found a vest, a pair of pants, and a pair of tennis shoes. I photographed them, took possession of them, and retained custody. They were later identified by Mr. Buie as belonging to Sabrina."

> Q. Did you ever go to the Red Springs Police Department when Mr. McCollum was there?
>
> A. Yes. That same Wednesday night with Agent Snead, when McCollum was picked up and he consented to be fingerprinted.

Allen then showed a fingerprint card with prints from the defendant's ten fingers on the front and two palm prints on the back.

The State had "no further questions" of this witness, and lunch recess was declared shortly before one o'clock.

Court resumed after lunch and Agent Allen took his place on the stand before the jurors were summoned. The defense established on cross-examination that latent prints had been lifted from the Schlitz Malt Liquor cans. Allen had taken inked fingerprints from Henry McCollum, Chris Brown, and Darrell Suber.

> Q. Did you take any fingerprint impressions from L. P. Sinclair?
>
> A. I don't believe I did, sir.
>
> Q. Did you get the fingerprint comparisons back from the lab?
>
> A. Yes, sir. I did.
>
> Q. Isn't it true that Mr. McCollum's fingerprints did not compare?
>
> A. Yes, sir.

Special Agent David Hedgecock was called to the stand. He had been with the SBI for eighteen years, and in September, 1983, he had been employed as a forensic serologist for ten years. Having obtained his B.S. degree in Chemistry from the University of North Carolina and having been qualified as an expert in the field of forensic serology "approximately seventy-five times in those ten years," this Court also qualified him as an expert. Agent Allen had personally delivered the evidence to him in Raleigh. His job was to "analyze substances for blood characteristics from fluids."

Gesturing to the rape kit, a small cardboard box, he said it contained a liquid blood sample, vaginal smear, anal smear, oral smear, vaginal swabs, saliva sample, a swabbing of the chest area, a known pubic hair sample, a known head hair sample, and a swab from the left thigh area. On the same day he had also received the plywood board and two sticks. The reddish brown stains on the plywood proved to be human blood, type A, but there was not that much to work with, and nothing further could be determined. The small stick had a reddish stain on "what I'd refer to as the blunt end, although both ends were, in fact, jagged," which was human blood, but not enough to determine any groups. The larger stick had two sharp ends, one more so than the others. The sharper end continued an inch or two from the point, and had "some reddish crust," which was determined to be type A human blood. Two other blood groupings were determined from the plywood and the larger stick, and upon analysis, all matched the sample of Sabrina's blood.

Agent Hedgecock told the jury that swabs are usually used to determine blood groups of any semen found on the smears, so the smears are examined first to see if any sperm are present. If semen is found, then the swabs are examined. No semen was found on the smears.

Q. Are there factors that determine how long semen stays in the body?

A. Yes. Time is the biggest factor. Once semen is deposited, in a living person, it is usually gone in eighteen to twenty-four hours. In a deceased individual, it may last a little longer, two to three days .... Other factors include the physical features semen is exposed to, such as deterioration of the body and, therefore, bacteria ....The length of lapsed time is definitely a factor as to whether or not semen can be found.

Q. What length of time?

A. Two or three days is a general range.

The witness stated that all items he received were returned to Agent Allen except the hair samples, which were sent to someone else for analysis. The State had no further questions.

Mr. Fuller conducted the cross-examination for the defense.

Q. Did any of the tests you did reveal any information about Henry McCollum?

A. I received no evidence from Mr. McCollum to compare these results with.

Q. Is your answer "no"?

A. I received no evidence from Mr. McCollum to compare these results with.

Q. I'll ask the question again. Is it true that none of the tests you did reveal any information about Mr. McCollum?

A. Again, I received no evidence from Mr. McCollum to compare these results with.

Q. No further questions.

Apparently, no samples had been taken from Mr. McCollum, therefore, none could be compared, and with none to compare, none could reveal information. The circular play of words was to confuse the jury. What the jury did know from this witness is that Sabrina had been on the plywood board and the two sticks had her blood on them.

Robert Clay Duncan was next to take the witness stand. Also in the SBI, he was assigned to the latent evidence section and specialized in fingerprints, palm prints, and foot prints. He had been given three prints, and of these, only one print was of value. He explained that fingerprints were composed of 98 percent water and 2 percent oils, and that the ridges on our fingers leave a residual pattern. Only a small percentage of latent prints are identifiable and even a smaller percentage can be linked to one individual.

"Some people don't secrete, and it depends on the surface touched. When the fingers are mashed, it flattens the ridges and leaves a smudge. For example, on raw wood or skin, the moisture sinks in and migrates. Plywood is tough [to find a print on], along with leather, vinyl, and human skin."

This was interesting, but the bottom line was that of all the items examined, there had been only one print of value, and that print had not matched the prints of the defendant.

Again, Mr. Fuller cross-examined.

> Q. Isn't it correct that no evidence or information was produced about Mr. McCollum?
>
> A. I'd say that was fair.

SBI Agent Kenneth Snead was called as the State's next witness. He told the court that during his career he had investigated over one hundred and thirty homicides. On September 26, 1983, he was called at 7:00 P.M. and told about the case.

Q. What day of the week was that? Do you recall?

A. It was on a Monday, I believe. I arrived at 8:10 P.M. at the Red Springs area and met with other officers.

Q. When did the name of Henry Lee McCollum come up?

A. On the twenty-eighth. An individual gave us that information, and I went to the defendant's residence with Agent Allen and Detective Sealey, arriving a little after 9:00 P.M.

Agent Snead said he had had no discussion with anyone, including Agent Allen, about the details of the items that had been found in the woods.

Q. After you and Detective Sealey went to the defendant's home, what, if anything, happened?

A. Detective Sealey stayed in the house six minutes and came out with the defendant. He was not under arrest and agreed to go with us to the Red Springs Police Department.

Q. Did you have any conversation in the car on the way?

A. Just small talk.

Q. During any conversation in the car, did he appear to understand?

A. Yes.

Q. What, if any, conversation did you have once you got to the police department?

A. We carried on a general conversation, and he had no problem understanding me, or I him. His responses were normal, and he had no trouble comprehending.

They had arrived at the police department at 9:20 P.M. The defendant was asked if they could take his fingerprints, and he said they could, so Agent Allen inked his hands and took impressions.

"At 10:15 or 10:20, I looked at the defendant and told him his name had come up in the investigation of Sabrina Buie. At that time, he became visibly upset, and I read him his rights. I told him he had the right to leave, that he was not under arrest. He agreed to talk to me and signed the waiver."

The prosecutor went over the standard Miranda rights waiver in detail with the witness who also told us that the defendant had given Agent Snead his Social Security number from memory.

The Assistant D. A. would want the jury to remember this seemingly inconsequential piece of information when the defense started their case.

SBI Agent Snead continued:

"He answered and initialed all of the rights on the form and then said, 'I'm going to tell you and then I'm going to tell it in court.' He did not appear to be under the influence of drugs or alcohol."

State's Exhibit Thirty-five was a five-page statement of the defendant in Agent Snead's handwriting.

"This was information provided to me by the defendant, Henry Lee McCollum. I looked at him--I knew him as 'Buddy'--I said, "Buddy, all I want is the truth. A lie won't help any of us.""

Agent Snead began to read the statement he had taken on that night. There was no sound in the courtroom, as the jury sat riveted, listening, but instead wanting to cover their ears and close their minds to this worst-nightmare story.

On Saturday, September 24th, I was standing at the intersection of Richardson Street and Old Maxton Road. This was about 9:30 P.M. Sabrina Buie and Darrell Suber came out of Sabrina's house and walked toward me. Louis Moore and Chris—I don't know Chris' last name--they walked up to the stop sign where we were. Just a few minutes later, Leon came up to the stop sign. All six of us walked down the road to the little red house near the ballpark. All five of us boys tried to get Sabrina to give all of us some pussy. She wouldn't do it. Darrell and Chris left and went to Harry's store and got a six pack of Bull Malt Liquor Schlitz, 16 ounce cans. A few minutes later, Chris and Darrell came back with the beer. Nobody messed with Sabrina at the red house. Darrell Suber, Chris, Louis Moore, Leon and me talked about taking some pussy from Sabrina. I agreed to do this. Chris said, 'I'm going to be first.' Darrell said he was going to be second and I was going to be third, and then Leon was fourth. Louis said, 'Fuck y'all. I'm leaving,' and left. Darrell talked Sabrina into going down in the woods behind Harry's store. Darrell, Leon, Chris, Sabrina and myself walked across the bean field to the woods behind Harry's store. We walked across the ditch and Darrell and Chris picked up this board about two or three feet wide and about six feet long and carried it to the woods at the edge of the field. All five of us went into the woods at the edge of the field. Me, Darrell and Sabrina still had our beer cans. We sat there in the bushes, heavy bushes, and drank our beer, and Darrell said, 'I'm sure going to get me some of that pussy.' Sabrina did not say anything. At this time, I grabbed Sabrina's right arm and Leon grabbed her left arm. Sabrina started hollering, 'Mommy, Mommy.' Sabrina was hollering and crying. Darrell took off Sabrina's shoes and then pants and then her panties. Sabrina had a little skinny belt on too. Chris picked up Sabrina's clothes, and Darrell jumped on the girl, took him some pussy. Sabrina was crying and hollering, 'Mommy, Mommy. Sabrina was saying, 'Please don't do it. Stop.' Sabrina kept on hollering, 'Don't. Stop. Mommy, Mommy.' Darrell finished screwing her and he got up. Chris got on top of Sabrina, raped her, screwed her, fucked her. Chris finished. Sabrina was laying there looking pitiful. I was third to get on her and fucked Sabrina. While I was screwing her, Chris held her left arm and Darrell held her right arm. I didn't shoot off in her. After I finished, Leon turned her over. Chris and Leon turned her over, and Leon screwed Sabrina in her butt. Leon finished.

When we all four screwed Sabrina, we had her laying on the board. After we all four screwed her, Darrell said, 'We got to do something because she'll go up town and tell the cops we raped her.' Darrell said, 'We got to kill her to keep her from telling the cops on us.' Sabrina had not been cut on. The panties had not been stuck in her throat. Chris picked up a stick and tied Sabrina's pink panties on the stick. I grabbed her right arm and held her. Leon grabbed her left arm and held her on that side. Sabrina was completely naked, laying on the board, crying. Chris knelt over Sabrina's head and took both hands and started jigging the stick in her mouth. Chris was trying to choke Sabrina to death with her panties on the stick. The stick broke. Chris got a bigger stick and kept pushing the panties down her throat. While Chris was using the stick, Darrell was cutting her with a knife he had. Darrell wiped the blood off his knife with some of Sabrina's clothes and put his knife back in his little case on this belt. The knife had black handles and was a fold-up type. Sabrina was trying to get up during this, but me and Leon held her down. After she was cut and the panties stuck in her windpipe, she stopped breathing and struggling, and we knew she was dead.

I grabbed her right arm and Chris had her left arm. She still had her top and bra on, but was naked on the bottom. Chris had thrown the rest of her clothes in the woods near where we killed her. We drug Sabrina up the edge of the woods toward the ditch and stopped in the edge of the woods. We drug her to hide her body. Chris said, 'We'll dig a hole and leave her here.' Chris started digging and dug a small hole a couple inches deep. Chris couldn't dig with his hands, so he quit. Darrell said, 'Let's take her up in the bean field and leave her.' I grabbed her right arm and Chris her left, and we drug her into the field and left her laying on her back. Chris took her blouse off. She had her bra on, pulled up over her breast. Her breasts were showing. Chris threw her white blouse in the ditch. The blouse had a little flower on it. The blouse was dirty and nasty. The sweater had blood, had the flower on it. We all went home. Chris said, 'We should never had raped and killed her.' We spent about one hour with Sabrina from the time we got her in the woods and left her body. Darrell had blood on his brown corduroy jacket and Nike gray tennis shoes with burgundy seal. Chris had blood on his sneakers, New Yorkers. While we were in the woods, Darrell was smoking Newport cigarettes. Chris smoked Newport also and had a box of small stick matches. After we killed Sabrina, I got home about 1:30 A.M. Sunday morning. We left three beer cans in the woods where we killed Sabrina. I was not drunk and knew what I was doing when we killed Sabrina.

"Signature at 1:37 A. M., September 29th, 1983. Witnessed by myself, Detective Sealey, and Chief of Police Haggin."

Detective Snead ended.

The entire statement was distressing, but the last few sentences seemed unbalanced or "not quite right." The cigarettes, beer cans, etcetera, were out of order, incongruous to the flow of the story, added as an afterthought or an attempt to "fit the evidence" by covering each detail. It was surprising that the defendant had remembered these tiny details--Nikes and New Yorkers, Newports and brown corduroy jackets--while taking an active part in such an outrageous atrocity. Yet...

> Q. Regarding the cigarette butt, stick matches and three beer cans--did you have any knowledge of those at the time of the statement?
>
> A. No. I did not.
>
> Q. Did you threaten him?
>
> A. No. In fact, he was given three cokes--the first at 10:25, the second at 11:15. He had a glass of water at 12:35, another coke at 1:37, and he smoked three-fourths of a pack of cigarettes. He never asked to see anyone or an attorney.

What Agent Snead had just recounted also revealed that the questioning had lasted over three hours. He explained.

The first time, Henry (Buddy) went through it orally. The second time, I wrote it down. I read it back to him, and he signed each page.

Minor mistakes had been made, and each time a word was added, the defendant had initialed the change except for one:

"Sabrina did not say anything.... I'd left out the 'not,' added it, and didn't have him initial it."

Agent Snead then identified a "basic map of the area and of the bean field" drawn by Agent Allen with the help of the defendant.

"X marked where they killed her, with a line to where they attempted to dig and another line to where they dragged her body and left it in the bean field. At 1:35 A.M. the conversation ended. I asked him if he would help me. I took him to where his brother, Leon, was in another room, and asked him, 'Have you told me the truth, Buddy?' He answered, 'Yes. I have.'"

The confession was passed to the jury. Most of the jurors just scanned or glanced at the five-page statement, but one juror on the front row read it word for word. The first two jurors on the back row, a young man with longish hair and an older white- haired woman held it jointly and carefully examined it together. In the previous trial, the defense had tried to suppress the confession, claiming the defendant had not understood, that he had been questioned too long, that he was coerced by the officers, and the statement would inflame the jury. They had lost their argument; the confession had been allowed by Order of the previous judge during pre-trial motions. And they had been right about the reaction.

The effect of the statement on the jury was devastating. That anyone could do such a thing was horrendous, and then to have that person sit in the same room and ask their help had to seem absurd.

But the defense was hoping the jury, once over the initial shock, would understand something more: that it was Chris who crammed the stick down her throat, and that Darrell was the instigator, leading their client, a follower.

Obviously, the defense did not have much to argue with; this statement alone nullified most defensive positions. So their tactic would be to show that Henry was not the main person to blame, and since Darrell had never even been arrested, why should Henry die and Darrell live as a free man? That they believed this argument had some validity was understandable--it was all they had. A man drowning in white-water rapids will hold on to a dandelion if that's all there is.

But, looking at the jurors' faces, I didn't think it would wash. While one course of action is not necessarily fair, the same can hold true for the alternative. Surely, the jurors would be incensed that Darrell was still not held accountable, but that didn't mean Henry was any less responsible.

The defense's argument could be compared to four bank robbers being chased by the police; If the officers caught two and the other two outran them, should they release the first two?

Agent Snead was still on the stand. The defense would cross-examine and try to convince the jurors that their defendant was not the main culprit.

> Q. At 9:00 or 10:00 P. M. on the twenty-eighth had you talked to Agent Allen," at that time?
>
> A. Yes, sir. At 9:10 we went to Mr. McCollum's home.
>
> Q. Had Agent Allen told you about the report from the autopsy?
>
> A. He had.

Agent Snead told the jury that the actual interview about Sabrina Buie had not begun until 10:27, even though they had arrived at the police department an hour before. One reason was the fingerprinting process; another one, "general conversation." What Agent Snead could not say, because it had nothing to do with this case, was that he had questioned Henry initially about two entirely different crimes (more than likely, rumors he had picked up in the investigation). What he did say was that the defendant had been "very co-operative," helping Agent Allen draw the map, and telling him what to place on it. The defense pointed out that the confession took three to three-and-a-half hours, and Agent Snead explained.

"The first time was oral, and the second time, I wrote it down, sentence for sentence. Then I had him look it over. He went through each page and signed the last page at 1:37 A.M."

The defense attorney read from the statement.

> Q. "Darrell suggested that they have sex with Sabrina," is that correct?
>
> A. The way I read it, they all agreed.
>
> Q. Chris said, 'I'm going to be first.' Darrell said, 'I'm going to be second.' On the second page, 'Darrell still had the plastic holder around his beer can'... 'Darrell took off Sabrina's shoes, then her pants, then her panties.' Third page, Darrell said, 'We've got to do something because she will tell.' Darrell said, 'We've got to kill her.' Chris knelt over Sabrina and poked the stick down her neck. Chris threw the rest of her clothes in the woods. Chris said, 'We'll dig a hole and leave her.' Darrell said, 'Let's take her and leave her in the bean field.' Isn't that what Darrell said?"
>
> A. No, sir. That's what your client said.
>
> Q. He said that's what Darrell told him?
>
> A. Yes, sir.

"Yes," Agent Snead said, he had written the statement himself, and he had read it to the defendant.

> Q. Did he read it?

A. I read it to him. He looked at the document. I have no idea if he read it.

Q. And then you asked him to go into the room where Leon was and tell him that he had told the truth about killing Sabrina?

A. I took him into the room where Leon was. I said, "Buddy, did you tell the truth about killing Sabrina?" He said, "Yes, sir." I walked out.

The first day of testimony was concluded, and Court was adjourned for the weekend.

There was no doubt as to our role for the next two days. Three of our four children would be home for the weekend, but, naturally, all on a different schedule. Craig would be home Saturday morning; Allen, late Saturday afternoon. Rob would come in on Sunday, not long before his brothers had to leave, and stay until Monday. I was happy that they all had busy and productive lives, but in recent years, getting all of this crew home at one time and on the same schedule had taken some organization and strategy akin to directing a play. This summer for Jack's birthday, I had sent invitations six weeks in advance with an "agenda of events." In the end, we all enjoyed our time with each other.

Monday morning, Ronnie Buie, Sabrina's father, was recalled to the stand.

He and the defendant were dressed alike--both were wearing a dark blue sweater over a white collared knit shirt.

Mr. Buie testified that Darrell Suber lived near him and that he knew him well.

Q. Did Sabrina ever visit at his house?

A. Yes.

Q. On a regular basis?

A. Yes .

Q. What, if any, relation was Darrell to Sabrina?

A. They were cousins.

Q. Was it unusual for Sabrina to go to Darrell's house?

A. Oh, no. She was over there about every day.

Q. Is Chris Brown known by any other name?

A. Izar.

Cross-examination was a chance for the defense to bring home their main thrust.

Q. Does Darrell Suber still live there?

A. Yes.

Q. He still lives near you?

A. Yes, sir.

Q. How about Chris--or "Izar?"

A. I don't know.

Q. Does he live in the Red Springs area?

A. I couldn't tell you. It's been so long since I've seen him.

Listening to this mild-mannered, polite man testify, the jury had to wonder how he must feel living so close to Darrell, his relative, who, according to Henry's statement, was the probable leader of this group of individuals who had taken his little girl's life in such pitiless, savage fashion. And whose only motive was instant self-gratification.

Lee Sampson was called as the State's next witness, but his testimony would be very brief. He was employed by the District Attorney's office in Robeson County, but in 1983, he had been a resident agent with the SBI for the same county.

> Q. Did you have an occasion to interview Christopher Brown?
>
> A. Yes, I did.
>
> Q. And do you know how old--

Mr. Fuller was on his feet.

"Objection. I'd like to be heard, Your Honor."

The jury was sent out, and Fuller argued.

"The State has sought and obtained an Order to prevent us from putting on evidence during the guilt/innocent phase about the other persons involved. Now, they are trying to put on that evidence. "

Mr. Carter stated that his purpose was "just to establish the age of the persons involved in the crime. That's all I'm going to ask."

"I don't see how that is relevant," Mr. Fuller argued.

"The State contends it has a great bearing as to who played what roles as leaders or followers."

Apparently, the State had their own ideas to combat the defense position that the defendant was a minor player, and it would concern the relative ages of the participants. But the jury would not learn what their ages were at this time. His Honor decided that what the State wanted to show was "premature in this stage of the evidence."

"I further observe that you may open the door for cross examination into a lot more about the co-defendants. So the objection is sustained at this point." Turning to the bailiff, the judge instructed, "You may bring the jury in."

Lee Sampson stepped down, and Doctor Deborah Radisch replaced him on the witness stand.

She was tall, attractive, blonde, and the Assistant Chief Medical Examiner for the State. In 1983, she had held that title only two months before Sabrina's autopsy, which had been performed on September 27th at 9:15 A.M.

> Q. Who was present when the autopsy was performed?

> A. Agent Leroy Allen, Mr. Brickhouse, an investigator and photographer, and Dr. Robert Thompson. I performed the autopsy under Dr. Thompson's supervision.

Dr. Radisch explained that both the body bag and white sheet were removed and an examination done for "trace evidence--apparent foreign materials." One hair was found on Sabrina's left buttock. Her fingernails were examined and clipped. On examination of her external genitalia, there was evidence of rape, and the doctor looked for injuries and took samples using a rape kit.

Employing photographs to illustrate her testimony, Dr. Radisch showed the jury the scratches and abrasions on Sabrina's neck.

> Q. What caused the abrasions?

> A. In my opinion, these injuries were caused by a blunt object coming into contact with this area of skin.... Here you see insect activity. There is evidence of fly larvae or maggots, especially in the left eye.

Objection.
Sustained. The jury is to disregard that last statement.

The defense had maintained all along that the occurrences and effects during decomposition were not the doing of the defendant, and such testimony could prejudice the jury.

The dark marks in the white of the eye indicated bleeding in the eyeball.

Q. Do you have an opinion as to what may have caused the bleeding?

A. In my opinion, the areas have been caused by the stopping of the blood flow to the head--or stopping of breathing, causing the vessels to fill up with blood and pop. There were a large number of blades or "wings," and the pigmented layer of skin had actually been rubbed away.

Q. Do you have an opinion as to how these abrasions may have been caused?

A. Yes, I do.

Q. And what is that opinion?

A. By dragging the body on the back over a rough surface.

Q. Were you able to determine the victim's health status prior to death?

A. Yes. She was perfectly healthy.

On examination, the doctor had noted a tear deep inside the back of the vagina. A small amount of bleeding in this area meant that the tear occurred before death.

Q. What could have caused such a deep tear?

A. A blunt object applied with force.

Q. Is the male sex organ considered such an object?

A. Yes. That would be included in that.

Taking samples from the victim's mouth, vaginal, and anal areas, Doctor Radisch had not detected sperm, adding that sperm can remain viable up to forty-eight hours and would be subject to destruction or decomposition after two or three days.

> Q. If Sabrina was killed on Saturday, and you examined her on Tuesday, would it be unusual not to find sperm?
>
> A. If sperm had been present, it would not be unusual for them to be absent at this time.

The doctor had also found "several short or small lacerations of the lining of the tissue" in the victim's anal area, which, in her opinion, had been also caused by a "blunt object."

> Q. Would that be consistent or inconsistent with the male sexual organ?
>
> A. That would be consistent.

After the body was "cleaned up" and the external examination complete, the body was opened for the internal examination, consisting of three primary areas: the skull, exposing the brain; the chest, involving the heart and lungs; and the abdominal area, containing the rest of her organs.

> Q. At that time, did you know the cause of death?
>
> A. It was not apparent, but at that time, I would be thinking of a blow to the head or strangulation because there was no gun or knife wound.... Because I was concerned about strangulation, the neck area was left intact. The neck organs were then dissected out and removed. The airway was completely obstructed by a pair of wadded-up panties with a stick wrapped within them....This would require a

large degree of force. The upper airway showed a hole in the back of it. The esophagus was perforated.

State's Exhibit Twenty-six, a photograph of the neck organs after they had been removed from Sabrina's body, was now shown to the jury.

"This shows the relationship of the panties and the stick. I kept the area intact until it was photographed, and this is as it would have appeared in her body."

There had been no external view of the panties and stick in Sabrina's throat prior to the internal examination.

Q. Doctor, do you have an opinion as to cause of death?

A. Yes. I do.

Q. And what is that opinion?

A. In my opinion, death was due to suffocation by airway restriction by the panties ....No air is going to be able to get into her lungs and no air could get out of her lungs....The whole body is deprived of oxygen ....Not enough oxygen to the brain can cause abnormality to the heart beating because of carbon dioxide that can't escape.

The doctor answered, "Yes" there would be pain associated with having one's esophagus perforated.

Q. Would you describe the throat area as far as the tissue where you found the stick and where it had perforated?

A. That tissue is soft and vascular--easy to bleed--and has nerves. It is a delicate area.

Q. Could you estimate the length of time it would have taken for Sabrina to die?

A. In my opinion, with this type of obstruction, unconsciousness would occur within a few minutes, with death or irreversible brain damage occurring in four to five minutes.

The defense team did not cross-examine this witness. They had no choice at this point in the trial but to sit there and take what they could not refute.

To the surprise of all save the jurors, Mr. Carter announced, "The State rests."

Everyone except the jury knew that a film had shown on at least one television newscast in which Henry McCollum had "confessed" to a news reporter, and we had assumed the State would present it as evidence. I had seen the film on Channel 11 a few weeks ago when this case had been originally scheduled, before the delays. The incident had taken place during the usual, everyday footage of a handcuffed suspect's being led down a police department corridor. What made it unusual is that when the news reporter asked the prisoner if he had any comment, to the amazement of all (including the reporter), the defendant had replied, "All I did was hold her arms down." The reporter had not understood what he said, and the defendant had repeated it. Apparently, the State had elected not to use the TV tape. The admission of guilt was not new, but they would be the only words the jury would hear from the defendant himself if he chose not to testify in this trial, an admission from the man himself as opposed to one in the handwriting of a law enforcement officer.

Mr. Fuller stood.

"Your Honor, the defendant chooses not to put on evidence, as is his constitutional right."

The guilt/innocence phase of the trial was abruptly over. The prosecutor had held a no-trump hand, with all the aces, kings, queens, and jacks. The defense hand had been dealt during pre-trial motions when their attempt to exclude the defendant's confession had been denied. If their client was found guilty, their evidence would be confined to the sentencing phase.

It was now time for the four attorneys and the judge to decide the jury charge, and instead of listening to pattern jury instructions referred to by number, I wandered the back halls, coffee cup in hand, and talked to Sherryl, the court reporter in the case. Henry's confession had mentioned blood on the shoes and articles of clothing of the two not arrested, and I wondered how far the investigation was followed up.

"You know," I said, "it really boggles the mind that the other two, Darrell and Chris, were never arrested. Was there any investigation of them that you know of?"

"Well," she replied, "there was more investigation back in those days than there is now, because they called in the SBI. But they couldn't tie it to those two without the testimony of Henry and Leon."

"So why didn't the then Assistant D. A. make a deal to get all four?"

"The assumption is that he wanted the death penalty for the two he had."

I was really asking what I thought I already knew. Joe Freeman Britt, the former District Attorney in Lumberton, had been legendary, even appearing on SIXTY MINUTES because he had won such a large number of death verdicts. He had been dubbed by the press as the "hanging D. A." I didn't know the other problems involved, but I had heard this reason before from someone closely connected to this case: he'd rather have two death verdicts and let two go free. It had not been my decision to make, but that course of action seemed like a high price to pay. Now that I knew Leon, Henry's brother, could not be tried for his life, that possibility might exist--

"Do you think they could make a deal with Leon to get the other two?" I asked Sherryl.

"From the little I've seen of him, he didn't seem the type to cooperate. He ranted and raved just during the two or three minutes he was in the courtroom for arraignment," she answered.

"If McCollum is convicted, do you think there is a chance he might testify against the others?"

"Not a chance," she laughed, *"He wouldn't have anything to gain. "*

The judge's charge had been agreed upon in part and ruled on in part. First Degree Rape would be admitted. The defendant had been nineteen at that time, and his victim had been eleven.

First Degree Murder would be submitted, but under two different theories: Premeditation and deliberation, and Felony Murder Rule. The jury could choose one or the other or both. Either way (or both) could mean the death penalty or life; this also, the jury's decision.

The State was opposed to Second Degree Murder being submitted for the jury's consideration. Sure of his strong case, the prosecutor didn't want to give the jury an "out" and did not see any possible way they could vote "not guilty." Mr. Fuller, however, wanted this choice included on the verdict sheet. The two attorneys had argued this point back and forth, pointing out the possible adverse appellate consequences if the jury was not given this choice, and the opposite: the adverse consequences if the jury was given this choice and should not have been--almost a "Catch 22" situation. The prosecutor submitted a case in support of his argument to exclude Second Degree Murder from the jury's choices, and the judge said that he would give them his decision after the lunch recess.

When Jack and I went to his office, he began reading the case.

"Do you know which case the State submitted?" he asked.

"Not really. I heard him say 'Strickland case.'"

"It's Andrew Strickland."

"The same one you prosecuted as D. A.?"

"The same."

"Well, you should be familiar with the facts."

"Strickland" had been a vicious case--another nightmare scenario. Three men had randomly attacked a young girl and her date, tied the boy to a tree and killed him, gang raped her, stomped on her head and throat, and left her for dead. She had lived, however, and had dragged herself naked to a residence to get help. Strickland, considered by all to be the leader and the most cruel of the three, had received life imprisonment; Chance, one of the other men had received the death penalty--different verdicts from different juries (and possibly backwards).

After Strickland's conviction, when the Governor's office inquired whether Jack, still District Attorney at the time, would be opposed to commuting Chance's death sentence to life, Jack had told them he had no objection. His feeling was that Strickland had been the most culpable.

After the lunch recess, Judge Thompson announced his decision. He would allow Second Degree Murder to be a jury choice.

Mr. Carter began his closing argument for the State. "America is a benevolent country, and everybody gives a little something... In this case, you can't give away anything. This case concerns what Henry McCollum did or didn't do to Sabrina Buie. What he did do constitutes first degree murder under felony rape and first degree rape under the theory of acting in concert. If two or more persons act together with the intent to commit rape and murder, they are just as guilty of rape.... When these men began talking about 'pussy' from an eleven-year-old--when these men got together talking about what they were going to do to Sabrina, were they acting in concert? Were they acting as a team? First Degree Rape is defined as intercourse with another person by force and against the will of that person.... The physical evidence testified to by Dr. Radisch was that the laceration deep in her vagina was consistent with damage that could be done with the male sexual organ.... All the testimony is that there was no semen found, but the law does not require ejection of semen. In his own words, he said, 'I didn't shoot off in her,' so they couldn't have traced semen to him anyway. In his statement, the defendant tells us that he grabbed one arm and his brother grabbed her other arm and they put her on the board. She cried and struggled and called 'Mommy, Mommy'.... Four men vented their sexual aggression against an eleven-year-old girl... This is not a case of

Second Degree Murder. Before you find him guilty of second degree murder, let him walk from this courtroom. This is as strong a case as you will ever see of First Degree Murder.... What just excuse did he have for holding her down while others raped and sodomized her, while others pushed her panties down her throat hard enough to penetrate her esophagus? Do you know how painful that was? At one point one of the sticks broke. He had the opportunity then to say, 'Stop this,' but he didn't. He held her down while they found another stick. Premeditation is defined as formed intent to kill the victim in some period of time, no matter how short. The N. C. Supreme Court has said that premeditation can occur in 'the twinkling of an eye.' These four men decided quickly, but they *did decide* that they had to kill her after they raped her so she wouldn't tell. At any time anyone of this crowd could have said, 'This has gone far enough,' when she was lying on that plywood and crying for them to stop.... The State never has to prove motive, but they had one. They went through a reasoning process: 'If we let her go, she'll tell on us... Deliberation means 'in a cold state of blood,' not an emotional state. First of all, you have not heard any evidence that he was in an emotional state, and second of all, there was no provocation. What did Sabrina do to provoke this? Premeditation and deliberation can be found on strangulation alone--it is not an instant process."

The prosecutor had been close to the jury box, walking up and down, presenting his argument passionately. Now he walked to the exhibits table and returned with the small stick, the larger stick, and the victim's panties and held them up to drive home the point of how she had been strangled.

"After they finished, they tried to dig a grave for that little girl to put her in the ground and bury her where her parents might never find her, where animals might get her. But the ground was too hard, so they laid her in the bean field like a piece of dead meat..."

"Another first degree murder theory is the felony murder rule, which is murder committed during the commission of another felony--in this case, rape. This case falls right smack dab in the middle of that theory....

I'm not asking you to do anything that hasn't been proved in the evidence. I ask you to find Henry McCollum guilty of First degree murder, felony murder, and first degree rape. If you do so, you would have done what is right, just and fair."

The jury was asked to leave the courtroom for five minutes; Mr. Fuller wished to address the court for the defense. He told His Honor that he had talked to the defendant about arguing for Second Degree Murder--in other words, that he not even suggest to the jury that Mr. McCollum was innocent, but to admit his guilt--and try to persuade the jury to the lesser offense; his client had given him permission to pursue this line of defense.

The jury returned to their seats, and Mr. Fuller stood.

He kept a greater distance than had the prosecutor, standing in the middle of the courtroom some fifteen to twenty feet from the jury box, and he spoke in calm, measured tones.

"As you were told in the opening statement, this is not a 'who-do-ne-it.' This is not a question of what happened, but a question of what's fair, based on what happened."

But before discussing the "what happened," Mr. Fuller wanted to make sure the jury understood some basics. He told the jury that he felt it was important to dispel some myths about trials; how real life-trials differ from what they see on television.

"It is myth that all trials last forever--that is not true... In a real trial, the lawyers stay seated instead of pacing to and from the witness. Lawyers don't yell objections; they quietly object, and the judge quietly rules." "This is no place for shenanigans or tricks... One reason the trial was so short is that there was so little evidence. You heard about a terrible crime--there is no denying that.... As Mr. Carter said, 'Most of the evidence will come from Henry McCollum.' Actually, *all* of the evidence came from Henry McCollum....The defendant has admitted that he, his brother, and two buddies were the ones that did this....After the defendant confessed, he went to another one and said, as you have heard from Mr. Snead, 'I told the truth.

Now, you tell the truth.' Think back on all the evidence in this case. Mr. Carter has asked, 'Why didn't Henry McCollum leave? Why did he do what he did?' But also, what didn't he do? He was not the one to stuff the panties down Sabrina Buie's throat. He did not get the stick... "

Referring to the decomposition of Sabrina's body shown in the photographs, Mr. Fuller warned the jury not to consider that.

"A lot of the worst evidence took place long after this young girl was dead, and these pictures were used to evoke sympathy. Some of this testimony we heard would have been true if a hunter in the woods had died of a heart attack. That has nothing to do with the legal case. The doctor testified that Sabrina Buie was probably unconscious after two or three minutes. That doesn't mean you shouldn't be upset, but when you are asked by the State not to decide on sympathy for the defendant, that should go both ways."

Mr. Fuller explained to the jury the differences between first and second degree murder. Second degree murder was still a killing that was intentional or with malice, but lacked the "element of premeditation or deliberation."

"I ask you to find Second Degree Murder. No one is asking you to let Henry McCollum off....Use your common sense and fairness to determine what he did and what he didn't do along with the evidence of what other people did....All the killing itself was done by someone else. I'm not asking you to excuse him, but to consider his role.... Let Darrell Suber and Chris Brown have their day in court and be held responsible.... Second Degree Murder is the second most serious crime under our laws. Nobody is asking you to wink.... Isn't justice served if you convict him of Second Degree Murder and he is punished for what he did and not for what others did? He's the one that told the story and tried to get others to tell the truth.... Be just and fair and consider this is his trial and let the others have their trial. "

After a twenty minute break, the jury returned at 4:05 for the judge's charge. Among other things, the judge defined "intent" as "a mental attitude seldom provable by direct evidence" which may be inferred, and that "motive was immaterial and does not have to be proved."

The jury listened intently, hanging onto every word, just as they had to the evidence. The husky young man with semi-long brown hair on the end of the back row sat on the edge of his chair and leaned forward when the judge started explaining the law concerning rape.

"The actual emission of semen is not necessary." The young man nodded and leaned back. *Obviously, this was a question in his mind, one that he had hoped would be answered.*

The judge explained to the jury that they could find First Degree Murder under two theories: premeditation and deliberation or felony murder rule (murder committed during the course of another felony--in this case, rape). The first theory for them to consider was "that the defendant acted after premeditation, that is, that he formed the intent to kill the victim over some period of time, however short, before he acted *or* before the actions of another person with whom he may have been acting in concert."

If the jury believed that Henry had not had time to contemplate what he was about to do, they could find him guilty of committing murder while committing the felony of rape (if, of course, they found him guilty of rape). Or they could find that the evidence fit both concepts.

The basic distinction in the two considerations centered on time--time to think and to form intent. These twelve people would have to try to put themselves in the defendant's place and decide if he consciously thought, "We are going to kill you" at any point before the act itself.

What the jury didn't know at this time was what an extreme difference the jury's choice of theories could make if they convicted him and chose life imprisonment instead of death.

It was now 4:30 in the afternoon, and the twelve jurors were sent to their jury room to begin their discussions. The three alternates were told to call the jury pool room at nine o'clock the following morning for instructions. If the defendant was convicted, there would be a second phase to determine sentence, and their services would be required.

The court personnel, grateful for the chance to stretch their legs, stood in the back hall behind the courtroom talking and waiting. At five o'clock, just thirty minutes after the jurors had retired, they heard a knock on the jury room door and resumed their seats in the courtroom.

The foreman of the jury was a nice looking, professionally dressed black man on the back row. He stood and answered, "Yes, we have" when the judge asked if they had reached a verdict. The verdict sheet was passed by the bailiff to Linda, the courtroom clerk, who read it aloud.

> Guilty of First Degree Felony Murder.
> Guilty of First Degree Rape.

No one was especially surprised, including the defense attorneys or the defendant himself. Henry Lee McCollum maintained the same posture he had throughout the trial, rocking back and forth in his chair, his legs casually spread in front of him, and looking at the floor. Even when the verdict was read, he never changed expression.

Judge Thompson asked the jury to return to their room for five minutes. Mr. Fuller stood and asked for some time to finish preparation for the sentencing phase.

"It's not like this stage of the trial was unanticipated, Your Honor, but we desire some breathing room. Two of our witnesses are in New Jersey, and we did not expect to need them this soon."

The judge inquired how long each side expected to take for their respective evidence. The State replied they would present none, and the defense said theirs would last "about a day." His Honor decided that he would suspend court for the next day, and that they would resume on Wednesday morning. Although he had asked for no scheduling delays, the trial had taken far less time than anyone had foreseen. In just two days,

Friday and Monday, the State had presented their evidence, the defense had presented none, the judge had charged the jury, and the jury had reached a verdict--lightning speed for a case this egregious.

I walked through the courtroom and into the back hall where the judges' chambers and lawyer/client conference rooms are located. On my way out of the courtroom doorway, I noticed that the court reporter looked astonished at whatever the prosecutor had just told her.

The clerk, Linda, turned to me and, thinking I had heard the conversation, said, "Can you believe that?"

"Believe what?" I asked.

"Because the jury found him guilty under only the felony murder rule, if they now decide life imprisonment instead of death, he can receive one life sentence. He can't get another life sentence for the rape because the rape was the felony."

"So under one theory, he can get half the sentence?"

"Right," Linda said, "Life means twenty years, and he's already served eight."

"So if the jury comes back with life, he will be eligible for parole in twelve years? Is that what you're saying?"

"You've got it."

Jack made a valiant attempt to explain the discrepancy to me at dinner. We had decided on Luigi's, a favorite local haunt, and my questions began.

"He has been found guilty. Now the jury will decide death or life, and if they decide life, they have several choices of premeditation, or felony murder theories to decide from. And depending on which "life theory" they decide, his sentence will be different. If he is convicted under premeditation, he can get life plus life, or forty years; if he is convicted under felony murder, that eliminates one life sentence, bringing it down to twenty years, and as he has served eight years already, he would be eligible for parole in twelve years."

"Yes, I can't impose a sentence for the rape--it's 'arrested.' You cannot use as an aggravating factor an element of the crime itself--in this case, rape."

"But one penalty carries double the life punishment?

"I know what you're saying, he replied, "but you're talking apples and oranges. The difference is in the concepts. There is a fine line between the two theories of First Degree Murder. Premeditation and Deliberation carries a higher burden for the jury; it's more difficult to prove. Felony murder was added as a way of elevating more circumstances into the First Degree category. For instance: a robber enters a grocery store with a gun, but not intending to kill anyone; the grocer pulls a weapon; the robber shoots the grocer: felony murder. You would have a hard time proving premeditation, even if it existed. But even if he didn't intend to kill the grocer, he took another person's life in an unlawful situation he created. If you did not have felony murder rule and could not prove premeditation, the jury choice would be either Second Degree Murder or maybe Voluntary Manslaughter. So with two concepts of First Degree Murder, even if the jury cannot determine premeditation based on the circumstances, they can still find him guilty of the most serious murder offense."

"So what makes felony murder rule different than Second Degree, which doesn't require premeditation either?"

"Different theory."

"I know the scenario is different, but as to sentencing? You can get life for second degree murder, can't you?"

"Yes. Actually, you can sentence up to fifty years or life. Life means twenty, but he can receive parole earlier than that for Second Degree. For First Degree, life means twenty years also, but it means a minimum of twenty, and that can be extended to life, literally, if they choose not to parole him."

I conceded that there were some apples and oranges. Not only that, I knew that one obvious hole in my argument was my careless dismissal of the eight years he had already served. A life sentence is a life sentence, and he would serve at least a total of twenty years if the jury chose not to give him death. This case had just sat so long that the discrepancy appeared larger than it was.

Still, the reality was that, as of this moment, Henry MxCullum could be a free man in twelve years, or he could be executed. The jury, of course, was unaware of this fact.

Although parole possibilities should not fall within the purview of the jury, it still seemed they were not being given the full story and may have chosen the premeditation theory if they had been informed of the sentencing differences.

At least, we would have the day off tomorrow.

Jack spent Tuesday "reading the law" in his study and taking a break to get a much-needed haircut.

I took the opportunity of a free day to start my preliminary scouting for Christmas gift ideas. Thanksgiving, just a week away, fell late in the month this year, giving me a week less time to do all those "extraneous but necessary" holiday chores I seem to put off until twenty minutes before the big day. I had made my list this past weekend and knew instantly that my task was humanly impossible. So I took some advice I had heard on one of the morning television news morning shows and made another list of what I was not going to do this year. I didn't believe I would adhere to the "don't do" list, but it made me feel better to look at it. At the end of the day, I sported one small package and no brilliant ideas. The shops I had counted on for multiple possibilities had offered the least selection. The escalating recession was leaving its mark.

On Wednesday morning, court opened a half hour before the jury was due at nine-thirty to rule on objections made during depositions taken earlier by the defense team. This chore took a little longer than the half hour allotted. At ten o'clock the jury was brought in.

"Does the State intend to present evidence?"

"No, Your Honor."

"The defense may proceed."

The defense called Mrs. Marinaro, a middle-aged woman with short brown, curly hair, to the witness box. Possessor of a Master's degree in Special Education, she had taught school in New Jersey before her retirement. "Yes," she knew the defendant, but she had known him as Henry Wallace. Henry had been in her classroom in Public School 32, a middle school in Jersey City.

"The first thing I remember was how clean he was. He always seemed to shine. He would come every day in a clean shirt that seemed to be ironed.

Q. Can you describe Henry's demeanor at that time?

A. Henry stayed apart from the other students. He was shy. But he enjoyed anything that the class did.

Q. Would you describe how Henry performed academically?

A. Academically, he was between a third and fourth grade level, but he did very well.

Q. How old was Henry when you first knew him?

A. I don't know exactly. I imagine he was thirteen.

Q. How did he get along with others?

A. Pretty good. But children will try to annoy one another from time to time. If someone annoyed him, he would mumble and tell me they better leave him alone. I would watch the situation, and, if necessary, tell the other child to leave Henry alone.

Q. What type of students did you teach, Mrs. Marinaro?

A. I taught the educable mentally retarded. Some were neurologically impaired, socially maladjusted, and emotionally disturbed.

Mrs. Marinaro identified a photograph of the school and a snapshot of herself with her class. She was asked to draw an arrow to Henry Wallace, and, with no hesitation, she did so.

"As you can see, for Henry this was typical--standing off by himself. The others had to invite him to join them. He would not impose himself.

Q. How did Henry perform in class?

A. He did as well as I expected. I tried to teach my students something they could do-- reading, writing, math, and fun things like art--mainly, things that would help them cope.

Mr. Carter cross-examined.

Q. Did you have access to the defendant's school record?

A. No.

Q. Were you aware of a behavior problem that the defendant had at PS-9 before he was transferred to PS-32?

A. No. I was not. I could have gotten the records if he had been a problem, but I would have had to go to the principal and request them.

Q. Are you aware that another instructor said that "it was necessary that he be helped now or incidents would occur and that he would do injury to others?"

Objection.
Sustained.

Q. Are you aware that he was described as "so violent he could almost turn you off. You could not get close to him?"

Objection.
Sustained.

Q. "Buddy would go off and explode in a split second?"

Objection. Your Honor, Mrs. Marinaro has testified that she didn't have access to the school records.
Sustained.

Q. Did Henry have any problem understanding you or the material?

A. Oh. All students have problems.

Q. But would you say he did as well as the other students in the class?

A. Oh, yeah.

Q. And would you say that Henry did know the difference between right and wrong?

A. Yes.

Q. And while he was in your class, he showed no violence and was always well dressed and cared for?

A. Yes.

Throughout her testimony, Henry McCollum sat with downcast eyes, rocking in his chair.

Mrs. Marinaro stepped down, and a male court reporter who had taken video depositions now wheeled a television into the courtroom and set it immediately in front of the jury. Two newspaper reporters who were present for the trial changed their positions to be in view of the television. The prosecutor, two law enforcement officers, and one defense attorney also moved to the side benches so they too could see the tapes. All of the depositions had been taken a month ago in New Jersey where Henry McCollum had grown up.

The first person on the screen was William Murphy, the principal of PS-32. He testified that Henry Wallace had come there from PS-9 when he was thirteen years old. He had been described as "overaggressive with his peer group in an educational setting," and it was suggested that he might fare better in a special class. A social worker had submitted his social history as part of a work-up for the referral, and a school psychologist had reported his IQ to be sixty-one. At age twelve, his reading level was third year, second month; his spelling level was third year, seventh month: and his arithmetic level was second year, eighth month. He was known as "Buddy" for the two or three years he was there. The referral recommendations included "counseling to diminish aggressive behavior."

Under cross-examination, Mr. Murphy said that most of what he knew about Henry was from the records. He had little independent recollection of him, only "that he seemed to be a good kid." The record described Henry as educable mentally retarded, "certainly able to understand" and "to know right from wrong."

"Although, Mr. Murphy added, "those students do have difficulty with value judgments."

"Would he know the difference between a criminal and noncriminal act?"

"Yes."

The prosecutor called Mr. Murphy's attention to other entries in Henry's file that were damaging. He had been known to have "an extremely bad temper," and one incident described Henry delivering a karate kick to someone's body while in a "thorough tirade with the foulest language imaginable." In the fifth grade, someone had noted that "the vehemence of his anger is frightening because of his age." One psychologist had found his IQ to be seventy-five, placing him in the higher range of educable mentally retarded, but others had disagreed.

The defendant was still rocking, eyes on the floor, with no visible reaction to what people were saying about him.

Judge Thompson declared a short recess.

We went to Jack's chambers in the back hall. I stood at the large window looking out and thinking about what I had heard. What should or could a school system have done to help those like Henry was not within my province to pronounce, and I wondered how many more potential Henry McCollums were in the fifth or sixth grades now and if the "powers that be" knew any more now than they did then. What was it we had to do to prevent another Sabrina Buie catastrophe? Our schools had more discipline problems now than in the past, so we were apparently moving backwards--not a hopeful situation.

The view from chambers, on the back side of the building, looked toward the Cape Fear River, and I thought of Tim MCLaurin, the author of a book I was reading, KEEPER OF THE MOON. A Fayetteville native, he grew up in a rural community on the "wrong side of the river," and his description of poverty and abuse, cock fights and pit-bull fights staged by hard-working, hard-drinking men who cruised dirt back roads in pick-up trucks, was not the side of Fayetteville I knew. I had never seen roosters bloody each other with razor sharp blades strapped to their legs or snarling dogs with icepick teeth goaded into gutting each other. Yet I knew and thought I understood the people he talked about, living out their days trapped in the disillusionment of their dreams, mimicking their fathers before them, their worst nightmare at eighteen. Too often they were the ones that appeared on the "wrong side of the rail" in the courtroom as well--but not for the more serious crimes--I realized abruptly. These men generally broke minor rules, not major ones. They were "deprived" in their own way, but they reported to work each day and tried to do the best they could for their families. Though not a huge fan of Thoreau, I acknowledged that he may have been right about most of us leading "quiet lives of desperation." Maybe despair is merely a matter of degree. Regardless of geographical location, New Jersey or North Carolina, it all seemed to boil down to varying layers of education, economics, and home-taught values.

Outside the window the day was as gray as my mood. Hundreds of small blackbirds darkened the overcast sky, having made it this far in their yearly Southern migration. Flying in formation, they resembled rhythmic rain-soaked clouds, then dove in a cluster to disperse and light on some vacant lot or among the highest branches of the leaf-stripped trees dotting the downtown landscape. Another flock filled the sky and followed the first group's lead. With the temperature reaching nearly eighty degrees on this late November day, they may have thought they had reached their winter destination, but they would not loiter long. The temperatures were forecast to plunge again, starting tomorrow. We had been playing see-saw with the weather since early October.

Back in the courtroom, the jurors listened to the next three video-tapes. We had been told the volume would be louder on these, therefore, the portable TV set could be moved farther back in the courtroom. But the volume was only slightly louder, and the set remained where it was, just three feet in front of the jury box.

Elizabeth Carmody was a learning disability specialist who, as part of a team, identified students for special classes. As a matter of routine, re-evaluation was required every three years, and she had tested Henry Wallace when he was fifteen. He was aging out of PS-32, and decisions had to be made as to where to place him. His reading recognition placed him at the fourth grade level. He could read the words and break down the sounds, but he couldn't abstract--that is, identify pictures and show he understood the words--he did not have reasoning skills. His auditory memory *(being able to remember what he heard)* was on the level of a nine-year-old.

Rosemary Williams had lived in New Jersey thirty years, although she had been born in Robeson County. She had worked at a nursing home for twenty-three years. Henry was her sister's child, but he had been raised by her mother.

"He loved my mother so much that he stayed when my sister got married and moved away."

Her mother and Henry had lived in Montgomery Complex, a publicly subsidized housing project in Jersey City.

> Q. How was the environment at the time Henry was staying with his grandmother?"
>
> A. Bad. Not as bad as it is now, but pretty bad."

She said that sometimes he liked to spend the night with her "because he loved me and I took him to church."

When Henry was twelve or thirteen, he had turned against her one day at her mother's house.

"He did get a pipe at me, and I called the police, and they took him to the youth house. He apologized later. He always loved and respected me, and he still writes me letters every week and calls me 'the greatest aunt that ever was.'"

Mrs. Williams said that presently she spends her vacations in Raleigh, staying in a motel and visiting Henry at Central Prison. On these visits, she brings him paper and pencils, because "he is the nervous type--he likes to stay busy, like writing or drawing." They talked mainly about his pending court case and "all the family news."

Henry's aunt further testified that while her nephew was growing up, he had avoided confrontation.

"He was not the type to want to fight. If he saw a fight, he would go away around the building to stay away from it."

He hung around with only three friends.

"The other boys were too fast and rowdy--the type who wanted to fight. He stayed out of the reach of the boys that carried guns."

Henry's neighborhood had been "a violent place to live."

> Q. What was the Montgomery Street building like on the inside?

A. There were all kinds of people--people shootin' up all day and all night, markin' walls. There was gambling--betting money and rollin' their reefers, or what have you, because they don't have locked doors to the building. Anyone can walk in. You could clean it up one day, and it'd be back the next."

In the early Eighties, Henry had moved to North Carolina.

Q. Why?

A. Henry had found some money at the fairgrounds, forty or fifty dollars. Some boys claimed the money the next day and told him it was their money for college. They threatened him, and he was sent to North Carolina.

Mrs. Williams also told the jury that Henry had been subject to bad headaches and he had received treatment for them.

Q. Do you know what caused his headaches?"

A. Well, no. They didn't say. He hit his head to the wall, or something like that."

She further noted that Henry had been spoiled by his grandmother.

"He was her pet--and if he didn't get money or something he wanted, he would get a little headache."

Chirley Lee Sellers, Henry McCollum's first cousin, had little more to add to the overall picture. She had grown up in Jersey City also and described the Montgomery Complex as a "basically pretty decent area" where "everybody got along."

"Henry used to ask me to help with his school work. He was basically shy and got his feelings hurt a lot. He stayed to himself, and people don't understand that."

Although she had attended the same schools, she was approximately eight years older than Henry and totally unaware of the discipline problems he had in school.

The last deposition was that of Henry's real father, James L. McCollum. He had never been married to Henry's mother, Mary Wallace, and he had married someone else when Henry was twelve or thirteen. He and his wife lived ten or twelve blocks from Henry in Jersey City.

"My wife, Priscilla, and I used to take him to church on Sunday and out to eat at McDonalds, and we used to buy him clothes."

Working two jobs, Mr. McCollum had not had much time for Henry, and his son was around ten when his father started taking him places on Friday nights and Sundays, mostly.

He had noticed Henry was "slow in doing things" around the age of eight and that he didn't like school; but he thought Henry was progressing. When Henry bagged at a supermarket, his father made that his "place of business" so he could tip his son.

"We had a very close relationship. My wife was understanding, and his grandmother was understanding. It was a family."

Nevertheless, he was totally unaware that his son was a constant truant problem or that he had been judged as an aggressive and hostile child or that he had threatened his aunt with a steel pipe.

"I never got a bad report on him for his behavior."

Mr. McCollum had stayed in contact with Henry while his son was in prison.

"I go down a couple of times a year to visit him. We mostly talk about the Lord. I say to him, 'The Lord Jesus God knows why you're here.' He would always say, 'Daddy, I don't know why I'm here. I hadn't done anything.'"

The jury was excused for lunch, and Jack and I found a place close by where we could get a quick salad bar while he read. The defense had presented him with a motion for special instructions they wanted included in his charge after they rested their case. Their motion was based on the Enmund case which had stated that the defendant had to have been an active participant in the murder with intent to be eligible for the death penalty. Since the jury in this case had not found the defendant guilty on the premeditation and deliberation theory, the defense contended that it was "a whimsical flight of fancy" to instruct now on the death penalty. Jack read their request, but wasn't sure he agreed.

Court resumed at 2:30.

The weather had become almost muggy at mid-day. The juror on the back row had removed his sweater and several of the women had abandoned their jackets.

Despite the prosecutor's strong objection, the defense attorney was allowed by the judge to read to the jury a one- sentence statement from the warden of Central Prison stating that the defendant had committed no infractions since his incarceration.

Dr. Faye Sultan, a clinical psychologist in Charlotte, took the stand for the defense. In addition to her private practice, she worked in conjunction with the Department of Corrections as part of a program funded in part by the State government and in part by private organizations. A listing of her academic publications filled the next five pages of her curriculum vitae, and a copy was provided to each juror. One-and-a-half pages told of her community work, honors and awards. She stated that she had testified for both the State and the defense in other trials, and she had been asked to conduct a psychological evaluation of the defendant by the defense attorneys.

In addition to reviewing available records and history, she had met with Henry McCollum twelve times in sessions ranging from forty-five minutes to two-and-a-half hours.

The formal psychological testing had been done by someone else in her office, however, because "it has been shown that it is best to have the tests done by a different person than the one who has developed a relationship with him."

Dr. Sultan stated that Henry fell into the educable, mentally-retarded range, that his mental age range was eight to ten years of age, that he was not able to understand instruction, that he had trouble controlling his impulses, that he assumed strange body posture and facial expressions, and that he would either under-react or over-react emotionally as a child would.

> Q. What you have described--was that confirmed by your formal testing?

> A. Completely.

Using the Weschler Adult Intelligence test in 1990, she had found his IQ to be 69. She compared this score with other scores from the past--61 on the Stanford Binet in 1975, and 56 on the child version of the Weschler test in 1978. Employing other tests for reading comprehension, she testified that he had improved only one year, from 1.9 (almost second grade) in the fifth grade to 2.9 (almost third grade) at his present age of twenty-seven.

> Q. Do you have an opinion on his ability to stay focused on a particular problem?

> A. He has two kinds of attention problems. He is unable to gather enough information in his head to pay attention, like a child of six, seven, or eight. Another attention problem is that he will take a piece of information out of context--latch on to two or three words and think that's what has been said."

The doctor told the jury that when she had met Henry McCollum, she noted that he had trouble understanding what she was saying. When she asked him to repeat back to her, the information was nothing like the original. She had found him highly suggestible, highly dependent, and anxious to gain approval.

"For example, if I said, 'the food is quite good here,' he will think the food is good here. He would agree that those were his feelings because that is what he thought I wanted him to feel."

Another test consisted of showing the defendant pictures and asking him to tell a story that must have a beginning, a middle, and an end.

"He was able to complete most of this request."

However, his stories had demonstrated "overall depression, a sense of helplessness, difficulty in personal relationships, and his view of male/female relationships was unrealistic."

"Yes," the defendant had been treated in prison with counseling by psychiatrists and with medication. The records indicated that he was found to be fearful, timid, extremely passive, highly dependent, and that he had periods when he was out of control, not physically, but mentally.

In her opinion, the defendant was "generally passive," as opposed to hostile, and he had significant psychological problems separate from his intellectual capacity. His perception of reality was distorted, as was his recollection of his school years, but he was progressing.

"He used to tell me that he used to be retarded, but isn't any more."

Mr. Fuller placed a large writing tablet on an easel in front of the witness and the jury and questioned Dr. Sultan regarding the eight entries, one by one.

1. Mental disturbance and retardation

2. Emotional disturbance

3. Subject to influence and influence of others

4. Difficulty conforming conduct to law

5. Difficulty understanding adult English

6. Difficulty with problem solving

7. Difficulty anticipating social consequences

8. Difficulty thinking clearly under stress.

She replied that the defendant had each of these problems.

Dr. Sultan stated that, in her opinion, part of the defendant's mental disturbance was due to post-traumatic stress syndrome from an incident that had happened to him between the ages of ten and twelve.

"When I first started interviewing Mr. McCollum, he had a degree of fearfulness that I could not explain by what I knew. I knew it was true that he was abandoned by his mother and left with his grandmother. He felt abandoned again when his mother moved to North Carolina. But this didn't explain him talking about his fear of being hurt by other men in prison."

Upon further questioning, the defendant told Dr. Sultan the following story:

> "When he was ten or twelve, he used to bag groceries for tips, as
> was the custom in his neighborhood. One man had asked him
> to carry his groceries home and he would give him a tip there.
> When they got to the man's apartment, the man hit him on the
> back of his head. He fell on the bed and the man raped him for
> a prolonged time--in his words, 'a long time, one or two hours.'
> Henry walked back to his grandmother's apartment and washed
> himself; he was bleeding. He remembers someone asked why he
> stayed so long in the bathroom, but he didn't tell because he said
> the man had threatened him and would hurt him worse if he
> told."

"He continues to have flashbacks of the rape and fantasizes that a person might be harmful to him in what we would consider normal situations. In situations where he feels he is in danger, he describes a numbness or feels paralyzed and is unable to respond. This is another documented symptom of post-traumatic stress syndrome."

In Dr. Sultan's opinion, the defendant did not possess the ability to plan and would be unable to formulate intent.

On cross examination, Mr. Carter asked Dr. Sultan whether or not the defendant had talked to her about the murder and rape.

> A. Yes. Henry told me that he was among five men who met together one evening. Darrell suggested they abduct Sabrina. He said, 'Count me out.' Darrell called him a chicken, and it made him feel like nothing. Chris called him a punk, and it made him feel like more than nothing. Henry told me that he was instructed by Darrell. He told me, 'I didn't mean for them to kill her. I was afraid of those guys.' He said at some point he grabbed Darrell's arm when Darrell was going to hit Sabrina. 'I should have died instead of her. I would have saved her if I knew how. I couldn't move. Something was holding me.' He said he wanted to do things--he thought them but he couldn't act.
>
> Q. Didn't he also tell you 'one of those devils pushed him on top of her' and he did not have sexual intercourse?
>
> A. That's what he told me.
>
> Q. And did he tell you he was the oldest one there?
>
> A. Yes. Chronologically, the oldest.

The witness added that despite Henry's physical age of nineteen, his mental age was between six and ten.

"When you tell me he was older, that has no significance to me." she added.

Mr. Carter pointed out that Leon, Henry's brother, had an even lower IQ level.

Q. But you didn't interview any of the other individuals?"

A. I never said they functioned at higher levels.

Mr. Carter asked the witness about testifying four times in the past year in Robeson County for defendants, giving the same tests, and in each case saying the defendant had a low IQ.

A. I can recall one where the defendant was mentally retarded.

Q. Dr. Sultan, these cases just happened a year ago, and you can't remember?"

A. I can't remember all the specifics in those cases.

Q. Did you ever talk to his mother, his grandmother, or his aunt?

A. No, sir. I did not.

Q. Even though these were the people closest to him?

A. I had a good bit of information provided from those people and I was able to read that information.

Under the law, the criterion for holding a person with mental illness accountable for his actions is whether or not the person knows right from wrong.

Q. In your opinion, does the defendant know the difference between right and wrong?

A. In a theoretical sense.

Q. Does he know it is wrong to kill an eleven-year-old girl?

A. Yes. He does.

Q. In your opinion, Doctor, would you agree that he could be dangerous to society later on because he can't conform his conduct to the law?"

A. I'm not in a position to predict the future.

She added that the defendant functions well, in a structured environment like prison because "he is passive and follows the rules."

Asked about the "steel pipe" incident, Dr. Sultan said she was aware of it and knew why it happened.

A. He said he wasn't given as many pieces of candy as the other children. But when he was told to put the pipe down, he did. His response was immediate.

Q. His aunt called the police. You don't think she was afraid of him?

A. She said why she called the police--to teach him a lesson. He also lived with his grandmother who was elderly and did not provide discipline.

Mr. Carter questioned Dr. Sultan about Henry's being involved in a fight with another inmate while in prison, trying to refute the statement by the warden.

"Yes," she knew about it.

Q. You forgot to tell that to the jury when they said he had no infractions, didn't you?

Objection: That was another witness.

Sustained.

Dr. Sultan calmly asked the prosecutor for a glass of water, but received no response. Mr. Fuller took her a glass.

Q. Dr. Sultan, are you familiar with an article written by a psychologist in Rhode Island that states that among his professional colleagues there is a 'tendency to seek abnormalities when a brutal crime has been committed'?

A. Some professionals might. I certainly don't.

Q. Were you aware that the defendant testified in the last trial and denied the rape and murder--that he said he was somewhere else? How could he follow the questions and answers and deny involvement if he doesn't understand?

A. I can theorize, but I don't know.

Q. Did you read the transcript from the first trial?

A. No.

Mr. Fuller asked a few more questions on redirect.

Q. Doctor Sultan, do you have an opinion of the differences in how Mr. McCollum functions in a structured and a unstructured environment?

A. Yes. I do. It has been shown that the defendant functions very well in a structured environment and sometimes quite poorly in an unstructured environment.

Mr. Carter re-examined.

Q. Doctor, you are opposed to the death penalty, are you not?"

Doctor Sultan paused, as if weighing her answer.

A. Yes, sir. I am.

Q. In fact, you are an advocate of alternatives to incarceration, are you not?

A. I am an advocate of alternatives to incarceration for nonviolent crimes. Yes, sir.

After a short afternoon recess, court resumed at 4:30, and the jury, filing in from their special room, took their seats.

Mr. Fuller stood.

"Your Honor, on behalf of Henry Lee McCollum, we rest."

Mr. Carter stood.

"Your Honor, I need to be heard out of the presence of the jury."

The judge smiled as he told the ladies and gentlemen of the jury to please go to their jury room. The jurors smiled back as they stood and exited the same door they had just entered.

The Assistant D. A. wanted to use the testimony of L. P. Sinclair as a rebuttal witness. Mr. Sinclair was deceased, but his testimony was preserved in the previous trial transcript.

The defense opposed this evidence:

"It goes to the state of mind at the time the rape occurred and whether the defendant had malice and intent to commit the crime and tends to discredit the testimony of the doctor and show the defendant's ability to understand what he was doing," the prosecutor argued.

"The question of malice was finished yesterday in the guilt phase. This has nothing to do with sentencing. The jury decided malice yesterday when they found him guilty," Mr. Fuller countered. "Some of the testimony contains references to another party that would be objectionable in this trial."

The "another party" was Leon, who had been tried jointly with his brother Henry the first time in 1984.

There was also a question of hearsay, but the State maintained that Dr. Sultan had opened that door when she testified to what Mr. McCollum had said.

After reviewing the transcript and what the testimony would be, His Honor allowed it, but the testimony would be edited to leave out references to Leon, and the lawyers and the judge would have to go line by line and decide what to delete.

The jury was sent home. It was 4:45 in the afternoon; there was no reason for them to sit and wait while this task was accomplished.

Thursday morning, we took separate cars because I had a noon appointment and some errands to run. By the time I left home, the rain was coming in sheets, the courthouse lot was full, and I finally parked at the Victorian-house law office. My umbrella was almost useless against the torrential downpour, my clothes damp and half wrinkled by the time I reached the courtroom. I hoped the farmers and ducks were happy.

The prevailing mood in the courthouse was as gloomy as the skies.

Mr. Sampson, the investigator with the D.A.'s office in Robeson County, took the stand. He testified that he had met L.P. Sinclair during the investigation of the rape and murder.

> Q. At some point during the investigation, did he testify?
>
> A. Yes.
>
> Q. Under oath?
>
> A. Yes.
>
> Q. Was Mr. Sinclair later killed?
>
> A. Yes. I believe it was in 1990.
>
> Q. Do you know the manner in which he was killed?

A. Yes. He was shot.

Q. Now, this defendant had nothing to do with that incident?

A.. No.

Mr. Sampson now read Mr. Sinclair's answers from the transcript as Mr. Carter asked the questions. The day of the murder, Mr. Sinclair had gone to Leon Brown's house, arriving around 7:30 P. M., and leaving ten minutes later with Leon. They walked to Lisa's house, where "they was playing music in the backyard in a shed." Buddy and Chris Brown arrived, and Buddy and Leon started arguing, almost getting into a fight. "We left at twenty after eleven."

> Q. Now, you say "we left at twenty after eleven." Who is "we?"

> A. Me, Buddy, Leon and Chris.

> Q. All right. And how were you traveling at twenty minutes after eleven when you left Lisa's house?

> A. By foot.

> Q. By foot? And what route did you take from there?

> A. We left there and went straight on across and went to a small path in front of the bus place behind the office, went on through the project, to the back of the playground, kept walking, got ready to separate, then we separated. Then Leon hollered, said, "Hey Man, do you want to go and watch Showtime?"

> Q. All right. What did you say?

> A. I said, "No."

Q. Then what happened?

A. Then all of a sudden Buddy and Leon huddle up. Chris Brown was with them, but he did not huddle up with them, and Buddy said, "I'm going first."

Q. Speak up, please. Buddy said what?

A. Buddy said, "I'm going first." Then Leon said, "I'm going first." They kept on saying that.

Q. How many times did it go back and forth between Buddy and Leon, each saying, "I'm going first?"

A. Five or eight times.

Q. What were you doing during this period of time?

A. Listening.

Q. Then what happened?

A. Then Buddy calls me over to where he is at, and he says, "Let's go get some pussy from Sabrina. We'll take her back there in the woods." I looked at them and I said, "Fuck it. Fuck all of you," and I got the hell out of there.

Q. Did they say what they were going to do to her when they took her back there in the woods?

A. No, sir, but they said they were going to get some pussy.

Q. After making your statement to them, you did what?

A. Went home.

Q. Did you see them anymore that night?

A. No, sir.

Q. Okay. So when you left that area, who was there at that time?

A. Who did I leave standing there?

Q. Yes.

A. Buddy and Leon and Chris.

Q. All right. The next day was Sunday, the 25th of September. Is that correct?

A. Yes, sir.

Q. What did you do that Sunday morning?

A. Sunday morning I went to church, Sunday School.

Q. Who did you go with?

A. My mother and, you know, little sisters and brothers.

Q. That afternoon did you have occasion to go anywhere?

A. Not right then, but I left home about 3:30.

Q. Where did you go, please?

A. I went down Baldwin Street, and as I was leaving, I met up with Buddy and Leon.

Q. Now, did you have a conversation with Buddy and Leon there in the street?

A. Yes, sir.

Q. Tell the jury about that, please.

A. We stopped in front of a big white house, and then they get ready to pass me, and then Buddy called and Leon walked up a little bit. Buddy called me to the side. He said, "Hey Man, don't tell." I said, "Tell what?" He said, "We got some of that pussy. We tore it up." Then he said, "We killed her." The minute he said that I struck out. I went to the Seven-Eleven, got a pack of cigarettes, and went home.

The courtroom was deathly quiet. The portrait the defense had tried to paint of a passive, child-like, go-along-with-the crowd, in-the-wrong-place-at-the-wrong-time defendant had just been severely smeared.

The defense lawyers also re-enacted a small portion of the cross-examination of this witness from the transcript to point that out. Mr. Sinclair had not originally told investigators of these conversations with Buddy because "I didn't want no part of it at all."

The State rested.

But the defense had come up with their own rebuttal to the State's rebuttal. District Court Judge Carmichael from Lumberton walked to the witness stand.

He testified that before he became a judge, he had known L.P. Sinclair as a client.

> Q. Were you able to form an opinion as to Mr. Sinclair's truthfulness and veracity?
>
> A. In my opinion, he was not a truthful person.

However, cross-examination revealed that he had not met Mr. Sinclair until 1989, six years after Sabrina Buie's death.

> Q. And is it true that prior to 1988, Mr. Sinclair had not been convicted of anything?
>
> A. Not that I'm aware of.

Mr. Fuller submitted a Certificate of Fellowship, showing it to the jury and explaining that Henry McCollum had earned this in prison for his religious studies.

The defense rested.

The jury was sent out for an extended break. Everyone else involved in the case took a shorter break and returned for the charge conference.

I left to meet my twelve o'clock appointment. The rain had slackened to a drizzle, but it was still warm. The cold weather had not reached us as predicted, so the confused blackbirds were probably still hanging around, doubting their built-in mile markers and wondering why their journey seemed shorter this year.

When I returned at two o'clock, I knew from Jack's easy smile that he had made his decisions on the issues he had to consider before charging the jury.

The jurors took their places for the final arguments. The defense would go first.

Bill Davis, the other defense counsel, from whom we had heard very little, stood at the podium and began.

"During jury selection, you promised to hold Henry Lee McCollum accountable for his own acts, not the acts of others. We are not asking you to excuse him. But Henry McCollum is not the only one involved--he identified three others. The court has told you that you may consider if he was acting in concert with Darrell Suber, Leon Brown, and Chris Brown....The General Assembly has set out guidelines as to whether you give him life or death.... They have recognized that the death penalty is not always appropriate, which gives you the opportunity to save someone's life. If you find that he was emotionally disturbed or mentally retarded, you may consider that and give it weight. This is a child in a man's body. He has the mental age of six to ten years, according to Doctor Sultan. Hold him accountable for what he did, but judge him as an individual."

After ten minutes, Mr. Davis sat down.

Mr. Carter's argument on behalf of the State would be much longer.

"This is an important case, not only to you as citizens, but also to the Buie family. Judge Thompson told you at the beginning of this trial that the death penalty was not always appropriate....The death penalty is reserved for cases that are so heinous, so atrocious, and so cruel, that the only appropriate sentence is death .... This case is special because a special person is involved--an eleven-year-old child who had a future .... The conscience of your community cries out. Sabrina's family cries out....The death penalty would not be revenge. Revenge would have been Ronnie Buie tracking down the ones who did it, but that too would be first degree murder....If you can't recommend the death penalty in this case, ladies and gentlemen, do you think you'll ever hear of a case in your life that it is appropriate? Sabrina Buie is not here to talk to you today. A stranger has to stand in front of you and plead for her ... Put yourself in Ronnie Buie's place. If you can truly do that and still say give him life, then do so.... Mrs. Marinaro loved all her students. Good. We need good teachers. But the individual she knew in her classroom is not the same individual that you see across the courtroom today.... The person you see across the courtroom is the kind of person that Doctor Sultan said could not conform his behavior to the law. But your values are different than Dr. Sultan's. You said you believed in the death penalty. She doesn't. Doctor Sultan tells you that this defendant has trouble focusing, yet on three different occasions, this defendant has taken the witness stand and said he had nothing to do with Sabrina Buie's death. He is able to focus on what he wants to when he wants to... Who's following who? Henry McCollum was the oldest one there, but now he's saying that all of them were making him do it... They say he is really a six to ten-year- old. How many six to ten-year-olds do you know who would commit rape and murder? They say he is depressed in prison. What do you think Ronnie Buie has felt? Do you think he likes the idea of seeing his little girl's picture and the clothes he saw her wearing when he went to work at 11:30 that morning?"

Mr. Carter held up the bloody blouse, blue pants, panties, and stick for the jury to see.

"This is the legacy of Henry Lee McCollum and his friends." The prosecutor held up the photographs the jury had studied before.

"How many of you would like to see your child looking like this... the skin scraped off her back after these defendants raped and killed her?"

Objection.

Overruled.

"Her throat laid out on a table--"

Objection.

Sustained. The jury will disregard that last statement.

"What does Buddy McCollum tell L. P. Sinclair? 'We tore that pussy up. We killed her.' Then he puts his hand on a Bible and denies it."

"When the defense attorney puts his hand on the defendant's shoulder, he is telling you, 'He's all right.' He's not all right. He's a dangerous, dangerous person. Dr. Sultan said he has the mind of a six to ten-year-old. 'He's all right.' He's not all right. He is a dangerous, dangerous person." "Twenty million people fall into a low 1Q range--"

Objection.

Sustained. The jury will disregard that last statement.

Going down the list of mitigating factors that would appear on the sentencing form for consideration by the jury, the prosecutor argued against them.

"He can't conform his conduct, not to rape and murder? Is that what they're saying? They say he didn't do well in school and has a low 1Q. That's true, but what's that got to do with killing a little girl? They say he couldn't communicate in English. But he talked to the officers and testified. His aunt said she didn't have any problem communicating with him.... They say he is unable to carry out a plan. But he carried out a plan to lie on the stand on three separate occasions... They say he doesn't anticipate consequences. If he doesn't know the consequences, why did he say, 'Don't tell'? They say he had limited contact with his father. That's not what his father said."

"The pathologist told you it would take approximately five minutes for her to die. Mr. Fuller said two minutes. Even if we use that lowest estimate, time two minutes on your watch when you go to the jury room. Can you imagine living two minutes while somebody stuck a stick wrapped in panties down your throat? And don't forget the rape--for an hour by four people. Are we supposed to disregard that?"

"They took more than 'pussy' that night. They took a daughter from her father. They took a daughter from her mother. They took a child from this earth. She is somewhere in a coffin in Robeson County, and I am the stranger that has to speak for her."

Mr. Carter slowly paced in front of the jury box reading aloud the defendant's five-page confession, dramatically, deliberately, in a clear, resounding voice that saturated every corner of the hushed courtroom. The jurors' faces were pained, as if pleading with him not to make them listen to this play-by-play description again.

Mr. Buie sat leaning over his lap with his head in his hands. The jurors looked as if they were having great difficulty maintaining their composure, and they had never loved Sabrina as he had. Each time they heard this graphic story, it conjured sharper, clearer visions, in vibrant color, as if it were happening right here in front of them and they were powerless to stop it. They sat like zombies, suffering through the grueling details.

Mr. Fuller stood and began his plea for Henry McCollum's life.

"This young man, emotionally disturbed and mentally retarded, told the truth, and he is being asked to take all the blame, not only for what he did, but for what others did as well.... This trial ended Monday, and I respect your verdict. I ask you not to ignore the law--this is not a call for sympathy, but it is not a call for revenge either. I'm asking you to follow the law."

At this point, Mr. Fuller placed two pages of enlarged photocopies on an easel in front of the jury. The poster-sized blow-ups were a portion of the N. C. Supreme Court's ruling in State v. Stokes on the subject of whether or not, dependent on the circumstances, the death penalty is the appropriate punishment. Using a pointer, the defense attorney read the pertinent passages, explaining to the jury that the "focus must be on the individual conduct of the accused and not on the conduct of the others."

"What you have just *heard* from Mr. Carter was an impassioned and transparent plea for sympathy for the victim and for the victim's father, whom we all have sympathy for ... Sabrina Buie's life was worth saving, and if there was anything we could do to bring it back, we would. Sabrina Buie has had justice. Henry Lee McCollum has been convicted of first degree murder, and that's justice. Throughout Mr. Carter's argument, whether it was on purpose or a slip of the tongue--I'll try to give him the benefit of the doubt--he used the word 'excuse.' I've come to know you, talked to each of you, watched you as you've watched me--have I ever asked you to excuse Henry McCollum for what he did? Instead, I ask you to honor the quality of life. I'm going to take some time, and I won't apologize for it. I'm scared. I've been practicing law for twenty years, although my practice usually involves car wrecks. But this time somebody's life is on the line and I'm afraid. It's late, you're tired, but I need you to reach inside yourself, because I need you. When you were selected for this jury, I told you that you would hear a gruesome case, and you said that in spite of that, you would go into the sentencing phase with an open mind. I ask you to consider all the evidence: his educators, his family, Dr. Faye Sultan, the letter from the warden, and his discipleship--his study of religion while he was in prison. Dr. Sultan's testimony, under oath, was that Henry McCollum told her that he was not only sorry, he was embarrassed--he was humiliated that he didn't do anything to save her life, that he should have been the one to die. "

Mr. Fuller, referring to Mr. Carter as a passionate prosecutor, complained that "perhaps, his passion got away with him in closing argument," and proceeded to dispute what the Assistant D. A. had told them.

"He told you that Dr. Sultan favored alternatives to incarceration, when in fact she said she favored alternatives to incarceration for non-violent crimes."

"He told you that the defendant testified on the stand on three separate occasions, when actually, it was three different times--there's a difference. He can't talk to you about what he knows not to be true. It's not proper."

Mr. Carter was on his feet, objecting and asking to be heard.

Mr. Fuller looked none too pleased. Arguments in and of themselves are not evidence, and customarily, opposing attorneys give each other a wide berth and do not object unless the subject matter is strictly forbidden, knowing that they want the same freedom when it's their turn.

The jury was sent out.

Mr. Carter objected strongly to the court that Mr. Fuller was not just misrepresenting what he said, but, in essence, "lying." His Honor not only disagreed, but objected himself to the prosecutor's use of that term.

"Overruled. Bring the jury back."

Mr. Carter was on his feet again, waving his arms and almost shouting:

"You mean he can stand up there and--"

"Mr. Carter, " the judge interrupted loudly, "I am telling you that at this point in time, I have ruled. Now, sit down."

Tempers had become frayed during the course of this trial. The guilt/ innocence phase had been a slam-dunk for the prosecution, the defense having to wait on the bench for the overtime. In the sentencing phase, although Dr. Sultan had been an effectual witness, Mr. Carter had effectively cross-examined, scoring some points. All in all, the case had gone well for the prosecution and only as well as could be expected for the defense, sufficiently explaining Mr. Fuller's frustration. But Mr. Carter had persisted in wanting everything his way, an impossibility in a trial. The nature of the crime itself was the culprit, the catalyst for his zeal.

That, and the fact that the prosecutor still had not learned that over-ruled means overruled.

Mr. Fuller continued after the jury returned.

"Dr. Sultan's testimony was so important that you have to disbelieve every word she says or bring in a verdict of life imprisonment... Ladies and gentlemen, this is not Fuller v. Carter. This case is about Henry McCollum. Dr. Sultan's testimony in other trials has not been only for the defense, but about half and half for the prosecution and the defense... You have also learned that Henry McCollum has had no infractions in prison since 1984--that's seven years, and the prosecutor brings up one scuffle that somebody else started.... The material we presented from New Jersey was meant to show a pattern of life... Did he get smart for a couple of years and then get retarded again? Both his retardation and emotional disturbance have been there for many years..."

He referred again to his listing of Henry McCollum's problems that he had gone over one by one with Doctor Sultan.

"You will see every one of these on the verdict sheet as mitigating circumstances. You've heard from Mr. Carter that there is no evidence of this and that, but Judge Thompson has to decide there is mitigating evidence for it to appear on the verdict sheet."

Mr. Fuller attacked the testimony of L. P. Sinclair, telling the jury it had nothing to do with sentencing, and, unable to recall Mr. Sampson's name, referred to him as the "bushy headed guy with a mustache who read from the transcript."

Mr. Sampson just happened to be out of the courtroom, but upon his return a few minutes later, Mr. Carter, smiling, whispered to him how he had been described.

"This State's witness was reading the testimony of a witness that had lied to him. He knew that twice Mr. Sinclair had not told him the truth, but now he's the one reading Sinclair's testimony as truth."

Mr. Fuller placed another enlarged document on the easel in front of the jury, a copy of the several-page verdict form they would fill out.

"Every mitigating factor was supported by believable evidence, some more than others, I grant you, but some evidence." For each circumstance, he penned a "Y" for "yes" in the answer blank, writing "Life" on the last line of the form.

Quoting the book of Matthew, he declared McCollum to be one of "the least of my brethren."

Reading lines from the defendant's statement, Mr. Fuller focused on phrases that included the names of McCollum's partners in crime, emphasizing their roles.

"Officer Floyd has told you that Darrell Suber is still living in the same neighborhood, and Chris Brown now lives somewhere in Red Springs. Well, you know where Henry McCollum lives."

The verdict form was removed from the easel, and in its place, Mr. Fuller displayed an enlargement of the statement itself, using a yellow highlighter to point out how many times Chris and Darrell's names appeared on each page, then counting them for the jury.

"Henry Lee McCollum is being asked to bear all the burden... Talk about justice--this retarded kid is facing the death penalty, while one is still running around the neighborhood and one lives across town .... Socrates said, 'Justice without mercy is revenge.' And then it is written in another book, "Vengeance is mine, sayeth the Lord." And in Deuteronomy 30:19, 'I set before you this day death and life; therefore, choose life.' I ask you to give justice, not revenge. I ask you to choose life. I ask each of you to follow the law, choose life, and spare his life."

The arguments concluded at ten minutes after six, and the jurors were excused until the following morning. Jack had work to do, so we decided on a quick omelette before he settled in his study. He finished composing his jury charge around nine. Tomorrow would probably bring a verdict.

Friday morning, the jurors were instructed on the law by Judge Thompson for an hour and sent to begin their deliberations.

We had all remarked how serious this jury had been from the very beginning. Usually, until jurors are allowed to talk about the case, you will hear laughter from the jury room as they get to know one another and engage in everyday conversation.

Not this time. As a group, intelligent and thoughtful, they had given each attorney and each witness their full attention, and there had been no noise at all during their sequestered sessions in the jury room.

There was no doubt that this was a heinous crime--no rhyme, no reason--and perpetrated against one of the most innocent among us, a child, one who would have had no perception of what could occur under circumstances you and I would warily avoid and no comprehension of why this was happening to her. But the evidence of McCollum's emotional and intellectual age would weigh heavily on the jurors' minds also. Even though they most probably believed that whoever executed this deed deserved death, they had to deal with the idea of putting another "child" to death.

We waited in the back halls, chambers, and Judges Office, changing locations for something to do, not knowing that Amanda, the Judges Office secretary, had plans for us. Judge Gore and Judge Brewer had recently had birthdays, and although belated for both of them, this was the first time that Amanda, who never forgot birthdays, had been able to catch them here on the same day. At the moment, three juries were out, one from each judge, so the timing was perfect. Clerks, court reporters, and other personnel were rounded up, and we shared cake and conversation in an empty conference room.

It was after one o'clock when Judge Thompson sent for the jury to dismiss them for lunch. *The only spectator present besides myself was Ronnie Buie. Two of the women jurors on the back row had been crying, still wiping their eyes as they took their seats.*

The jurors were told to return no later than two-fifteen on this Friday afternoon, but all came back early, and they began again at two-ten.

At two-forty, less than thirty minutes later, the knock came. They told the bailiff they had reached a verdict.

The judge warned that there were to be no outbursts of any kind when the verdict was announced. The foreman stood, answered "yes," they had a verdict, and passed it to the bailiff, who passed it to the judge. After looking at each page, he handed the form to Linda to read aloud. Besides the jury, the judge and clerk were the only two that knew what the verdict was.

The tension built.

Linda stood and addressed the jury foreman.

"You the jury have unanimously found from the evidence beyond a reasonable doubt the answer to Issue One-A, (that the defendant himself: Killed the victim; or Intended to kill the victim; or Was a major participant in the underlying felony and exhibited reckless indifference to human life) as 'Yes.'"

"Yes," answered the jury foreman.

"You the jury have unanimously found from the evidence beyond a reasonable doubt the answer to Issue One, (the existence of one or more of the following aggravating circumstances: Murder committed for the purpose of avoiding or preventing a lawful arrest; and Was this murder especially heinous, atrocious, or cruel) as 'Yes.'"

"Yes."

"You the jury have found from the evidence the answer to Issue Two (the existence of one or more of the following mitigating circumstances) as 'Yes.'"

"Yes."

"You the jury have unanimously found beyond a reasonable doubt the answer to Issue Three (that the mitigating circumstance or circumstances found is, or are, insufficient to outweigh the aggravating circumstance or circumstances found) as 'Yes.'"

"Yes."

We knew.

"You the jury have unanimously found beyond a reasonable doubt the answer to Issue Four (that the aggravating circumstance or circumstances you found is, or are, sufficiently substantial to call for the imposition of the death penalty when considered with the mitigating circumstance or circumstances found by one or more of you) as 'Death.'"

"Yes."

Henry Lee McCollum sat looking at the floor. He had stopped rocking.

Three members of the defendant's family were present, and while their faces were grim, no tears were shed. They had been through this before.

Two of the defense attorneys had their hands to their mouths. Mr. Fuller shook his head. He was pale.

Judge Thompson asked that the jury be polled, and each juror was asked individually if this was his verdict. Each answered that it was.

The judge excused the jury and, with agreement from the attorneys, said he would impose the sentence now.

The defense attorneys stood with the defendant to face the bench.

"The prisoner, Henry Lee McCollum, having been convicted of Murder in the First Degree by verdict of the Jury duly returned at the term of the Superior Court of Cumberland, North Carolina, and the Jury having unanimously recommended the punishment of death."

"It is, therefore, ordered and adjudged that the same Henry Lee McCollum be, and he is hereby sentenced to death, and the Sheriff of Cumberland, North Carolina, in whose custody the said defendant now is, shall forthwith deliver the said prisoner, Henry Lee McCollum, to the Warden of the State's Penitentiary at Raleigh, North Carolina, who, the Warden, on the 24th day of January, 1992, shall cause the said prisoner, Henry Lee McCollum, to be put to death as by law provided."

"May God have mercy on your soul."

Mr. Fuller gave notice of appeal.

"Any further matters?" the judge inquired.

"No, Your Honor."

"He is in custody."

The defense attorneys were visibly shaken. Intellectually, they knew this result was a real possibility--even probability--but emotionally, this moment is impossible to prepare for. Mr. Fuller had just watched one client die, the after-shocks still reverberating. The effect is lasting and takes its toll on any man. Now, he may witness Henry McCollum's death, and each day for the next few years, this thought would haunt his psyche.

But Henry Lee McCollum would not be executed on January twenty-fourth. The defense had appealed--not entirely their decision, but mandatory for every death case. The N. C. Supreme Court would examine this trial again with "strict scrutiny," the highest standard of review. Necessarily, the date would be changed until all appeals were exhausted.

Although this was Judge Thompson's third capital case this year, this was the first time he had had to sentence someone to death and affix his signature to the Order for execution.

He looked a little paler too.

Later, I kept asking if he was all right. He kept saying he was. I wasn't, not really, and I had done nothing but observe.

The stark reality of having to look at a living, breathing, human being face to face and tell him he was going to die is sinister under any circumstances. The prosecutor had argued that if this was not a death case, there were none, but that rationale was not comforting at this moment.

The holidays were upon us, and we had a social function we had promised to attend that night. Engaging in cocktails and chatter was going to require an effort, an about-face switch in mood. We would have difficulty sloughing the somber side-effects this trial had brought about, but seeing other people could be the best thing we could do to get our minds off the case.

Jack thought it best, and I agreed, that we not discuss the trial, at least, not bring it up.

But for now, and as we went through our rituals of preparing for a large party, our thoughts were still in the courtroom.

I wondered what the jurors would think if they had known that a verdict of life imprisonment might have meant twelve more years. But, rightfully so, they did not know. How a sentence is administered is not within their expertise or power, and what they thought could or might happen--tossing about "what-ifs"—should not influence their decision.

The parole possibilities, however, were now moot. These twelve people had concluded that this particular murder ranked among those considered the most vile, and, therefore, deserving of the supreme punishment--termination.

AFTERWORD

In September of 2014, after almost 31 years on death row, Henry McCollum, along with his brother Leon Brown were released from prison.

The reasons are as follows:

The two prisoners filed a Motion for Appropriate Relief and an investigation by the North Carolina Innocence Inquiry Commission found DNA from a cigarette butt near the scene of the crime did not match either of them, but did match someone else convicted of committing a very similar crime one month after McCollum and Brown were arrested. His name was Roscoe Artis and he lived beside the field where Sabrina was found.

A hearing was held in September of 2014. A member of the Innocence Commission was the only witness. The Court granted the Motion for Appropriate Relief which entitled them to a new trial.

The District Attorney dismissed the 31 year old case, and the Court ordered their immediate release.

Following their release, they applied to Governor McCrory for Pardons of Innocence, which were granted. They were also granted clemency and each were written a check for $750,000.

The former defendants filed a civil action alleging False Arrest, Deprivation of Due Process of Law, and Malicious Prosecution against the six law enforcement officers, each acting in concert and aiding each other claiming that Henry McCollum and Leon Brown's arrests and convictions were obtained through fraud, perjury and coercion.

The County of Robeson and Town of Red Springs are included in the suit.

EPILOGUE

December, 1991

This last week of December, there is no court, the children have departed after our Christmas celebration, and our house is unnaturally, but pleasantly, quiet.

I have learned to cherish these special times with no schedule.

Jack is up early, waking me later with a cup of coffee and the paper- -only the sections he has perused, of course. Our bedroom is on the east side of the house *(having no sense of direction whatsoever, the only way I know this is that the sun rises outside the bedroom window)*. On the opposite wall from the window, a heavy, brass mirror hangs above our dresser. When the morning light streams across the room, the beveled edge of the mirror acts like a prism, splaying red, yellow, green, and purple rays across my white comforter. I can linger for a while, drinking my coffee with rainbows and reflecting on the last twelve months.

This had been quite a year, and not just for us.

Nineteen ninety-one had opened with the most dreaded word in our vocabulary, "War," and the world had watched in horrified fascination. After its swift conclusion, we felt reassured, proud, and grateful that "all that money" we had spent on defense had paid off. Space-age technology actually worked, sparing the lives of our young men while they liberated another country from the evil clutches of a fiery-eyed madman, who looked like a clone of another monster fifty years past. The madman was still loose, however. We would keep a close eye on him.

The Berlin Wall was literally torn down by a people feverish for the taste of freedom, a people resolved to salvage the rest of their lives, even if it meant starting over with nothing.

Russia, our most feared opponent for generations, giving up on Communism as a concept and world domination as a goal, was now our friend. The immediate effects and future ramifications for both our nation and theirs staggered our collective imaginations.

Now, at the end of the year, we were plunging even deeper into the pit of a recession we had not wanted to believe was happening.

And it was once again time to listen to campaign-trail politicians who aspired to the one and only Oval Office.

The events of this one year were profound and too complex for my mind to digest. Fortunately, Americans more intelligent and more perceptive than I would attempt to sort it all out.

Our own little world had been complicated enough for me.

In September, we had suffered a close personal loss. Jack's sister and my friend, Irene, had died. We would miss her quick wit and caring ways for a long, long time.

And, lastly, we had known joy. On Christmas Day, our daughter, Kathy brought us the glad tidings that we would have a new life in our family this coming August.

Jack has completed a year on the bench, a year that now, in retrospect, seems like three or four months. He has borne the duties of his new position by doing his best, comfortable with the responsibilities his long, black robe represents.

My year has been successful as well. Law school ambitions have subsided, at least for now. I have grown content with my added role as "the judge's wife." But that will be my supplement, my fill-in for whatever I choose to do next.

Postscript:

As I sit at my desk on this late March day, almost a year from the date when I started jotting down my adventure, I am nearing the conclusion of my written account of last year's events.

Pausing to gather my thoughts, I glance out the window.

Today is officially the first day of Spring; yesterday we wore short sleeves.

This morning, true to the unpredictability of our North Carolina weather, snow is softly falling on my blooming azaleas...